More Praise for *A Lasting Promise,* New and Revised Edition

"Finally, a practical, easy-to-read book that deals with real marital issues from a Christian perspective! Soundly based on both biblical principles and marital research, *A Lasting Promise* is a must-read for any couple who wants to upgrade their marriage and make it a promise for life."

—David and Claudia Arp, coauthors, *The Second Half of Marriage*

"Every couple wants 'a lasting promise' but the tragic reality is many of the promises made at the alter don't last and many of those that do become impoverished relationships that are a far cry from what God had in mind when He designed marriage. This is much more than a second edition—in many ways it's a new book. With cutting-edge research, the theological integration is deeper, it is biblically richer, and at the same time even more practical. The chapters on prayer and jars of clay alone are worth the price of the book. *A Lasting Promise* will help you see marriage from a new perspective and free you to enjoy the deep levels of passion and intimacy that God designed us to enjoy in a healthy marriage relationship. Whether you are a newlywed couple, a graduate student, a pastor, or a counseling professional, you will benefit personally and professionally from this resource. It's a book you'll give to friends and one you'll refer to often. Invest in yourself or someone you love by giving the gift of this book!"

—Gary J. Oliver, PhD, executive director, The Center for Relationship Enrichment; professor, psychology and practical theology, John Brown University, Siloam Springs, Arkansas

A Lasting Promise

A Christian Guide to Fighting *for* Your Marriage

Scott Stanley
Daniel Trathen
Savanna McCain
Milt Bryan

New and Revised Edition

JB JOSSEY-BASS™
A Wiley Brand

Cover design: JPuda
Cover image: rings © Doug Armand/Getty; couple © Yuri Arcurs/Getty
Copyright © 2014 by Christian PREP, Inc. All rights reserved.

Published by Jossey-Bass
A Wiley Brand
One Montgomery Street, Suite 1200, San Francisco, CA 94104-4594—www.josseybass.com

Jossey-Bass books and products are available through most bookstores. To contact Jossey-Bass
directly call our Customer Care Department within the U.S. at 800-956-7739, outside the U.S.
at 317-572-3986, or fax 317-572-4002.

Wiley publishes in a variety of print and electronic formats and by print-on-demand. Some
material included with standard print versions of this book may not be included in e-books or
in print-on-demand. If this book refers to media such as a CD or DVD that is not included in
the version you purchased, you may download this material at http://booksupport.wiley.com.
For more information about Wiley products, visit www.wiley.com.

Unless otherwise noted, all scripture quoted is from the *Holy Bible: New International Version*
(North American Edition). Copyright 1984 by the International Bible Society. Some passages
as noted are from the New King James Version (NKJV; copyright by Thomas Nelson, Inc.,
1982) or the King James Version, where rendering makes the points clearer.

**Library of Congress Cataloging-in-Publication Data has been applied for and is on file at the
Library of Congress.**
ISBN 978-1-118-67292-1 (paper); ISBN 978-1-118-69051-2 (ebk.);
ISBN 978-1-11869058-1 (ebk.)

Printed in the United States of America
SECOND EDITION
PB Printing V10002145_070318

Contents

Acknowledgments

This book is founded on the contributions of many others who have studied to better understand marriage and how to help couples. First and foremost, we acknowledge our friend and colleague Howard Markman. Dr. Markman had the pioneering vision in the late 1970s to take emerging understandings from sound marital research and apply this information to helping couples prevent divorce and preserve lasting, loving marriages. His impetus has born much fruit over many years in this field. Over the past thirty years, Dr. Markman and Dr. Scott Stanley (coauthor of this book), along with a host of distinguished colleagues, have worked to refine both our understanding of marriage and effective strategies for couples who want to make their marriages all they can be.

We specifically acknowledge a core group of colleagues who have worked at various stages over many years on research or foundational principles and strategies that lie behind all our efforts to help couples. The list of centrally involved colleagues includes Natalie Jenkins, Susan Blumberg, Frank Floyd, and Galena Rhoades. The list of other colleagues and researchers who have provided an endless stream of useful studies that inform what we do to help couples is too long to include here, but we acknowledge the immense value of that body of work.

We also acknowledge the dedicated team at PREP, Inc. who continually make important and creative contributions to the efforts to develop and distribute thoughtful, research-based materials for helping people build healthy and happy marriages. The team has included many talented people over the years, and we list here the current and recent team members who have done so much for others: Todd Boyd, Lawrence Ramos, Nick Thayer, Jeff Erlacher, Lucinda Young, Sarah Healey, Lief Noll, Miranda Egger, Judi Metz, Jessica Jenkins, and Maggie Corcoran.

We also have had the good fortune to connect over the years with many people who have supported us in meaningful ways as our work has developed. Bill Coffin has been a deep and longtime advocate of efforts to help couples in marriage. He was instrumental in encouraging us to get our work out of the lab and into the world where it could make a difference. It is hard to imagine anyone who has known more people and connected more dots in this field than Bill. We also thank Diane Sollee for her pioneering national efforts to put marriage education on the map. She has been a great supporter of those who seek to strengthen marriages.

Over the years, we have been assisted by an incredible number of research colleagues, assistants, and students at the University of Denver. The list is truly too long to construct, but we are deeply thankful to you all for your work.

Our editor for the original version of this book, Alan Rinzler, has always been a great advocate and supporter—as well as a wonderful editor. He found us, first publishing the original *Fighting for Your Marriage* and then the first edition of *A Lasting Promise*. Now we add our thanks to our new editor, Marjorie McAneny, without whose efforts this new edition would not have happened. We also express our appreciation to Nana Twumasi, for all her help in reviewing drafts, giving advice on content, and preparing the book for production. We are also grateful for the excellent work of the copyeditor, Michele Jones, and to Carol Hartland for all her work in moving this book through production. The entire crew at Jossey-Bass/Wiley have been fantastic to work with in every phase of this project.

Finally, we express our deep appreciation for the couples and families who have shared their lives in various research projects at the University of Denver and elsewhere. These couples have opened their hearts and their relationships to our interviewers and video cameras, and have endured long questionnaires—some couples doing so for many years. They have shared in a way that allowed researchers on our team to learn more about all aspects of marriage and romantic relationships in ways that inform the strategies we share in this book. Thank you.

We should clarify that the stories and examples of couples that we use throughout this book are based on composites of the experiences of many couples. The stories are "real" because our understanding of what goes on in marriages is deeply informed by our research and other experiences with couples over the years. However, none of the stories or dialogue presented here is from any specific, real couple, but the events and challenges described here are just like those that scores of real couples have experienced.

Finally, we thank God for life and marriage. As we explain in Chapter One, it's His idea. That's pretty amazing.

Introduction

Welcome to the new edition of *A Lasting Promise*. This edition is fresh and greatly expanded in many ways, including updated research and all-new chapters on subjects we did not address in the first edition. The time-tested strategies included in this book are for all couples—from the newly engaged to longtime marrieds—who want to make their marriage the best it can be. Some of you may be having significant problems at this time in your marriage. Some of you may have a great relationship and want to keep it that way. Either way, this book is for you.

Most people truly want a great marriage, but they don't know how to get there (or stay there). No book will give you all the answers, but we believe that you'll find this one full of practical ideas and principles that you can use. *A Lasting Promise* is similar to many other books about marriage written from a Christian perspective in that it is founded on the teachings of scripture. In fact, in a number of chapters, you will find that it goes quite deep into what is taught in scripture. In other chapters, we will present a general biblical principle and then focus almost entirely on the nuts and bolts of how to handle things well in marriage. The Bible and historic Christian teaching about marriage serve as the plumb line for all we have to say. But at least two features in this book are not typical of many other books on marriage from a Christian perspective.

First, in addition to being thoroughly scripturally based, *A Lasting Promise* has a strong foundation of university-based research about what leads to marriages' failing or thriving. Throughout, you will find scores of insights from sound research. At times, we specifically cite studies, and at other times we do not—just to keep things flowing well. We want you to enjoy working through this book and not get bogged down. If you are interested, Appendix C is an abbreviated list of some of the studies and papers that help inform the points we make in this book, and we mention how you can access a far larger list of research studies if you are interested.

Second, *A Lasting Promise* is focused on practical strategies. Unlike many books that are more theoretical or insight oriented, this one is designed for action. Sure, you'll find many things to contemplate—some we hope deeply—but much of what we have to say is about getting up and doing what you can do to keep your marriage strong and happy. Not only that, the things we will encourage you to do have been shown to make a difference for many couples. We want to equip you to develop the full promise of your marriage.

Many ideas and strategies presented here are based on the internationally recognized program called PREP (the Prevention and Relationship Enhancement Program). Based on decades of university-based research, the PREP approach focuses on specific attitudes and ways of acting that can make a difference in your marriage. Some of the most important and specific strategies in this book are based on PREP and also the secular book on PREP called *Fighting* for *Your Marriage*, written by Howard Markman, Scott Stanley, and Susan Blumberg. Markman and Stanley (and their colleagues) have worked on PREP and the research underlying it for over thirty years. The first edition of *Fighting* for *Your Marriage* was published in 1994; it is now in its third edition (Jossey-Bass, 2010).

All works for couples based in whole or in part on PREP incorporate principles founded on extensive research conducted in the United States and around the world. That is one of the things that make this book different from most other resources for marriages. For example, there is a great deal of evidence that, compared to happier couples, distressed couples show major differences in their ability to handle conflict. Such findings have led us to a number of specific strategies that address how couples can handle issues more constructively—the strategies that we will teach you here. But this book is not just about communication and conflict. We also focus on such topics as commitment, forgiveness, spiritual intimacy, friendship, sensuality, and fun. This new edition updates those themes and extends the book into new territory, including the meaning and impact of having a physical body, prayer for your mate and marriage, emotional support, and how to manage technology in your marriage.

Many studies underlying this book have been conducted at the University of Denver by Howard Markman, Scott Stanley, Galena Rhoades, and their colleagues. However, we've also developed strategies for you based on scores of published studies from around the world. We focus on the good stuff—that which is most clear, and research that is well conducted. Because of its roots in solid research and its straightforward approach, PREP has received a great deal of attention from couples across the country, professionals in the field of marital and relationship education and counseling, and the media. You may have been exposed to some of the coverage about PREP (or various studies from the University of Denver) on CNN, *Fox News*, or MSNBC and on such programs as *20/20, 48 Hours, Good Morning America, Focus on the Family, The Today Show, Moody's Midday Connection, Oprah, Family Life Today*, and so forth. This work has also been covered in newspapers and magazines such as *USA Today*, the *New York Times*, the *Washington Post, Woman's Day, Redbook, Psychology Today*.

One of the things that research helps us identify is patterns that are associated with success or failure in marriage and family life. Prevention experts call these protective factors and risk factors. Knowing more about why and how marriages are more vulnerable (and most are) and how some marriages come apart (and many do) gives us clear ideas about where couples should focus their attention to make marriage all it can be. Here we will direct your attention to dimensions identified in scripture and in research, but we focus on areas where you can make changes. From our work at the University of Denver, we have learned to emphasize what we call "dynamic" risk factors, as opposed to "static" risk factors. Both matter, but static risk factors are things like your parents' having divorced when you were a child, and you cannot go back in time and change something like that. We focus our attention here on dynamic, changeable dimensions, such as communication, conflict management, strategies for protecting and enhancing depth of connection, and commitment—all factors that you can do something about to make your marriage strong, happy, and lasting.

Before beginning, we want to mention how we think about the integration of research findings with revealed truth from scripture. To highlight the approach to integration taken, we quote from two sources associated with Christian PREP, which was the forerunner to the theological integration you will experience in this book.

> Thomas Aquinas, a Dominican monk, labored in the 13th century to integrate reason and revelation. Believing strongly that there was one source of truth (God), he believed that "nothing discovered in nature could ultimately contradict the Faith" (quoting Chesterton, 1956, p. 93). Essentially, truth discerned by observation and reason (e.g., science) should not be incompatible with truth given by God through revelation. Revelation can be considered to be special (e.g., Scripture) or general (revelation discerned about the creator from studying creation, e.g., truth discerned through research).[1]

> This approach is based on the belief that God has provided guidelines for marriage in Scripture. Furthermore, he allows us to learn more about the workings of relationships through sound research. The belief guiding the integration of Scripture and research is that "all truth is God's truth," with Scripture being preeminent.[2]

In other words, sound marital research can discover truth because all truth comes from God. Through scripture, God reveals His thoughts on the essence of marriage and truth about relationships. Our desire is to present clear truth from scripture and also present research findings that can further illuminate patterns associated with marriages of lasting promise. Whenever and if ever research reveals findings that are inconsistent with revealed truth, we choose to follow scripture. One of the great blessings to us has been just how wonderfully scripture and sound marital research point in the same direction.

How to Get the Most out of This Book

This book starts with the basics, presented in a step-by-step manner, and builds to incorporate a variety of specific strategies. With each skill or principle, we'll also tell you about the underlying theory and research so that you'll understand why it works. We give specific instructions for exercises that can be done at home in order to help you learn and practice new patterns where needed. If your mate is not interested in reading this book with you, that is OK. In fact, that's pretty common. You will have to use wisdom in how you apply various strategies, but we believe that valuable changes can begin with just one partner in many cases. There is a lot one person can do to improve his or her marriage. If your mate is up for your sharing some of your favorite ideas as you go through this book, just focus your work together on those specifics. You can decide how to implement other strategies as you do your part to make your marriage all it can be. When you are both working on learning new strategies and skills taught here, practice will add to the value of your efforts. By practicing and trying out new ideas, you put your love in action. We hope that you will realize the full blessing and *lasting promise* of your marriage.

PART ONE

Foundations

1

Naked and Unashamed

So they are no longer two, but one.
MATTHEW 19:6

God designed marriage to be a relationship in which trust, openness, and vulnerability can thrive. He designed the first relationship to be nourishing, enriching, and fruitful. Adam and Eve were the first to experience the joys and miseries of marriage. Let's see what we can learn from this very first couple.

As God was creating matter, light, and life, He declared everything He made to be good. There was one notable exception: "The LORD God said, 'It is not good for the man to be alone'" (Genesis 2:18). Sin and the fall had not yet happened. But still it was not good for man to be alone. Why? Simply because God created man for relationship: with Him, in marriage, and with others. But relationships, especially close relationships, are difficult. In fact, it seems that our relationships with those we love most are the relationships most difficult of all to manage. Why is this? Let's look at what happened between Adam and Eve in the Garden of Eden for some clues.

These two people were the last creations of God. They were the pinnacle of His work, a perfect man and a perfect woman, joined together and living in perfect harmony in a perfect world. We don't know exactly what Eden was like, but we can imagine there being no limits on time or money or any other resource.

Imagine you are in the most relaxed and beautiful setting and experiencing total enjoyment and peace of mind. Our imaginary Eden is as close as we will get to Eden this side of heaven. Here were Adam and Eve in this wonderful setting, anticipating a wonderful life together, knowing God intimately, and without a care in the world. The Bible says,

> For this reason a man will leave his father and mother and be united to his wife, and they will become one flesh. The man and his wife were both naked, and they felt no shame.
> (Genesis 2:24–25)

This passage is quoted by Jesus and by the apostle Paul as the foundation for understanding marriage. By letting Jesus and Paul amplify our understanding of it, we can learn a great deal about what God intended marriage to be.

Oneness and Intimacy in Marriage

In Matthew 19, the Pharisees were questioning Jesus about divorce. "Is it lawful for a man to divorce his wife for any and every reason?" they asked (Matthew 19:3). The Pharisees and scribes had been debating about the conditions under which a man could divorce his wife. In asking Jesus, they weren't really interested in the right answer; they were merely hoping to trap Jesus into giving a "politically incorrect" response that would diminish His popularity with the people. As on other occasions, this attempt to trap Him failed. In answering them, Jesus went straight to Genesis to reveal the essence of what God was thinking about marriage:

> "Haven't you read," he replied, "that at the beginning the Creator 'made them male and female,' and said, 'For this reason a man will leave his father and mother and be united to his wife, and the two will become one flesh'? So they are no longer two, but one. Therefore what God has joined together, let man not separate.
> (Matthew 19:4–6)

Although this passage is frequently cited to emphasize the seriousness of divorce in God's eyes, what Jesus says about being joined together in oneness speaks to the core of what this book is about. In fact, there is something about oneness versus separateness that runs through the heart of Christian theology.

Although oneness is a major theme in Christianity, it's far from easy to describe. In fact, there are very different manifestations and forms of oneness presented—among others the Trinity, the members of the church as the body of Christ, the relationship between Christ and the church, and, of course, marriage, the most fundamental of human relationships.

Oneness means many things to many people, but in His conversation with the Pharisees, Jesus appealed to the ideas of *oneness* and *permanence* in answering their trick question regarding divorce. He seems to be telling them that divorce is not God's perfect plan because marriage is fundamentally about two people mysteriously becoming and remaining one for the rest of their lives. Put another way, God's design for marriage is that it be a covenant of spiritual unity in which the souls and hearts of a man and woman are joined before Him and with Him into a "three-fold cord" providing direction and meaning in the bond of love (Ecclesiastes 4:9–12; Ephesians 5:31–32). How does that happen? How do two people somehow become one? The Bible says it is a mystery.

The Mystery of Oneness

Historically, Christians have talked about oneness in marriage as a diamond having several facets: spiritual, emotional, intellectual, and physical. We will focus on these dimensions in many ways throughout this book. The foundational teaching about oneness, of course, rests in the physical union of husband and wife, but much more is implied. What it means for two people to become "one" is a rich and wonderful mystery. Paul quotes the Genesis passage, then refers to the concept of mystery as he describes what marriage is all about:

> For this reason a man will leave his father and mother and be
> united to his wife, and the two will become one flesh. This is a
> profound mystery but I am talking about Christ and the church.
> (Ephesians 5:31–32)

The Greek word for "mystery" comes from the idea of astonishment or a "shut mouth." When something is a mystery, what can you say? Paul is referring to the mystery of the relationship between Christ and the church, but we believe he is also making a more general point about oneness—that it is inherently mysterious. What do *you* think oneness in marriage means? Stop reading for a moment and ponder this. What might be so wonderful about it that it cannot be easily described?

One thing seems absolutely clear. Biblical oneness in marriage does not mean that one person's identity becomes lost in the other's, forming one big blob. Some people fear that this will happen in marriage, that they will somehow lose track of themselves if they grow truly close to another. We've heard it said this way: "The two shall become one—but which one?" That is not the concept presented in scripture. In fact, one of the most powerful examples of biblical oneness conveys diversity in unity that is quite the opposite of "blobness." Paul describes the body of Christ as being one but made up of many individual parts, each unique in its own function (1 Corinthians 12 and 14). It's a unity (one body), but a unity made up of many unique parts. Although it is mysterious, the concept of oneness lies at the very core of Christianity.

The following diagram conveys a healthy view of oneness in marriage. Note that there are two distinct persons coming together in the marital union: a "you" and a "me." But there is also a third identity of "us" that is born out of the connection between "me" and "you." One person's identity is never to be lost in the other, but God's design is that the two come together in a powerful way to form a new entity that is unique in and of itself. Beyond this limited understanding, oneness really is mysterious. You can't quite describe it, but you probably know when you and your mate are experiencing it and when you're not.

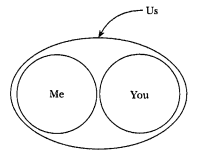

The concept of mystery implies that something is not specifically defined. This suggests great freedom in the way you express the unique oneness of your marriage. Because oneness is mysterious, there is not one "cookie cutter" way you *should* develop it. You can be creative in the ways you express it over the years. Research on successful and happy marriages reveals a great diversity in the ways happy couples relate. But there's very little diversity in how unhappy couples relate—usually with cold distance or chronic conflict. These patterns are quite common and not at all unique from one unhappy couple to another. Simply put, couples are very different in the ways they express oneness, but they fall into well-worn ruts in the ways they destroy it.

We will help you keep out of these ruts by teaching you how to avoid the attitudes and behaviors that destroy the experience of oneness and intimacy. In Chapter Sixteen, we will focus on ways to help you develop spiritual oneness, the most mysterious oneness element of all.

Permanence in Oneness

When Jesus said, "what God has joined together, let man not separate," he clearly conveyed the sense that marriage is to be a relationship of permanence (Matthew 19:6). "Until death do us part" is the way this is commonly expressed in marital vows. Scripture leaves us with no doubt that God loves all people, including those who divorce, even though He hates divorce (Malachi 2:16). But this is not a book about the theology of divorce. It's about preventing divorce and enabling you to realize the full promise of your marriage. It is a book for couples who want to make their marriages all they can be—marriages that will last and that fully express the mystery of oneness with joy, confidence, growing love, and fruitfulness.

In Chapter Fourteen, "The Power of Commitment," we will talk more in depth about permanence and maintaining a marriage through good times and bad. For now, consider this one crucial fact about the need for the kind of commitment that supports lasting love in marriage: it is the sense of permanence based in a healthy and strong commitment that allows a marriage to thrive even though it is made up of two imperfect beings. One of the greatest problems for marriages these days is that people have grown to expect more than is possible from their relationships. Should you aim high for what your marriage can be? Sure. Are we arguing for settling for mediocrity in marriage? Not at all. But we do want you to grapple with the fact that people have come to expect levels of sustained attraction to, and acceptance from, their mates that are rare if not impossible. The unrealistic expectations hurt perfectly good marriages. Marriages can be great, but will not be perfect, and marriages that succeed provide a huge number of benefits in life for the spouses and their children. The reality of two people thriving through the trials and imperfections of life trumps the fantasy of perfection.

One of the greatest benefits of having the type of commitment that fuels a belief in permanence is that it provides the foundation for true, deeper intimacy and acceptance, to which we now turn.

The Nature of God and Marriage

There are many reasons why marriage matters in society. That has been a topic of many books and discussions, but it is not our focus here. Closer to our focus is the question, "Why is marriage so important to understanding life?" The answer lies in the depth to which marriage signifies important characteristics about God.

Consider the fact that marriage plays a central role throughout the Bible. First of all, marriage is the main event in the Genesis account of creation. Further, the marriages of major figures of the Bible are prominent throughout the Old Testament—including all the elements of joy and beauty, conflict and misery. In the Old Testament, marriage is a metaphor for the relationship between God and Israel (for example, Isaiah 54:5f; Jeremiah 2:3). In the New Testament, Jesus performed His first miracle at a wedding by changing water into wine (John 2:1–11). He taught about marriage numerous times during his ministry (Matthew 5, Matthew 19, Luke 16). In addition, the apostle Paul wrote a great deal about marriage (Ephesians 5, 1 Corinthians 7, and Colossians 3:18–19). And one of the final events described in the Bible is the future wedding supper of the lamb, described in the book of Revelation. What that depicts is the full union of Jesus Christ and the church. The Bible both begins and ends with marriage.

All this emphasis on marriage throughout the Bible makes clear that marriage matters because marriage reflects who God is and how He relates to us. Now combine this thought with the teaching in Genesis 1:26–27:

> Then God said, "Let us make man in our image, in our likeness, and let them rule over the fish of the sea and the birds of the air, over the livestock, over all the earth, and over all the creatures that move along the ground." So God created man in his own image, in the image of God he created him; male and female he created them.

It was important to God to make us in His image and sustain us in marriage through the process of oneness with Him and each other. This is a deep and wonderful truth that holds meaning far beyond what we can explore in this book. Here we want to note two truths based on the teachings we have cited. One, in some important way, we all bear the image of God. Two, in marriage, God reveals essential truths about His nature and His relationship with us. Through your marriage, and as two people made in the image of God, you are taking part in something much bigger—how God chooses to reflect who He is to the world.

Naked and Unashamed: The Deep Longing in Us All

Now we get to the really interesting part. Here are Adam and Eve, living in the Garden of Eden, enjoying their honeymoon, and experiencing something really amazing. Think about this verse again:

> The man and his wife were both naked, and they felt no shame. (Genesis 2:25)

Naked and no shame. What does that mean to you? We commonly hear these ideas expressed when we ask people to think about it:

| Closeness | Fearlessness | Acceptance |
| Vulnerability | Accessibility | Innocence |

No one can say what that was really like for Eve and Adam, but this passage captures something powerful, something most people really want in their relationship. Although many marriages end up in great pain and frustration, most people seem to genuinely desire the kind of closeness and acceptance implied in God's original model. When looking for a mate, were you looking for someone to argue with? Of course not! Like most couples, you were looking for someone to be your best friend and support—a mate for your soul. You were drawn to your partner not because of the inevitable conflicts you would have but because you sensed in him or her the possibility of a shameless relationship with absolute acceptance—something few of us have ever known, but all of us have longed for.

So Adam and Eve, the perfect couple, were created perfectly for one another, and were able to experience the joy of knowing one another in an awesome and perfect world. How long did that last? No one knows. But it didn't last forever. Something happened that is described in Genesis 3. Most couples start out with an experience that feels something like the experience of Adam and Eve. But then something happens to them as well. Barriers to oneness begin to overtake their sense of connection. They become wall builders instead of bridge builders.

Barriers to Oneness

Although we are created for relationship, and marriage is the most fundamental of human relationships, things don't always go the way we want them to. In marriage as in other relationships, we are frustrated by barriers that limit our ability to fully enter into the blessings we've longed for. Let's look at several kinds of barriers that get in the way.

The No-Trespassing Tree and the Fear of Rejection

The events described in Genesis 3 include the perfect couple's temptation, their sin, and their fall from the perfect state. These are important topics to be sure, and they lead theologians to explore weighty matters beyond the scope of this book. Because this is a book about relationships, we will focus on what happened to Adam and Eve in their relationship. They had been created for each other to live freely and fruitfully in paradise. They had only one limiting admonition to observe: they were not to eat from the tree of the knowledge of good and evil (Genesis 2:17). They had a world of exciting possibilities open to them. Only this one choice was off-limits. That one limit became the point for temptation. Think of Adam and Eve's whole world (or yours, for that matter) as a compass, with 360 degrees of possible directions they could go. It was as if God said, 359 degrees are fine, but just don't take this one path. Much more was open to them than was out of bounds. People often think of God as limiting us; they don't see that He wants us to know of the limits we must observe in order to fully partake of the wonderful diversity of life that is in bounds!

Satan tempted the first couple to doubt what God had said (Genesis 3:1) and to doubt that God really had their best interests at heart (Genesis 3:4, 5). They doubted God's goodness and sinned—they ate from the tree that they were not to touch.

Once they had sinned, the couple did a very curious thing. They immediately covered themselves up.

> Then the eyes of both of them were opened, and they realized they were naked; so they sewed fig leaves together and made coverings for themselves. (Genesis 3:7)

Consider this. They had seen this tree with their *eyes*, grabbed the forbidden fruit with their *hands*, and eaten it with their *mouths*. So why were they covering what they covered? Tradition and some translations say they made loin coverings. Why did they cover that part of their bodies? Why not make fig-leaf blindfolds because they had seen the tree with their eyes, or fig-leaf mittens because they had touched the fruit with their hands, or fig-leaf gags because they had eaten the fruit with their mouths? There are two answers to this question. First, they covered up the part of their bodies that was probably one of their most wonderful ways of expressing their intimacy. In fact, because the whole picture of oneness is rooted in the expression of physical union (one flesh), what we see is the shattering of sexual oneness in this story.

Second, the couple no longer felt the glorious freedom of utter acceptance, so *they covered up where they were most obviously different.* Let that one sink in a bit. Isn't that what we all do all the time? We cover up our thoughts, feelings, and opinions more when we are with someone who might see things differently from us. There's no fear of rejection when people see things the way we see them. It's our differentness that leads to our fear of rejection. In marriage, it's the same way. The very differences that are so much a part of our attraction to begin with eventually become the basis for our friction and frustration. For far too many couples, their poor ways of handling these differences create barriers to oneness that keep growing and eventually destroy the whole marriage. Careful research solidly confirms this.

In the next part of the story, God confronts Adam and Eve about their sin. Their reply is noteworthy:

> Then the man and his wife heard the sound of the Lord God as he was walking in the garden in the cool of the day, and they hid from the Lord God among the trees of the garden. But the Lord God called to the man, "Where are you?" He answered, "I heard you in the garden, and I was afraid because I was naked; so I hid." (Genesis 3:8–10)

Do you think God somehow lost track of Adam and Eve, needing to ask where they were hiding? It seems more likely that God wanted them to think about the question, as in "What have you done? Where are you now?" Adam's answer is even more interesting as he displays his motive for hiding—fear. After they sinned, it was the fear of rejection that drove them to cover up from one another and hide out from God. This was a fear they had not known before their disobedience. Along with sin and shame come a sense of separateness and a terrible fear of rejection.

Fear lays the foundation for many barriers in marriage, as couples seek to protect themselves from rejection, rather than recklessly give themselves to one another in love. By fear, we are referring to the fear of being close because of the hurt and rejection that might come. Couples fear the danger of the thing they most long for! Such fear works against showing love, but, at the same time, love is also the most powerful antidote to it. As the Apostle John wrote, "perfect love drives out fear" (1 John 4:18). Our hope in this book is to help you use active love to drive out fear in your marriage.

The Barriers of Sin and Selfishness and the Power of Love

The barriers of sin and selfishness are embedded in the story of Adam and Eve. We like to call special attention to these two things as we consider the common barriers to oneness in marriage. A marriage brings together two imperfectly motivated people who strongly desire intimacy but are afraid of being hurt. When they do hurt each other, it is because they have been motivated by these selfish and self-protective desires. James pinpoints such selfish desires as a root cause of destructive conflict:

> What causes fights and quarrels among you? Don't they come from your desires that battle within you? You want something but don't get it. You kill and covet, but you cannot have what you want. You quarrel and fight. You do not have, because you do not ask God. When you ask, you do not receive, because you ask with wrong motives, that you may spend what you get on your pleasures. (James 4:1–3)

As believers in Jesus Christ, we have been set free to love and serve one another. It is this love that enables us to overcome our basic selfishness. Look how Paul points out that love is the essential message of the law, and then contrasts such love with the corrosiveness in relationships where love is not leading the way.

> You, my brothers, were called to be free. But do not use your freedom to indulge the sinful nature; rather, serve one another in love. The entire law is summed up in a single command: 'Love your neighbor as yourself.' If you keep on biting and devouring each other, watch out or you will be destroyed by each other. (Galatians 5:13–15)

Paul contrasts servant-hearted love with self-indulgence and hurtfulness that destroy relationships. Scripture is filled with such warnings and admonitions because such patterns are so very common. But your God-enabled ability to love in other-centered ways will affect every relationship you are in—with your spouse, family, church, and coworkers, and with God. We want you to see the ideas and suggestions in this book as tangible ways to put your love in action. A true lasting promise is rooted in a love that acts. It is in motion, and it is this kind of love that keeps a marriage protected from self-destructive danger and more open to its fullest blessings.

This brings us to another important point. This book is not primarily about discipleship in the broader sense of that word. Our focus is not on what you can or need to be doing to know Christ more deeply or to follow Him more closely in your own life. Although those actions are absolutely essential, we are focusing on that aspect of discipleship that has to do with living biblically in marriage. We believe this will result in a healthy, joyous, loving, and lasting marriage that will bring honor to God. And if you are sincere about growing in your capacity to "serve one another in love," what we share with you will be that much easier to put in action. There is no substitute for growing spiritually when it comes to fueling great relationships, especially your marriage. The desire to change patterns in your marriage begins at a place deep in your own heart, with a commitment to learn how to improve the ways you relate to your mate. Before moving on to the next chapter, which reveals patterns that can destroy or build up marriages, there's one final barrier to oneness and intimacy that needs to be discussed.

Not Knowing What Better to Do

One of the most beautiful things Jesus ever said was "Do to others as you would have them do to you" (Luke 6:31). Known as the Golden Rule, this statement from His Sermon on the Mount embodies the call to love in the simplest of terms. It also puts the emphasis on the word "do." But wanting to do what's right and knowing how to do it are two different things. There is a common belief among Christians with which we take issue: it's the belief that if your heart and soul are in harmony with God, you'll somehow automatically know exactly *what* to do in your marriage and how to do it. We don't buy that. Prospering spiritually does not mean that you know how to do the things that nurture a marriage. For example, do you know *how* to really listen to your mate, even when tensions are high or you disagree? More important, can you stop an argument before damaging things are said? Do you know *how* to problem-solve as a team, *how* to work through the process of forgiveness together, *how* to clarify your deepest expectations, and *how* to enhance and deepen commitment? These are valuable "how-to" things you can learn, and when learned well, they can help you develop and keep the kind of marriage you want most. They are practical ways to put your love in action.

Perfection is not possible, of course. We will never restore ourselves to Eden. Heaven will more than take care of that. But it is possible to avoid many of the pitfalls that snag far too many couples. In the rest of this book, we hope to teach you a number of concepts and techniques that can help you stay together, stay happy, and more fully enter the blessings God intends for your marriage.

Doing Your Part

Oneness requires that we do our best to break down the barriers in order to open up the paths to intimacy. Spend some time thinking over what you've read in this chapter. What do you think about when you think of oneness? intimacy? barriers? being naked and unashamed? What are some of the barriers you are more concerned about in your relationship? What do you think Christian marriage is all about? Why does marriage, especially your own marriage, matter to God?

2

Communication Danger Signs
Damaging Conflict

> *Reckless words pierce like a sword, but the tongue of the wise brings healing.*
> PROVERBS 12:18

Learning constructive ways to handle your differences is one of the most powerful things you can do to protect the promise that your marriage holds. Much of this book is designed to give you specific ways to do just that. In the chapters that follow, we'll teach you some specific tools you can use to preserve and protect positive connection and to control negative patterns that can damage your relationship. That latter goal of managing negatives starts here in this chapter, where we will describe the four Communication Danger Signs that can wreck all of the good stuff in marriage. We call these escalation, invalidation, negative interpretations, and withdrawal and avoidance.

The Power of the Negative

You might be thinking, "Why focus on the negative?" According to research conducted by our team at the University of Denver as well as by other researchers around the world, the kinds of negative communication patterns we describe in this chapter are associated with marriages that do not make it or that are chronically unhappy. Some couples start out with a lot of these negatives; for others, the negatives develop over time. If you don't control the negatives, they can erase the good effects of just about everything else you have going for you. You cannot be positive enough to erase a lot of negatives, so reining in these patterns is crucial.

Risk Factors for Marital Failure

Researchers have found that the likelihood of divorce is associated with a variety of factors—many of which are there for couples when they walk down the aisle to say "I do." For example, some things that put couples at risk are historical, such as either one of you having parents who never married or who divorced. The belief among researchers is that that history plants a seed in a person's mind about commitment in marriage, weakening it. You can counter a risk factor like that by being more decisive and clear about your commitment to your mate. Other patterns that increase risk for divorce may or may not have such a clear historical reason for existing, but they are patterns very much with you now. Some of these factors that put marriages at risk have to do with how a person thinks, communicates, and handles conflict. That's our focus in this chapter. What's most important is that if you can focus on the things that can be changed, the unchangeable factors are much less likely to get in the way of a lifetime of blessing in your marriage.

Both scripture and research make it very clear that how you treat one another when disagreements and conflicts arise says a great deal about how your marriage will be in the years to come. The kinds of negative patterns we describe here can wipe out a lot of positive. In fact, marital researchers Cliff Notarius and Howard Markman, as well as John Gottman, have estimated that one verbal negative can wipe out the effects of five or even twenty positives. It's much like what Solomon said ages ago: "As dead flies give perfume a bad smell, so a little folly outweighs wisdom and honor" (Ecclesiastes 10:1).

Trying the "Not"

We believe that when it comes to how we treat one another (in all relationships, including marriage), scripture says far more about what *not* to do than exactly what to do. Sure, there are global passages such as 1 Corinthians 13 on the wonderful positive aspects of love, but think of the scores of passages that warn us how not to relate to one another (for example, Proverbs 12:18, 20:3, 29:11; Matthew 5:22, 7:1–5; Galatians 5:13–15; James 4:1ff). The reason there are so many passages warning us about these kinds of destructive behaviors is that these patterns are extremely corrosive in all relationships.

Escalation: The Crazy Ladder

Escalation occurs when partners respond back and forth negatively to each other, continually upping the ante so that the conversation gets more and more nasty. In escalation, negative comments spiral into increasing anger and frustration.

Escalation is like a ladder. With each rung you go up, there is less stability. As you escalate, you make it more likely that the whole ladder will fall over and take you both down with it. Although one person can sometimes escalate without the other having to take part, what we're talking about here is mostly a two-person deal. One of you takes a step up one rung higher, and the other matches it, maybe passing, going up one higher still. It's a crazy race up a wild ladder. There is nothing good at the top waiting for you. The thing about ladders is that they are not only less stable as you move higher, but they are a lot harder to climb down than they are to climb up. You can go up fast, but safely getting back down on the ground is a much more difficult. It's better not to race up this ladder that will leave you wrung out. Yes, that's a bad pun, but it's also one that expresses an important reality.

Ted, a thirty-four-year-old construction worker, and Wendy, thirty-two, who runs a catering business out of their home, had been married for eight years. They had already racked up a lot of nastiness. Like many couples, their fights started over small issues:

TED: *(sarcastically)* You'd think you could put the cap back on the toothpaste.
WENDY: *(equally sarcastically)* Oh, and you never forget to put it back?
TED: As a matter of fact, I always put it back.

WENDY: Oh, I forgot just how compulsive you are. You are right, of course!

TED: I don't even know why I stay with you. You are so negative.

WENDY: Maybe you shouldn't stay. No one is barring the door.

One of the most damaging things about arguments that are escalating is that partners tend to say things that threaten the very lifeblood of their marriage. As frustration mounts, partners often try to hurt each other by hurling verbal (and sometimes physical) weapons. As Proverbs 12:18 says, "Reckless words pierce like a sword." You can see this pattern with Ted and Wendy, where the battle quickly heats up to include threats of ending the relationship. Once very negative comments are made, they are hard to take back. As we said, it gets harder to climb back down from the ladder, the higher up you go. These reckless words do a ton of damage to oneness and intimacy and a sense of safety in the relationship.

Even though partners can say the nastiest things during escalating arguments, such remarks usually don't reflect what they generally feel about each other. You may believe that people reveal their "true feelings" in the midst of fierce fights, but we don't believe that this is usually the case. Instead, what is said is mostly focused on the immediate goal of piercing the other as a way to protect oneself. People can slide rapidly into saying things that should not have been said in the first place.

In Ted and Wendy's argument, Wendy mentions his being compulsive because she really wants to hit him where it hurts deeply. At a more tender moment between them, he had shared his concerns about being so driven, and explained how he had always felt that he had to try harder to please his father. The escalation of this argument led Wendy to use her intimate knowledge of Ted to strike deeply into his soul. When escalation leads to the use of such knowledge as a weapon, the damage to the future likelihood of "tender" moments is grave. Who is going to share deeper things in a relationship if that intimate knowledge is going to be used as a weapon later?

You may be thinking, "We don't fight like cats and dogs—how does this apply to us?" Damaging escalation isn't always this dramatic. It can be subtle and still do its nasty work. Voices don't have to be raised for you to get into the cycle of returning negative for negative. Consider the following conversation between newlyweds Max and Donna.

MAX: Did you get the rent paid on time?
DONNA: That was going to be your job.
MAX: You were supposed to do it.
DONNA: No, you were.
MAX: Did it get done?
DONNA: No. And, I'm not going to do it, either.
MAX: *(muttering)* Great. Just great.

Being newlyweds, Donna and Max are very happy with their marriage. Imagine, however, the cumulative effect of years of small arguments like this one, gradually eating away at the positive things they now share.

For the future health of your relationship, it is very important to learn to counteract whatever tendency you have to escalate as a couple. If you don't escalate very much, great! Your goal is to keep things that way. If you do escalate a fair amount, your goal is to do whatever you can to stop it now. The apostle James addresses this issue rather bluntly: "If anyone considers himself religious and yet does not keep a tight rein on his tongue, he deceives himself and his religion is worthless." (James 1:26). You can't get a lot plainer spoken than James.

You can't say anything you feel anytime you feel it and have your marriage stay healthy. Nor can you really follow Christ well without learning to rein in your tongue. It's just a fact.

Stop It! (For High-Conflict Couples with Children)

For those of you who have children, the stakes involved with your managing conflicts well are high. Research such as that conducted by Robert Emery and colleagues at the University of Virginia and by Mark Cummings and colleagues at Notre Dame has documented strong links between parents' conflict and adjustment problems for children. Kids become more sad, angry, and fearful when regularly exposed to destructively handled conflict. This is one of the clearest and most consistent findings in the social science literature. Also, children are usually more aware of what is going on between their parents or stepparents than the adults think, and they are not eager to see their parents' high-wire act. Get off the ladder, or they will learn to follow you up.

Another downside to poorly managed conflict around children is that the parents teach their children to negatively interpret the motivations of others. No parent means to do that, we're sure, but that is what happens. Further, for some couples, escalation takes them closer to the line between nasty emotional patterns and physical aggression. These patterns thus raise the stakes for everyone in the home.

So, what can you do? Disagree, but don't fight nasty. If you have a conflict in your children's presence, use Time Out (a technique we describe in Chapter Four) to bring things to a better place as quickly as possible. Also, when you've calmed down, let your children see you coming back together—they often can't see how you do that because many couples make up behind closed doors. As far as your children's well-being is concerned, coming back to some point of emotional harmony is more important than resolving whatever it was you are fighting about. So do your kids a favor and work together to manage your conflicts with respect.

Staying off the Top of the Crazy Ladder

All couples escalate from time to time, but some couples get off the ladder a lot faster, while they are lower to the ground. Compare Ted and Wendy's argument, earlier, with Maria and Hector's. Maria, a forty-five-year-old sales clerk for a jewelry store, and Hector, a forty-nine-year-old attorney who works for the Justice Department, have been married twenty-three years. Like most couples, many of their arguments are about everyday events.

MARIA: *(annoyed)* You left the butter out again.
HECTOR: *(irritated)* Why are little things so important to you? Just put it back.

MARIA: *(softening her tone)* Things like that are important to me. Is that so bad?

HECTOR: *(calmer)* I guess not. Sorry I was so negative.

Notice the difference. Like Ted and Wendy, Hector and Maria tended to veer into escalation, but they quickly got back down while on the lower rungs. When escalation sequences are short-circuited, it is usually because one partner backs off and says something to de-escalate the argument, thus breaking the negative cycle. Often this takes the simple humility of choosing to soften your tone and put down your shield. Remember, "A gentle answer turns away wrath, but a harsh word stirs up anger" (Proverbs 15:1). Often a gentle answer is all it takes. That one verse, put into practice, would make the whole world a much better place to live.

Invalidation: Painful Put-Downs

Invalidation is a pattern in which one partner subtly or directly puts down the thoughts, feelings, or character of the other. It can take many forms. Here are two other conversations, one between Ted and Wendy and the other between Maria and Hector:

WENDY: *(very angrily)* You missed your doctor's appointment again! You are so irresponsible. I could see you dying and leaving me, just like your father.

TED: *(bruised)* Thanks a lot. You know I'm nothing like my father.

WENDY: He was a creep, and so are you.

TED: *(dripping with sarcasm)* I'm sorry. I forgot my good fortune to be married to such a paragon of responsibility. You can't even keep your purse organized.

WENDY: At least I am not obsessive about stupid little things.

MARIA: *(with a tear)* You know, I'm really frustrated by the hatchet job Bob did on my evaluation at work.

HECTOR: I don't think he was all that critical. I would be happy to have an evaluation as positive as that. Why don't you just give it to the Lord?

MARIA: *(with a sigh and turning away)* You don't get it. It upset me.

HECTOR: I think you're overreacting.

These examples are as different as night and day. With Ted and Wendy, you can feel the contempt seeping through. Long-time marital researcher John Gottman finds that contempt is one of the greatest destroyers of marriages. The argument has settled into an attack on character. Jesus taught strongly against such attacks on the character of another:

> But I tell you that anyone who is angry with his brother will be subject to judgment. Again, anyone who says to his brother, "Raca," is answerable to the Sanhedrin. But anyone who says, "You fool!" will be in danger of the fire of hell. (Matthew 5:22)

The translation note for the New International Version says that "Raca" is an Aramaic term of contempt. It's something like telling a person he or she is worthless or empty-headed (an airhead). So you have Jesus and tons of research saying that invalidation is not OK. It's very damaging.

Although Maria and Hector do not show the contempt displayed by Ted and Wendy, Hector is nevertheless subtly putting down Maria for the way she is feeling. He may even think that he is being constructive or trying to cheer her up by saying, "It's not so bad," and "give it over to the Lord." Nevertheless, Maria feels even more hurt now because he has said, in effect, that her feelings of sadness and frustration are inappropriate—worse, that she's not being spiritual enough.

The contemptuous invalidation displayed by Ted and Wendy in the first example is more obviously destructive than Hector's more subtle form of invalidation. But any kind of invalidation can set up barriers. Invalidation hurts. What couple can maintain the ability to be "naked and unashamed" when two people are putting each other down? As we will repeat in future chapters, you want to make it safe to connect in your relationship. We have a lot of strategies to help you do that.

Validation: An Antidote to Invalidation

In either of the conversations here, the couples would have done better if each partner had simply shown respect for the other by acknowledging his or her viewpoint. Note the difference in how these conversations could have gone:

WENDY: *(very angry)* I am very angry that you missed the doctor's appointment again. I worry about you being around for me in the future.

TED: *(soft)* It really upset you, didn't it?

WENDY: You bet. I want to know that you're going to be there for me, and when you miss an appointment that I'm anxious about, I worry about us.

TED: I understand. It makes you worried for us when I don't take care of myself.

MARIA: *(with a tear)* You know, I'm really frustrated by the hatchet job Bob did on my evaluation at work.

HECTOR: That must really tick you off.

MARIA: Yeah, it does. I worry about whether I'll be able to keep this job. What would we do?

HECTOR: I didn't know you were so worried about losing your job. Tell me more.

We have replayed the discussions with similar beginnings but very different endings. Now there is acceptance of feelings, respect for each other's character, and validation instead of invalidation. You don't have to agree with your partner to validate his or her feelings.

You Make Me Sick

Janice Kiecolt-Glaser of the Ohio State University College of Medicine has been studying the physical reactions people have to conflict in marriage. In her own and others' work, poorly handled marital conflict has negative effects on the functioning of the cardiovascular, immune, and endocrine systems. This seems to be especially true for women, but it can cause these problems for either partner in a relationship.

Do you want to live long and prosper? Look for ways to show your partner that you are concerned about how your relationship is doing. Try not to pull away from discussions when your partner is concerned. Actively respond to your partner as a teammate, not as an enemy. By doing so, you will be protecting both of you and your marriage. If you tend to be the one who pursues talking about issues, recognize that your partner is your teammate. If he or she pulls away at such times, consider that your partner may simply want to avoid arguing with you, not that he or she doesn't love you. Both of you need to commit to talking without fighting about important issues under your control.

Negative Interpretations: When Believing Is Seeing

Negative interpretations occur when' one partner consistently believes that the motives of the other are more negative than is really the case. This pattern makes any conflict or disagreement harder to deal with constructively. Margot and David have been married twelve years, and they are generally happy with their relationship. Yet their discussions have at times been plagued by a specific negative interpretation. Every December, they have trouble deciding whether to travel to her parents' home for the holidays. Margot believes that David dislikes her parents, but in fact, he is quite fond of them in his own way. She has this mistaken belief because of a few incidents early in the marriage that David has long forgotten. Here's how a typical discussion around their issue of holiday travel plans goes:

MARGOT: We should start looking into plane tickets to go visit my parents this holiday season.

DAVID: *(thinking about their budget problem)* I was wondering if we can really afford it this year.

MARGOT: *(in anger)* My parents are very important to me, even if you don't like them. I'm going to go.

DAVID: I would like to go, really I would. I just don't see how we can afford a thousand dollars in plane tickets and pay the bill for Joey's orthodontist.

MARGOT: You can't be honest and admit you just don't want to go, can you? Just admit it. You don't like my parents.

DAVID: There is nothing to admit. I enjoy visiting your parents. I'm thinking about money here, not your parents.

MARGOT: That's a convenient excuse. *(storms out of the room)*

Given that we know that David really does like to go to her parents, can you see how powerful her negative interpretation has become? He cannot penetrate it. What can he say or do to make a difference as long as her belief that he dislikes them is so strong? A great many studies show that humans are strongly biased to see what they already believe to be true. Researchers call this "confirmation bias," and it makes is really hard to realize when we are seeing things unfairly.

No Doubt, No Benefit

When stressed out, most people will give their mate (and everyone else) less benefit of the doubt. We are all quicker to react to frustration with anger and criticism when stressed. Stress leads to more of the Communication Danger Signs. That negativity, in turn, diminishes the happiness and closeness in your relationships. All kinds of stress can fit this pattern. One that has been studied particularly well is economic strain. When couples are under financial pressure—such as feeling that there is just not enough money coming in to pay the bills—the partners become more negative with each other, and that in turn damages marriages. Rand Conger, a sociologist now at UC Davis, and his colleagues have demonstrated this pattern conclusively in long-term studies of how stress impacts families. Just when you need to be most supportive of each other, stress can turn you against each other unless you work against this tendency.

Mind Reading

Negative interpretations are a good example of mind reading. You are mind reading when you assume you know what your partner is thinking or why he or she did something. When you mind-read positively, it tends not to cause any harm. But when your mind reading includes negative judgments about the thoughts and motives of the other, you may be in real trouble, both in your marriage and in your spiritual life. Paul directly warned against attempting to judge the thoughts and motives of others (1 Corinthians 4:5). Jesus also issued a stern warning about this tendency to look more for the flaws in others than in ourselves.

> Why do you look at the speck of sawdust in your brother's eye and pay no attention to the plank in your own eye? How can you say to your brother, "Brother, let me take the speck out of your eye," when you yourself fail to see the plank in your own eye? You hypocrite, first take the plank out of your eye, and then you will see clearly to remove the speck from your brother's eye.
> (Luke 6:41–42)

As you can see, we are strongly warned to be on guard for the tendency to view or judge others harshly. A marriage would truly be in terrible shape if either partner routinely and intentionally did things just to frustrate the other. But this is seldom the case. Much more frequently, the actions of our partners that annoy us are either well intended or done with no conscious intention at all.

Seeing Through Your Negative Interpretations

You may need to reconsider what you think is true about some of your partner's motives. Your negative interpretations are something you have to confront within yourself. Only you can control how you interpret your partner's behavior.

First, ask yourself if your own thinking might be overly negative about things your partner does or fails to do. Second—and this is hard—you must push yourself to look for evidence that is contrary to the negative interpretation you usually make. For example, if you believe that your partner is uncaring, you need to look for evidence to the contrary. Does she do some things for you that you like? Could it be that he does nice things because he cares enough to try to keep the relationship strong? Ask God to help you clear your vision.

Withdrawal and Avoidance: Hide and Seek

Withdrawal and **avoidance** are different manifestations of a pattern in which one partner shows an unwillingness to get into or stay with important discussions. *Withdrawal* can be as obvious as getting up and leaving the room or as subtle as "turning off" or "shutting down" during an argument. The withdrawer often tends to get quiet, look away, or agree quickly to his partner's suggestion just to end the conversation, with no real intention of following through. Avoidance reflects the same reluctance to get into certain discussions, with more emphasis on the attempt not to let the conversation happen in the first place.

Let's look at this pattern as played out in a discussion between Paula, a twenty-eight-year-old realtor, and Jeff, a thirty-two-year-old loan officer. (Guess how they met!) Married for three years, they have a two-year-old baby girl, Tanya, whom they adore. They were concerned that the tension in their relationship was starting to affect their daughter.

PAULA: When are we going to talk about how you are handling your anger?

JEFF: Can't this wait? I have to get these taxes done.

PAULA: I've brought this up at least five times already. No, it can't wait!

JEFF: *(tensing)* What's to talk about, anyway? It's none of your business.

PAULA: *(frustrated and looking right at Jeff)* Tanya is my business. I'm afraid that you may lose your temper and hurt her, and you won't do a single thing to learn how to deal better with your anger.

JEFF: *(turning away, looking out the window)* I love Tanya. There's no problem here. *(leaving the room as he talks)*

PAULA: *(very angry now; following Jeff into the next room)* You have to get some help. You can't just stick your head in the sand.

JEFF: I'm not going to discuss anything with you when you are like this.

PAULA: Like what? It doesn't matter if I am calm or frustrated—you won't talk to me about anything important. Tanya is having problems, and you have to face that.

JEFF: *(quiet, tense, fidgeting)*

PAULA: Well?

JEFF: *(going to closet and grabbing sweater)* I'm going out to get some peace and quiet.

PAULA: *(voice raised, angry)* Talk to me, now. I'm tired of you leaving when we are talking about something important.

JEFF: *(looking away from Paula, walking toward the door)* I'm not talking, you are; actually, you're yelling. See you later.

Many couples do this kind of dance when it comes to dealing with difficult issues. One partner *pursues* dealing with issues (Paula) and one *avoids* or *withdraws* from dealing with issues (Jeff). Although common, this scenario is very destructive to the relationship. As with the other patterns presented, it does not have to be this dramatic to mean that more problems are to come. Even subtle withdrawal is associated with increased risks of a marriage not making it.

Pursuing and Withdrawing Dynamics: The (Sometimes) Gender Dance

The *pursuer* is the one in the relationship who most often brings up issues for discussion or calls attention to the need to make a decision about something. The *withdrawer* is the person who tends to avoid these discussions or pulls away during them. Studies show that men are more likely to be in the withdrawing role, with women tending to pursue. However, there are many relationships where this pattern is reversed. And in some relationships, the partners switch these roles depending on the topic. Simply reverse the points we make here if the gender patterns are reversed between the two of you.

Why do men tend to withdraw? Some say it's because they are less interested in change, and that they pull away to avoid dealing with the issues. Therefore, for some, it may be a power move. That may be the case for some men (and women, too), but we believe that something else is happening much of the time: the one who withdraws tends to do so because it does not feel safe to stay in the argument—meaning that it's not emotionally safe. Or the withdrawer may even fear that the conflict will turn physical. (If you have concerns about physical conflict and aggression in your relationship, please see Appendix A, "Getting More Help with Serious Problems.")

When this pattern gets going, it tends to be very frustrating for both partners. When their partners withdraw, pursuers feel shut out and begin to feel that the withdrawer doesn't care about the relationship, figuring that a lack of talking equals a lack of caring. But that's usually a negative interpretation of what the withdrawer is doing—which has more to do with trying to stop the conflict than with not caring about the relationship. Likewise, withdrawers often complain that their pursuing partners get upset too much of the time, griping about this or that and picking fights, as if they want to fight. That is also a negative interpretation, because what pursuers really want is to stay connected and resolve issues.

Avoiding Withdrawal

If you are seeing this pattern in your relationship, keep in mind that it will likely get worse if you allow it to continue. That is because as pursuers push more, withdrawers pull back more. And as withdrawers pull back, pursuers push harder. Avoiding issues will only lead to greater problems.

One thing to try to do is to refrain from taking the most negative interpretation of what your partner does when he or she is either withdrawing or pursuing. Also realize that you are not independent of each other. It takes two to do this tango. Withdrawers are not likely to reduce avoidance unless pursuers pursue less or pursue more constructively and gently. Pursuers are going to find it hard to cut back on pursuing unless withdrawers deal more directly with the issues at hand. Do a better dance. We can teach you the steps.

When you and your mate are not handling differences well, your relationship begins to feel unsafe. When it's not emotionally safe to be around the very person you had wanted to be your best friend, real intimacy and a sense of connection die out. Then the barriers grow into loneliness and isolation—a far cry from being naked and unashamed. There's no lasting promise in a marriage thick with fig leaves. The exercises that follow are a first step toward protecting your relationship from these damaging patterns.

Doing Your Part

The first step in changing patterns is to understand your part in them. Write your answers to the following questions independently from your partner, using a separate piece of paper. When you have finished, we suggest that you share your perceptions. However, if this raises conflict, put off further discussion until you have read the next few chapters and have learned more about how to talk safely about tough topics.

Before getting into specific questions about the four Communication Danger Signs, ask yourself what typically happens when you have a conflict with your mate. Think about the patterns described in this chapter in answering this question: escalation, invalidation, negative interpretations, and withdrawal and avoidance.

Escalation

Escalation occurs when you say or do something negative and your partner responds negatively, and off you go into a real battle. In this snowball effect, the two of you become increasingly angry and hostile as the argument continues (for example, Proverbs 12:18, 15:1, 20:3, 29:11; Matthew 5:22).

1. How often do you think you escalate as a couple?
2. Do you get hostile with each other during escalation?
3. What or who usually brings an end to the fight? How does it usually end?
4. Does one or the other of you sometimes threaten to end the relationship when you're angry?
5. How do each of you feel when your arguments are escalating? Do you feel tense, anxious, scared, angry, or something else?

(continued)

Invalidation

Invalidation occurs when one partner subtly or directly puts down the thoughts, feelings, actions, or worth of the other. This is different from simply disagreeing with one's partner or not liking something he or she has done. Invalidation includes belittling or disregarding what is important to the partner, out of either insensitivity or outright contempt. The partner usually feels hurt, discounted, or unimportant (for example, Matthew 5:22; Ephesians 4:29; 1 Corinthians 13:5).

1. Do you often feel invalidated in your relationship? When and how does this happen?
2. What is the effect on you? How do you feel when this happens?
3. Do you often invalidate your partner? When and how does this happen? How do you feel when doing this?
4. What do you think the effect is on your partner? On the relationship? What are you trying to accomplish when you do this? Do you accomplish that goal?

Negative Interpretations

Negative interpretations occur when you interpret your spouse's behavior much more negatively than she or he intended (for example, Matthew 7:1–5; 1 Corinthians 13:6, 7). Your partner can do little to change negative interpretations that you hold. These questions will help you make this change, if you are willing to work at it.

1. Can you think of some areas where you consistently see your partner's behavior as negative? What are the advantages to you in making these negative interpretations?
2. Reflect on this awhile. Do you really think that your negative view of your partner's behavior is justified?
3. Are there some areas where you have a negative interpretation, but where you're open to considering that you may be missing evidence to the contrary?
4. List two issues where you're willing to push yourself to look for the possibility that your partner has more positive

motivations than you thought. Next, look for any evidence that is contrary to your negative interpretations.

Withdrawal and Avoidance

Men and women often deal quite differently with conflict in relationships. Males are more often prone to withdraw from discussing issues in the relationship, and women more prone to pursue. But keep in mind that it could be different for you. Perhaps neither of you tends to withdraw or to avoid issues—which is most often the best pattern. Withdrawal and avoidance just don't work well over time in relationships (Matthew 5:23, 24; Ephesians 4:25–27).

1. Is one of you more likely to be in the pursuer role? Is one of you more likely to be in the withdrawer role?
2. How does the withdrawer usually withdraw? How does the pursuer usually pursue? What happens then?
3. When are you most likely to fall into this pattern as a couple? What particular issues or situations bring out this pattern?
4. How are you affected by this pattern?
5. With some couples, one or both partners may both pursue or withdraw at different times. Is this true of your relationship? Why do you think this happens?

3

Asking God

Praying for Your Marriage

*Ask and it will be given to you; seek and you will
find; knock and the door will be opened to you.*
LUKE 11:9

We could have put this chapter anywhere in this book, but we
decided to put it here because we believe that praying wisely for
your mate and marriage will make it much more likely that the
rest of the book will have an impact in some powerful ways.

But you may not be ready to benefit fully from the message
of this chapter right now. Maybe yours is a marriage struggling
greatly with how to talk constructively and not lash out in arguments. If that's the case, you'll probably want to skip to Chapter
Five so you can begin to work on those issues first. After that, you
can come back to this and the other chapters that take our
methods a lot deeper. Others would argue that you have the best
chance of changing your outward patterns after you have been
asking God to change you on the inside. We are not going to
resolve that question for you. If you are not sure what to do, try
praying about it right now. And if you have no clear direction
from God otherwise, go ahead and dig into this chapter now.

What You Can Do

Great power and peace can come from praying regularly for your
mate and marriage. This chapter is focused on how you can, by

yourself, strengthen your marriage and spiritual life. This chapter is *not* about what the two of you are to practice together (we discuss praying together in Chapter Sixteen). This chapter is about something you—the individual—can do for your marriage through prayer.

Think of your marriage as a tree. Prayer for it nourishes it to keep its roots going deeper, its branches growing stronger, and its fruit becoming more abundant. Prayer will anchor your marriage in the everlasting promise of God's great love.

Why Pray for Your Mate and Marriage?

You are probably not skeptical about the idea of prayer, but you may need encouragement to see that God desires prayer, and means for it to make a difference. Or perhaps you just need a reminder that it is a wise thing to do. Let's look at a few biblical examples of people praying for others.

- Isaac prayed for his wife, Rebekah (Genesis 25:21).
- Moses prayed for his brother, Aaron (Deuteronomy 9:20).
- When concerned friends approached the prophet Jeremiah, he prayed for them (Jeremiah 42:4).
- Jesus Christ prayed for all his disciples and for us (John 17:9–26).
- The members of the early church came together to pray for one another (Acts 14:22–24).
- The apostle Paul asked for the prayer of the saints on his behalf (1 Thessalonians 5:25).
- The apostle James gave us all kinds of reasons to pray for one another, such as for healing (James 5:13–16).

We should pray for many people, of course, but who could pray more wisely and more deeply for your mate than you? And who could pray better than you about how you treat your mate?

Peyton and Britta have been married fourteen years, and life has been good. Most things have turned out well for them. They tend to make good decisions together when it matters, rather than letting things slide and just happen. When their first child, Ingrid, was born, they decided together that Britta would shift to half-time at her job as a bank teller. That has worked out pretty well, but with the arrival of twins—Angela and Berger—life got more challenging.

Many couples struggle somewhat through the early years of child rearing. There are so many extra tasks and challenges, even when everything is going smoothly. Sleep becomes more difficult, and tempers can get shorter. Britta and Peyton started to argue more, saying some nasty things sometimes. They were growing apart, and both of them were aware of it.

Without either knowing what the other was doing, each decided to start praying more intently and daily for their marriage. Both approached this with genuine humility, too. Peyton started praying about a number of things, but two really stood out. First, he started consciously thanking God for the good things in their relationship. This began to change his attitude about the stress and strain of an overly busy family life. He began to appreciate Britta more, and that led to his making more regular comments to her about how much he appreciated her and all she was doing. He got back in touch with what was special about their relationship.

Second, Peyton prayed specifically that God would make him aware of ways and times he was being harsh or negative in his views of Britta's behavior and motivations (see the discussion of negative interpretations in Chapter Two). Here's the deal on this one: we believe that if you pray for God to show you where and how you are being a doofus (that's a technical term) with your mate, He is going to be really pleased to honor that prayer. Note that Peyton wasn't praying for God to show Britta all her faults. He was praying instead for God to show him his own faults and blind spots—at least as many as he could handle at the time.

Peyton started to be more aware of the times he was unkind and even nasty with Britta. For example, on days when he had worked the hardest, he'd come home and be short with everyone, which especially meant with Britta. This went over poorly. Britta would be pretty wiped out herself, and here came the children, doing what young children do, needing time and attention and care. Peyton started checking his attitude at the door and asking Britta how her day had been. He started to look for at least one thing he could do in the evening that he otherwise might not do to make the family routine run more smoothly.

Britta was praying, too. What resonated most for her was a desire for things to go well or for good things to happen to her husband through the day. In addition to praying for him, she also started to text him several times a day just to say she was thinking of him. That little act reminded him that she cared deeply for him.

What you can see in this example is that both Britta and Peyton were being changed by their praying. God was using it to help each to boost the emotional safety in their marriage. This regenerated their sense of being teammates. Their marriage was stronger, and both regained the joy that they were together.

Although you won't know exactly where daily prayer for your partner and your marriage will take you, it is sure to help you grow and change. When you pray for your partner, you see him or her in a different way. You are reminded that your partner is a child of God, part of His wondrous creation, and that he or she, just like you, is a frail human being. Praying for your partner requires you to think about his or her needs, hopes, struggles, and shortcomings, not with a view to be critical but with a sincere desire to see God work in your partner's life. It helps you gain a new perspective about your partner, and that can reignite deeper intimacy and passion in your marriage.

Praying daily for your relationship will help deepen your trust in God and allow Him to lead your marriage to the place He wants it to go. As you see God work in your marriage, and begin to view it the way He wants you to see it, you will gain a new appreciation for ways you need His power in your life.

You may find that going deeper in praying for your mate and marriage leads to many good things. Prayer can help you find new ways to love or to show love. It can help you focus God's love, acting through you, into your mate's life. Prayer can soothe an angry heart. It can heal. Prayer is a key way to see and support your mate's point of view. It can strengthen your awareness of God's care for you, your mate, and your marriage.

Enough said on why to pray. Next, let's talk a bit about how *not* to pray for your mate and marriage.

How Not to Pray for Your Mate

It is very easy to focus prayer on requests asking God to change your mate rather than asking God to change you. Don't get us wrong—there may be many changes God wants to make in your mate. But we are encouraging you to pray for blessings for your mate and changes in yourself. Consider praying, "Lord, change my mate's partner!" There is nothing wrong with praying that your mate would be improved, but we think more time and energy should go into how God can use you to strengthen your marriage.

Praying for your mate is especially tricky when you are upset. For example, when angry with our mate, it's very easy to fall into wanting God to judge him or her and to justify ourselves. We want God to take sides—our side, in fact. But His love transcends our judgments and heals our divisions. His love is a bridge, not a barrier. Focus your prayer on what the Lord can do in and through you from the depths of His love.

Here are some examples of prayers that are off track. Prayers like these could be the right thing to pray at times, but only if one's motivation is really open and genuine. Too often, one's motives are just not going to be that pure.

- "Lord, help her to see why I am right and where she is wrong in how we are handling this issue."
- "Lord, I commit him to you. Only you can help him see his problems clearly so he can change and be the husband you want him to be."
- "Lord, show her how she can follow you more fully, and how she can do a better job meeting my needs."
- "Lord, if he will not change, please discipline him and force him to change. Please cause him to undergo whatever pain and consequences are needed to help him seek you."

Be cautious in how you pray about your partner and what you want to have happen in your relationship. Let's look at a number of principles for praying wisely and effectively for your marriage.

How to Pray Well

One of the surest ways to pray more effectively is to focus on asking God to change you, not your mate. Here are some short prayers that counter the tendency we can have to pray for the wrong things in our relationships:

- "Dear Jesus, I ask you to help me to see where I've let my wife down and how I can be more fully supportive of her."
- "Lord, please make our marriage all you want it to be. Change me and guide me in being part of the change you want to bring to our home."
- "Dear God, thank you so much for our family. Help me to appreciate what we have and to tell my husband more often what I appreciate about him."
- "Father God, help us both to be more sensitive, less reactive, and more gentle with each other. Use me to be make constructive changes that will bless my mate and our marriage."

You get the idea. We don't know how exactly God would lead you in praying for your marriage, but we believe that if you pray with an attitude of humility and a desire to love your partner, God will help you. Not always in the way or the time frame that you think is best, but somehow He will come along beside you.

In the rest of this chapter, we focus on some very specific ideas about how you can pray more meaningfully for your marriage.

Praying Thankfully

> *Be joyful always; pray continually; give thanks in all circumstances, for this is God's will for you in Christ Jesus.*
> 1 THESSALONIANS 5:16, 17, 18

We are reminded throughout scripture to give thanks. Why not give thanks for your mate? This is clearly something that should please God because He delights in thankfulness. We believe that you will be blessed for expressing gratitude to Him for your marriage.

Being thankful as you pray for your marriage is going to change you. You are probably taking some of the good things in your marriage for granted. No marriage is perfect, but the odds are that there are many good things in your marriage and in your mate that you are not regularly aware of. You forget—we all do. There are many ways your life would be worse if your mate didn't have some of the characteristics that he or she has and didn't do some of the things that she or he does. Expressing thanks helps you be aware of these things about your mate.

You can even give thanks for the things that you are not wild about in your mate or in how your marriage is going. God may be using some of those things to knock off some of your own rough edges. Giving thanks to God is an expression of faith that the Lord understands you and what is happening in your marriage, and that He can work through the hard parts to bless your life and the life of your mate. He can work through you, even through your weaknesses, to bless him or her. And your mate's being blessed is pretty likely to bring more joy to you than your own being blessed. God is into giving to us and transforming us, and if expressing more thanks to Him for your mate leads you to give more of yourself, you are likely to experience more joy and peace. Remember, "it is more blessed to give than receive."

In the example given earlier, Peyton decided to give thanks for Britta. This was a big part of how his attitude and actions toward her changed to produce deep healing and renewed strength in their marriage.

The Power of Gratitude

In recent years, there has been a lot of solid research on thankfulness or, as researchers often call it, gratitude. This is part of a general explosion of research on things related to positive thoughts and feelings and how they impact the quality of emotional and physical life. A number of studies show that being grateful—and expressing it—is associated with all sorts of positive impacts, such as having a greater sense of well-being and an increase in willingness to help others. In fact, thankfulness in the heart and in action boosts all sorts of positive emotions in ways that are believed to broaden one's ability to cope creatively with challenges in life.

Two researchers who have conducted a lot of research in this area are Robert Emmons and Michael McCullough. In one of their studies, published in 2003, they had a group of participants practice gratefulness by listing things they were grateful for each week for ten weeks. Their research revealed that people who intentionally boosted their awareness of things to be grateful for had an increase in overall positive emotions.

Being more grateful can directly improve relationships. McCullough, Emmons, and their colleagues (Kilpatrick and Larson) have suggested that gratitude primes one to give to others, suggesting that gratitude is a moral motivator. Increases in gratitude are associated with doing more for others and, as a colleague of ours, Erica Ragan, suggested, motivate people to "pay it forward."

Do you see why the Bible might stress thankfulness? Thankfulness is something you can decide to increase in your life, and in doing so, you will likely end up acting more like Jesus in giving to others—including your mate. What we want you to think about here is how you can combine the power of prayer with the power of thankfulness by spending some regular time prayerfully thanking God for your mate. And it won't hurt to tell your mate some of the things you are thankful for about him or her, either!

Praying for Wisdom

We are invited in James 1:5 to ask God for wisdom. In fact, James said that God gives "generously without finding fault" when we do. That seems to mean that God is certainly not going to find fault with you for asking for direction out of humility. Asking for wisdom is wise, and by doing so, you can become wiser still.

Are you ever confused by what's going on in your marriage or how to best respond to your mate? You can try to ignore your confusion or what is going on in your marriage, but that's not going to turn out very well. If you are determined to start praying more for your mate and your marriage, include regular requests for wisdom and insight about what you should do to be a better mate or how to understand what is going on between you and your spouse. God loves this kind of prayer because you are expressing your willingness to recognize your weaknesses and to rely on Him to lead and enable you.

Praying About Temptation

One of the things you can decide to pray about is protection from temptation. This amounts to praying for the protection of your marriage. When the disciples asked Jesus to teach them how to pray, his model prayer included the phrase, "lead us not into temptation" (Matthew 6:13). That's pretty direct.

Let's start with the obvious temptations related to marriage. Are you ever attracted to people other than your mate? We don't mean that you simply notice others who are attractive. Everyone does that, of course. We are referring to when you start to think seriously about "what ifs" and what it might be like to be with someone else. Perhaps there is a specific person you are tempted to think about in this way. Or perhaps you are tempted to let your thoughts dwell on a type of person you might want to be with. Maybe pornography is a temptation for you. Just on the sexual level alone, there are many kinds of temptations that affect a lot of people. This must become a matter of prayer.

When you ask God to help you with temptation, you are acknowledging that the temptation exists, owning up to it with God and with yourself, rather than pretending it's not there and isn't affecting anything. Prayer is an important starting point for resisting temptation.

Temptation comes in all shapes and sizes. What other things tempt you that are not good for your marriage? If you know what path you should be on, any area of your life that encourages you to stray from that path is temptation. Maybe you are tempted to spend most of your free time in an optional activity that is otherwise a fine thing to do (for example, golf, exercise, even ministry), but you realize that if you spend more and more time in that activity, there is no time left for your marriage. Maybe you have to work a lot of hours, but if you admit it to yourself, you are tempted to work more than you actually have to, neglecting the time and attention you could give to your spouse.

If you are not sure what marriage-diminishing temptations are affecting you, ask God to show you. That's like asking for wisdom and for strength to resist the temptation at the same time. Pretty efficient praying!

Prayer, Commitment, and Relationship Satisfaction

There is a growing field of research into prayer, including prayer within marriage. Scott Stanley (coauthor of this book) has worked with a number of colleagues who have been leading the field in doing conceptual and research work in this area. Those researchers include Steven Beach, Frank Fincham, Nathan Lambert, and Scott Braithwaite. They come from all sorts of backgrounds in their beliefs and thinking about prayer. What unites them in their work is the knowledge that most people pray, that marriage is the most important relationship in the lifetime of most individuals, and that prayer can make a difference in people's lives.

In research published in 2008, Fincham, Beach, Lambert, Stillman, and Braithwaite found that prayer for one's partner was associated with relationship satisfaction in the future. Prayer had effects on relationships above and beyond various other positive and negative behaviors in the relationships. So, for example, prayer was associated with more satisfaction over time even after controlling for other things that matter in a relationship, such as good communication.

These researchers went on to show that one of the ways prayer influenced relationship happiness over time was through reinforcing commitment. Praying for one's partner strengthened commitment, which in turn made for greater happiness in relationships.

In another study headed up by Steven Beach, Tera Hurt, and their colleagues, couples took a workshop based on the
(continued)

content of the earlier edition of this book. Some of the workshops included an additional focus on prayer for one's mate and marriage. (Both of these groups did better, over time, on marital quality than those who did not attend the workshops.) The couples in the workshops with the strong prayer emphasis responded very well to teaching about prayer. Furthermore, there was an edge in marital quality, over time, for those in that workshop. This was especially true for wives' ratings of marital quality. In such studies, it's hard to know exactly what specific things change to bring the positive results. But it should not be hard to imagine that it's going to be a good thing when both partners are praying for their mate and marriage.

It is probably sufficient for you to know that prayer for your marriage is a good idea because praying for others is encouraged throughout the Bible. But we thought you'd also like to know that research backs up the idea that prayer for your marriage is a pretty smart thing to do.

Praying for Forgiveness

Have you treated each other honorably and respectfully through all your time together? There are some couples for whom the answer is pretty close to "Yes, we have." But that's probably pretty rare. Most of even the best of marriages have gone through tough times when one or both partners were not at their best. Things have been said or done that hurt and that left emotional wounds.

It would clearly be valuable to pray that God would forgive you for the ways you've fallen short in your marriage. As with so many other aspects of prayer, asking the Lord to forgive you for your sins in your marriage is an expression of faith and humility. If you see yourself as nearly perfect and believe you've been the nearly ideal mate for your spouse, you'll have trouble praying for forgiveness.

One word of caution: some people are so hard on themselves that they see far more ways they have fallen short in their marriage than either their mate or God sees. If you tend to have strong feelings of guilt and are pretty hard on yourself, we'd like to suggest that you ask God (and a close friend or pastor) to help you be reasonable in how you seek forgiveness for things you've said, done, or not done in your marriage.

Most people will benefit (as will their marriages) from asking God for help in being forgiving toward their mates. The degree to which you hold your mate's flaws and past actions against him or her is the degree to which your marriage is going to be limited into the future. As you'll see in Chapter Fifteen, "Forgiveness and Restoration," we're not talking about excusing the inexcusable or giving up on the need for your partner to be more responsible in some way. But what we are suggesting is that many people continue to hold things against their partner and, in doing so, damage their marriage further.

What do some people hold against their spouse that they need to ask God for grace to forgive? The list is potentially endless, and your list would be different from what others store up against their mate, but here are a few possibilities:

- Being messy
- Being out of shape
- Leaving you alone at a time when you really needed help
- Not always following through on commitments or family obligations
- Spending too much time with his or her friends
- Accidentally breaking something very valuable to you
- Doing so much to help others that there is little left over for the family
- Not being fully involved spiritually, or not being involved at all
- Being too much involved in church, Bible study, and so on
- Being unsupportive of you in something you really want to do in life
- Being prone to criticize
- Not staying focused in conversations,
- Being incapable of parallel parking (Just checking that you are reading this!)
- Yelling at you for spending time with your friends
- Being a poor cook
- Being less interested (or too interested) in sex
- Talking with his or her mouth full at dinner

- Interrupting during conversations
- Being the life of the party or being dull and withdrawn at a party
- Not liking to travel or wanting to travel all the time
- Having had an affair in the past
- Not liking the same music
- Failing to appreciate the wonder of your collection of . . .

That list long enough? We could go on and on, and so could you. Note that this list includes some things that are clearly significant transgressions. Most things on the list are ways in which your partner isn't who you wished they would be. We're suggesting that you spend some time asking God to help you forgive your partner both for things they have actually done wrong and also for missing the mark in not being the ideal mate you thought they would be.

In Chapter Fifteen, we'll talk more about forgiveness, consequences, and responsibility, including the differences between forgiveness and reconciliation. For now we are assuming that you are not in an abusive relationship. We are urging you to ask the Lord to give you a more forgiving spirit toward your mate so that you can more fully accept him or her. This kind of grace-based forgiveness and acceptance are essential in making it safe to stay connected.

Praying for Better Communication

Pray for God to help you have good communication in your marriage. Much of this book has to do with negative patterns of communication, better ways to communicate, and strategies for effectively dealing with difficult issues. Here, our point is simply this: ask the Lord to help you keep it emotionally safe in your marriage, or, as we'll say in the next chapter, make it safe to connect. Ask Him to help you listen carefully and completely to your mate about his or her day-to-day interests and concerns. Pray also for the ability to speak the truth in loving ways about the concerns that are on your own heart.

Regina and Gil were going through some very tough times in their thirty-fourth year of marriage. The children were grown and out of the home, and this left the couple somewhat at a loss for how to deal with each other. They never were great at communicating, but the responsibilities of life and the mutual joy of raising their children smoothed over all the rough spots in their relationship.

Now that they had more time alone, their communication difficulties came to the surface. Gil had trouble listening to Regina when she'd talk about anything that was bothering her and especially when she talked about problems that had to do with him. He believed that she was not a generally negative person, so he didn't think she was being critical of him. But that didn't mean he knew how to handle her comments well. For example, one day she decided to tell him that it had upset her the night before, when they were with her parents, that he took off right after dinner to watch television in another room. She had been embarrassed, and she'd wished he'd stuck around to pay attention to what they were sharing about the important trip her parents were planning.

The more Gil thought about it, the more he realized that Regina was right. He was not a great listener, to her or to anyone else, for that matter. Gil decided to pray about this. He started to ask God to help him be a better listener. He prayed pretty specifically, too. He prayed for better attention during conversations. He prayed for awareness of when the opportunity was right in front of him to listen better, especially to Regina. He prayed for increased ability to understand his wife when she was talking about something with feelings involved. He prayed that he'd be able to stop shutting down and pulling away.

And it worked. His prayers became quite regular about this very specific thing. He had ways to remind himself to keep at it. In asking God to help him in this, and in sticking to it, Gil changed. Actually, God changed him. Gil started noticing when listening would really mean something to Regina. She noticed it too, although she had no idea where it was coming from. She wasn't going to second-guess what seemed to her a wonderful transformation. She was thrilled, and he could tell. That felt good because he really did love her, and he could see her opening up right before him, thanks to the answers to his prayers and his willingness to change.

Moving Forward

You either believe that prayer makes a difference or you do not. If you are skeptical, give it a try. You could even start by asking God to help you overcome your skepticism about prayer—and perhaps about God Himself.

Maybe you have no difficulty believing in the power of prayer, but you might still have trouble doing it. What do you need to do to help yourself give this some serious effort? And what do you need to do to stay at it? We do not know your answers to those questions. We just know they are good questions.

Persistence is important. Jesus taught His disciples to pray without giving up, to be committed to prayer for things that mattered (Luke 18:1–8). The apostle Paul told the members of the church at Thessalonica to pray continuously (1 Thessalonians 5:17). One of our favorite parables is the one Jesus told to drive home the importance of persistent prayer.

> . Then Jesus told his disciples a parable to show them that they should always pray and not give up. He said: "In a certain town there was a judge who neither feared God nor cared about men. And there was a widow in that town who kept coming to him with the plea, 'Grant me justice against my adversary.' For some time he refused. But finally he said to himself, 'Even though I don't fear God or care about men, yet because this widow keeps bothering me, I will see that she gets justice, so that she won't eventually wear me out with her coming!'" And the Lord said, "Listen to what the unjust judge says. And will not God bring about justice for his chosen ones, who cry out to him day and night? Will he keep putting them off?" (Luke 18:1–8)

This is such a great passage. In it, God welcomes you to persist in crying out to Him—or in whispering if you need to. He's better than the judge who needed to be pestered. He's waiting and eager to hear when you come to Him. He even invites you to come boldly into His very throne room of grace (Hebrews 4:16). Go ahead and go for it. He's up all night, open all day, and He loves you.

Doing Your Part

To help you deepen your prayers for your marriage, we are adapting what follows from the first activities in a prayer journal we created just to help couples pray for their marriages. It is called *Like a Tree Planted by the Water.* (Appendix B will tell you how to get it.) There are twelve sections, the first of which we have included here. We recommend that you think through each of the following paragraphs for a day or two and then move on to the next one. It will get you started in praying seriously for your marriage.

As you begin to pray for your mate, think about the first line of the Lord's Prayer: "Our Father who is in heaven, Hallowed be Your name," as well as Psalm 127:1.

Take out a piece of paper and write down a few sentences about how praising God through prayer can help your marriage.

Think about Hosea 6:3, along with these words: "your kingdom come, your will be done on earth as it is in heaven." As you pray for your mate today, ask God to make known His will for your life and your marriage, now and over time. Write down a few ideas about where you think God is leading you.

Be still for a moment. Think about Psalm 34:10 and this line from the Lord's Prayer: "Give us this day our daily bread." As you pray for your mate today, ask God to give you clarity about what your mate's true needs are. Write down three things that you think your mate needs, and pray about those things.

As you pray for your mate today, quiet your mind so that you can focus on this phrase: "And forgive us our debts, as we also have forgiven our debtors." How do you see, or feel about, forgiveness being included in your prayers for your marriage and your mate?

In the Lord's Prayer, Jesus tells his followers to pray: "And do not lead us into temptation, but deliver us from evil." In Proverbs 3:5–6, God promises to guide us toward the right track if we trust in Him. Keep these ideas in mind as you pray for your marriage. Are there ways that you think you are

(continued)

susceptible to temptation? Don't write anything down, but think and pray about what comes to mind. Ask God for wisdom and help.

Consider the final words of the Lord's Prayer: "For Yours is the kingdom and the power and the glory forever." As you pray for your mate today, ask God to show you how your marriage can be used to advance His kingdom. How can He show His power and glory to both of you as well as to others? Meditate on ways your marriage fits into God's larger plan for His kingdom here on earth.

There are also sample prayers in the journal to help you get started. They are not something to memorize or build into a ritual of some sort. They are just solid prayers that can give you some examples of how you can pray for your mate and marriage. Here's one example:

> Dear Lord, please help me seek and find opportunities to express my love and show understanding to my mate. Help me find ways both small and large to express a love that is rooted in you. I know that nothing is too small for you to notice or too large for you to accomplish. Help me see the moments and the ways to shine for you and display your loving nature—even when I know you are the only one who is watching. Please grant me the great gift of being a vehicle of your love and understanding for my mate. Help me to act on concrete ways to express love to my mate. Help make our marriage an example of warmth, acceptance, and respect in a cold world.

Try writing out your own prayer that asks God to help you show love to your mate.

4

We Found Your Keys

If it is possible, as far as it depends on you, live at peace with everyone.
ROMANS 12:18

This book has many strategies for building and keeping a strong and happy marriage, and this chapter is about three keys that will help you remember the book's most important principles. We will also suggest a couple of ground rules that can make a real difference if you use them.

Three Keys

These key principles can help guide you whenever you are not sure about what to do. If you apply them, you will seldom go wrong. They are powerful, simple, and easy to remember.

1. Decide don't slide.
2. Do your part.
3. Make it safe to connect.

Key 1: Decide Don't Slide

This principle is a result of research on commitment and relationship transitions conducted by coauthor Scott Stanley at the University of Denver with colleagues Galena Rhoades and Howard Markman. Stanley and his colleagues believe that couples form their relationships these days by "sliding" through all sorts of transitions without even realizing what they are doing, much less talking about it. For example, many couples now cohabit before marriage even though study after study shows that cohabitation doesn't have the benefits people think it does. Most people who live together before marriage start off doing so without so much as a serious talk about what it will mean. They just slide into it—often gradually, not realizing that living together will make it a lot harder for them to break up if they decide later on that the relationship is not working out. This happens before they actually decide whether they want to be with each other for a lifetime. That's where the phrase sliding vs. deciding® originated.

These days, couples are making all kinds of important, potentially life-altering changes, such as moving in together, without clearly choosing to make them. This matters because commitments are, at the foundation, decisions. Commitment is making a choice to give up other choices. Sliding now rules the day in how relationships develop, and this probably undermines the solidity of the commitment many couples will make later on. In the rest of this book, we will use the concept of sliding versus deciding more broadly. The principle applies to all sorts of important moments and issues in a relationship.

Strive to thoughtfully decide about the things that matter. When you're taking a journey, it's necessary to make a clear decision about where you want to end up, instead of just driving around hoping to eventually end up somewhere you like. Sliding through—just letting things happen—is fine in noncrucial situations. For example, if you like the evening's routine together, just letting things slide will usually work out just fine. But when something important is at stake, make a decision.

Living Together Before Marriage

Lots of people wonder if they should live together before they get married. Traditional Christian beliefs have long held that couples should marry before living together. Obviously, the question would not even have been raised in prior generations, but we know that couples are much more likely to do so now.

What does the research show? Does cohabiting before marriage improve the odds of marital success? Coauthor Scott Stanley, along with colleagues Galena Rhoades and Howard Markman at the University of Denver, have conducted a lot of research in this area, and there are several decades of studies available across the entire field. It comes as a surprise to most people that there is almost no evidence that couples who live together before marriage tend to have better marriages. In fact, over the past few decades, most studies in this area have shown just the opposite—that living together is associated with less happiness in marriage and greater odds of divorcing. Stanley, Rhoades, and Markman have repeatedly shown that the risks are greatest for those who live together *prior to* being engaged.

When so many people believe that living together before marriage will improve their odds, how can it be that studies do not show this great benefit? People miss a very important detail. Living together makes it harder to break up—harder to break up compared to dating, that is. Sure, many cohabiting couples do break up. In fact, couples who cohabit are increasingly likely not to marry when it used to be that cohabitation was almost always a prelude to marriage.

Stanley and his colleagues believe that the inertia of cohabiting leads some couples (who otherwise would have broken up and moved on to a better-matched mate) to marry or at least remain together far longer than they otherwise would have. For many, this also means having children together even though the relationship does not have a strong foundation of commitment. Inertia is a powerful explanation for why the practice of living together before marriage does not demonstrate the benefits that people expect. It has some serious risks many people do not see until it's too late.

The fact that most couples who live together outside of marriage slide into doing so adds to the risk. In fact, research by Wendy Manning and Pamela Smock and the work of Stanley and colleagues shows that most cohabiting couples did not talk

(*continued*)

about the implications of living together beforehand. More than half just sort of slid into it. Yet commitment is all about clearly choosing a path based on free will; it is not something formed on the basis of transitions without decisions.

If you have not yet married and you want to assess whether your relationship really has what it takes, why not choose a way to inform your decision that doesn't make it harder to break up? For example, take a workshop for couples or go carefully through Chapter Nine, which discusses expectations. Those are the type of activities that can help you decide if you are right for each other without your running the risk of getting stuck in a relationship you might end up wanting to leave.

As you read this, some of you who are married may be thinking, "Uh-oh. We lived together before marriage. Are we at greater risk because we did?" We don't know, and very likely you will never be sure either. What we do know is that you picked up this book and are reading it. You clearly care about protecting your marriage and keeping your promise to your partner. Our advice is pretty simple: even if you slid all the way to this point in your lives together, it's not too late to start making decisions. It's not too late to decide to make your marriage all it can be.

Decisions take effort, energy, and teamwork. Do you need to decide where you will live in terms of the best work options? Are there major transitions coming up in your children's lives? What about how you manage money? Who does what around the house? How do you treat each other when you are upset? Do you just let things slide and let whatever happens just happen? Making a thoughtful decision supports a stronger commitment to follow through on whatever has been chosen.

You will see that we refer to sliding a lot throughout this book. We want you to recognize not only the value of making key decisions at the right moments but also all the ways in marriage that it's easy to let things slide, where sliding does not make for very good outcomes. For example, in Chapter Two, we described all sorts of negative patterns that are very easy to slide into. You can "do conflict" differently. Where it matters, don't slide—decide to take control of your issues rather than letting them control you.

Key 2: Do Your Part

You are headed for trouble if you focus on your partner as the source of your problems. Your partner obviously plays a role in your marriage. But you have no control over what he or she does. You do, however, have control over what you do to keep your marriage on track. We're asking you to think about what *you* contribute to your marriage rather than what you get out of it or what your partner does.

This means that when conflicts arise, for instance, or when you perceive your partner as being unfair, you take the responsibility to do the most constructive thing you can do, as opposed to blaming your partner. Far too often, when people believe that their partner is doing something hurtful or unfair, they feel relieved of their own responsibility to be the best partner they can be. Don't wait for your relationship to feel as though it's 50-50. We're here to tell you that you need to hold up your end of the relationship even when you think your partner isn't doing his or her share. (The major exception to this is if there is ongoing victimization of one partner by the other. That usually calls for strong actions of a different sort. See the section on domestic violence in Appendix A, "Getting More Help with Serious Problems.")

Take responsibility for what you say. If what you are about to say to your mate can pass the standard given to us by the apostle Paul, you are in great shape:

> Do not let any unwholesome talk come out of your mouths, but only what is helpful for building others up according to their needs, that it may benefit those who listen. (Ephesians 4:29)

You might have just thought to yourself, "You have got to be kidding me!" Rest assured, we doubt that Paul's point was that we need to always be saying something serious and meaningful, but we do think he meant that our goal should be to speak in ways that will bless others. And we think that's especially applicable between you and your mate. Handling issues well sometimes comes down to an act of obedience to the Lord. You can make a choice to "edit out" your negative responses and take control of the things you say and the way you say them. This goes back to a key point of Chapter One: most relationships can withstand only so much negative interaction. All the nasty stuff makes it next to impossible to be naked and unashamed. It pushes us toward the fig leaves, if not fig-leaf parkas. Jesus Christ, the apostles, Solomon, David, and many others all gave very significant warnings about the destructiveness of certain ways of treating others. We will all blow it sometimes. But if you really strive to limit the "reckless words that pierce like a sword," you will create a climate that fosters openness and closeness in your marriage.

You are already doing a lot to foster intimacy by reading this book and trying some of the things we recommend. In addition, it is important to recognize your partner's efforts to communicate well. Your encouragement can go a long way in keeping both of your efforts on track. For example, you can give your mate positive feedback when you think he or she is trying to bring up an issue constructively. Saying little things like "It really helped me the way you brought that up" or "Thank you for taking the time to listen to what I was upset about" is doing your part to make it easier for your mate to do his or her part.

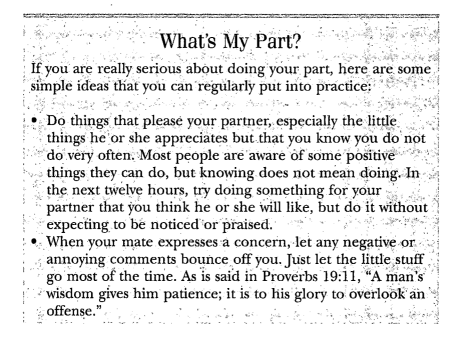

What's My Part?

If you are really serious about doing your part, here are some simple ideas that you can regularly put into practice:

- Do things that please your partner, especially the little things he or she appreciates but that you know you do not do very often. Most people are aware of some positive things they can do, but knowing does not mean doing. In the next twelve hours, try doing something for your partner that you think he or she will like, but do it without expecting to be noticed or praised.
- When your mate expresses a concern, let any negative or annoying comments bounce off you. Just let the little stuff go most of the time. As is said in Proverbs 19:11, "A man's wisdom gives him patience; it is to his glory to overlook an offense."

- When you have concerns of your own, bring them up without any of those little digs that might trigger your mate to become defensive. And bring them up at a time when you are both calm and can give attention to them constructively.
- Take good care of yourself physically. When your health is the best it can be—at least to the degree that this is under your control—you will be giving your best self to your partner.
- Manage your own stress level. Those who do so are going to find it much easier to manage the Communication Danger Signs.
- Be the best you can be as a person. Take responsibility for staying mentally healthy and growing spiritually. Your relationship with your mate is strongly connected to the quality of your relationship with God.

One last word on doing your part: people sometimes think they can't bring their behavior under better control until they first understand it. Although it can be beneficial to have insights into why you and your partner do some of what you do, you don't have to have it all figured out make important changes. If you're waiting for more insight and are not getting after doing what you can choose to do today to make a difference, you are not being wise. Actually, that's far less than wise. It's foolish. Start doing what you know is right or beneficial as soon as you can. The point is to take personal responsibility to do your part.

Key 3: Make It Safe to Connect

We began with Adam and Eve in Chapter One because that's where a biblical understanding of marriage begins. The Genesis phrase "naked and unashamed" conveys the deepest desire of the heart: to be loved and accepted for who one is, warts and all. When we say "safe," we are referring to how you talk to one another and the emotional tone you cultivate when together. Throughout the rest of this book, we will focus on keeping your relationship emotionally safe, especially when dealing with conflict. All too often, couples in counseling have told us that being together is like walking on eggshells, saying, "I can't be myself." When you are confident that you can do something to handle disagreements more skillfully, you are better able to relax and be yourself, opening the doors to emotional and physical intimacy.

One of the clearest findings in research on marriage is that the ways couples handle conflict are strongly related to how they will do in the future. Because conflicts are a common and expected part of relationships, many couples think that it's their differences that cause the greatest problems in their marriage. Strong differences in backgrounds and viewpoints do make conflicts more likely. But more than thirty years of research tell us that success in marriage is about how partners handle the differences they have, and not just the nature of the differences they have. Differences can be part of what draws two people together and also part of what makes it difficult for them to get along once they are together. Some differences, such as those in core spiritual beliefs, can be especially tricky to handle well. Whatever your differences, the part you have the most control over is how you keep it emotionally safe.

Ground Rules

In addition to the three keys, we want to introduce two ground rules that we believe can help you enact the three keys when it comes to protecting your marriage from conflict. The concept of ground rules comes from baseball. The idea is that each field where professional baseball is played has its own quirks, such as a wall that is higher here or further out there, or the way the stands are shaped. Because of its idiosyncrasies, each field has its own ground rules that apply to how things will be handled on that field. Using rules that add to the peace and harmony of your home is a great example of deciding rather than sliding.

There are a number of rules you could make about the ways things will be handled on your home field. The two we present here are among the most crucial for many couples to attempt to live out.

Ground Rule 1

When conflict is escalating, we will call a "Time Out" and either try to continue to talk more constructively or agree to talk later, after things have calmed down.

If we could get every couple to agree to one change in how they relate, this would be it. It's that important. This one simple rule on its own can protect relationships. Why? Because, as Solomon wrote, "A fool gives full vent to his anger" (Proverbs 29:11). Scripture clearly teaches us that escalating and venting at one another are foolish and harmful. Furthermore, research on marital health, mental health, and physiological health simply does not support the idea that "letting it all hang out" is healthy. In fact, careless venting is deadly for your relationship.

Feel Better Now? Thoughts on Blowing Off Steam

Many people believe that getting one's anger out—catharsis, it is often called—is good for the mind, body, and one's relationships. Wrong, wrong, and, well, wrong.

Screaming, punching something (like a pillow), or otherwise letting out all that negative energy is believed to work, but it doesn't. As Lilienfeld, Lynn, Ruscio, and Beyerstein point out in their book *50 Great Myths of Popular Psychology*, research just does not support this idea. There are also many studies showing that venting damages one's health. As we point out throughout this book, mismanaged anger and frustration can do great damage to your relationships as well as to your body and mind.

What works? First off, learn how to calm down if you do not already know how to do so. Work on the relaxation techniques in Chapter Seven. Calm yourself with prayer (Chapter Three). When you are calmer, find a constructive way to raise your concern or express your feelings (for example, by using the TIP statement explained in Chapter Six). Expressing your frustration and anger well, without attacking and with respect, is doing your part to keep it safe to connect.

This ground rule gives you an agreed-on way to stop arguments. Why should you keep going in an argument that you both know will damage your marriage? Worse, if you are really angry and upset with one another around your children, you are damaging them. The research is very clear on this (see Chapter Two). Your marriage and your children are going to benefit from following this one little rule about taking Time Outs.

You can also use Time Outs for talks that are off track but have not yet escalated. For example, "I'm not sure we're really hearing each other right now. Maybe we should take a break."

To really use this ground rule effectively, we suggest that you refer to it with a specific term such as Time Out or Stop Action. That way you'll both know what is going on—that what your partner is doing in saying "Time Out" is positive and not just avoidance of an issue. When you use Time Out, you are taking a stand against destructive behaviors and deciding to do something constructive instead, keeping yourself under the Lord's control.

Signaling to Detour Around Dangerous Places

Here's a secret. It's something happy couples do that all couples, happy or not, can learn to do: use an agreed-on signal to take your interaction in a different direction when it's not going well. Studies by pioneers in couple communication, such as John Gottman, Howard Markman, Cliff Notarius, and Robert Weiss, have shown that couples who are more likely to struggle do not exit damaging arguments as effectively as other couples. One way that couples rein in negative feelings and exit an argument is to agree on a special signal they will use. The clearer your cue and the more firmly you agree to use it, the better your odds of escaping an argument before it gets out of hand.

One couple we worked with used names of food for their conflict management cues. "Hamburger" came to mean "Let's pause and take a break from what is happening." So if they were escalating and getting snippy, one would say, "Hey, let's grab a burger." Sometimes this not only would help them cool it but also could get them laughing. Humor is great if you can get it working for you. That can be tricky, but some couples are able to use humor to help manage conflict.

Another couple we know has learned to catch things really early, before the situation gets too hot, so that they can get back on track. As soon as they start to get riled up, one of them will say, "Let's pump the brakes." It's as though they're in a car that's starting to go downhill too fast for the curves ahead, and it's time to pump the breaks to keep things under control. You may think that sounds corny, but this kind of thing can be powerful.

When you start to give a signal to your partner, use it also to remind yourself to start calming down. Mutually agreed-on signals are not an excuse to control your partner. They are a way you can work as a team to take control of your conflicts.

It is important to approach Time Out as something you are doing *together* for the good of your relationship. Sure, one of you may call Time Outs more often than the other. You can't stop escalation effectively without working together. You are calling Time Out on the destructive communication, not on your mate. The bad conflict—not your partner—is the enemy. Don't simply say, "Time Out" and leave the room, unless you absolutely have to in order to cool things down. It is much better if you can say something like, "This is getting hot. How about we take a Time Out and talk about this after dinner, OK?" By including your partner in the process ("How about *we* take a Time Out"), you are using this skill as a team to de-escalate frustration and anger.

Time Out Is Not Avoidance

Anybody can just walk out of an argument, but that usually fuels more escalation and hostility later on. Walking out is withdrawal, but taking an intentional Time Out is a skill. When you ask for a Time Out, you don't always need to delay talking about the subject until later. You might simply need to cool it and keep moving. But if there is something important to talk through, do so after you have cooled off. If you are a pursuer, this part of the ground rule—the agreement to come back later so that you can talk more effectively—addresses your concern that Time Outs could be used by your partner as a tool for avoidance. Time Out can also give the one who is prone to pull away the assurance that things won't get out of hand. Withdrawers become much more able to tolerate conflict when they know they can stop it at any time. This ground rule is designed to stop unproductive arguments, not to stop all dialogue on an issue. You do need to discuss difficult issues—but in productive ways. The next chapter is about how to do this more effectively. Using the skills in that chapter can make a huge difference.

When you do decide to talk later, try to set the "Time In" right then, perhaps in an hour. If things have already become too heated before the Time Out is called, you may find that you can't continue to talk about the problem right then. That's OK. You can agree on a specific time and place the next day. There must be enough time to allow things to cool down between you. In the NBA, when one team is starting to get far behind, they call a Time Out. At times, they surely wish they had more time out to reset how they are playing. In your marriage, you are using Time Out the same way, except that you are keeping the other team (conflict) from running up the score on your relationship.

While you're waiting for the Time In, you have a great opportunity to think and pray about what really concerns you. It's also a great time to do some relaxation work (see Chapter Seven) as you pray for the Lord's wisdom and grace to work together on the problem.

Luke and Samantha have been married for twenty years and have two teenage sons. Before learning these techniques, they would have frequent arguments that escalated to shouting and making threats about the future of the relationship. Both came from homes where open and intense conflict was relatively common, so changing their pattern was not easy. As you will see, they still escalate rather easily, but now they know how to stop when the argument gets going.

SAMANTHA: *(annoyed and showing it)* You forgot to put the trash out in time for the garbage man. The can is already full.
LUKE: *(also annoyed, looking up from the paper)* It's no big deal. I'll just stuff it down more.
SAMANTHA: Yeah, right. Then the trash will be overflowing in the garage by next week.

LUKE: *(irritated)* I can't do anything about it now. So just leave it alone.

SAMANTHA: *(very angry now, voice raised)* You aren't getting a lot of things done around here that you are supposed to.

LUKE: Let's call a Time Out. This isn't getting us anywhere.

SAMANTHA: OK. When can we sit down and talk more about it? How about tomorrow night after we get back from the school meeting?

LUKE: OK. That will work for me.

Although they had already begun to escalate, they used Time Out very effectively to stop an argument that was going to be destructive. Later, they did sit down and use the Speaker-Listener Technique, which we will teach you in the next chapter, so that they could talk constructively about Samantha's concern that Luke was not keeping up with his commitments around the house.

Time Out Can Save Your Best Moments

In this next example, another couple uses Time Out to save an important evening from potential disaster. Byron and Alexandra have been married for six years and have no children. They want kids, but have had trouble getting pregnant. This has added plenty of strain to their marriage. They had decided to take a weekend trip to a cabin in the mountains to get away and spend a relaxing—perhaps romantic—couple of days together. They had both been looking forward to this time for months. This conversation transpired on their first evening, as they got into bed together. Note that they had been practicing the skills we will describe in the next chapter, so they were able talk very effectively.

ALEXANDRA: *(feeling romantic and snuggling up to Byron)* It's so nice to get away. No distractions. This feels good.

BYRON: *(likewise inclined, and beginning to caress her)* Yeah, should have done this months ago. Maybe this relaxed setting can help you get pregnant.

ALEXANDRA: *(bristling at his words)* "Help YOU get pregnant"? That sounds like you think it's my fault we're not getting pregnant. Why did you have to bring that up?

BYRON: *(anxious and annoyed at himself for spoiling the moment)* I don't think it is your fault. We have been through that. I just meant—

ALEXANDRA: *(angry)* You just meant to say that there is something wrong with me.

BYRON: Hold on. Let's take a Time Out. I'm sorry that I mentioned getting pregnant. Do you want to talk this through now, or set a time for later?

ALEXANDRA: *(softening)* If we don't talk about it a little bit, I think the rest of the evening will be a drag.

BYRON: OK, I'll listen first.

ALEXANDRA: I got all tense when you brought up pregnancy, and I felt like you were blaming me for our infertility.

BYRON: *(reflecting what Alexandra has said)* So mentioning that subject raised unpleasant feelings, and more so because you felt blamed.

ALEXANDRA: Yes. That whole thing has been just awful for us, and I was hoping to get away from it for the weekend.

BYRON: It's been really hard on both of us, and you wanted to just forget about it this weekend.

ALEXANDRA: And I wanted us to focus on there being some romance here instead of just trying to get pregnant. Like it used to be.

BYRON: Yep, just you and me making love without a care. I remember those days!

ALEXANDRA: *(feeling really listened to and cared for)* Yes. Your turn.

BYRON: Boy, do I feel like an idiot. I didn't mean to mess up the moment, and I see how I hurt you by what I said.

ALEXANDRA: *(reflecting Byron's feelings)* You feel bad. You didn't mean to mess things up between us tonight.

BYRON: Yes, and I really don't think it is your fault we are not pregnant. Whatever is not working right in our bodies, I don't think of it as you or me messing up. When I said what I said about you getting pregnant, I thought of "us" getting pregnant. But really, it's you that will actually be pregnant. That's all I meant.

ALEXANDRA: *(with a smile)* You didn't mean to be such a doofus!

BYRON: *(chuckling back)* That's kind of blunt! But yeah, that's what I'm saying. I think we should just avoid that whole topic for the weekend.

ALEXANDRA: OK, you think we should make infertility an off-limits topic this weekend. I think that's a great idea. What else can we do, then, with all this time?

BYRON: *(moving closer to kiss her)* I have some ideas.

Notice how effectively they used the Time Out to stop what could have ruined the whole weekend. Alexandra was too hurt to just shelve the issue. She needed to talk right then, and Byron agreed to allow it. By focusing on it and having a good talk, they were both doing their part to make it safe to reconnect. In addition, they made a clear decision that was smart—to put the topic of infertility off-limits for the rest of their time away. By handling it the way they did, they actually felt closer and made it much less likely that they would slide into that danger zone again while they were away.

Ground Rule 2

We will make time for the blessings of marriage: fun, friendship, physical connection, and spiritual connection. We will agree to protect these times from conflict and the need to deal with issues.

You can't be focusing on issues all the time and have a really happy and connected marriage. You need nurturing and safe times for relaxing—having fun, talking as friends, making love— times in which conflict and problems are always off-limits.

We want to emphasize the two points that are embedded in this ground rule. First, set aside time for these positive activities together. You have to do this very intentionally. For most couples, letting this slide means you will have fewer positive experiences in your marriage. Second, when you are alone together for the purpose of enjoying your relationship, agree never to use that time to bring up issues. And if an issue does come up, agree to table it for a later time. Schedule a special meeting to focus on an important issue later, but don't let problems intrude on the times you've to set aside to enjoy one another.

Alexandra and Byron, who took the wonderful Time Out, were out to have a relaxing and romantic weekend, and it wasn't a good time to focus on one of their major issues. They were able to use Time Out to turn their weekend around when it started to get off track. But they could have also protected the weekend before it started by using this ground rule. How might that have looked? Imagine this conversation while they were driving away for the weekend.

BYRON: Hey, Alex. I've got an idea. We've been thinking and talking about how to get pregnant for a while now, and it's worn us both down.

ALEXANDRA: *(looking a little wary)* Yes, it's been a drag. What's your idea?

BYRON: I think we should agree right now to just forget all about it for the entire weekend.

ALEXANDRA: I'm not sure I can forget about it.

BYRON: I know. Me either. It's important to both of us. But what I mean is, how about we just agree to try to put it aside for the weekend. No talk about it, and we both try not to think about it and just relax.

ALEXANDRA: Byron, I think that is a fantastic idea. I'm in.

BYRON: OK, that's a deal. Let's just have some fun.

How much effort does it take to have a conversation like this? Not much. It does take some mindfulness. It requires a decision and an awareness of how letting things slide might not yield a good result.

When Only One of You Is Pursuing a New Strategy

Quite often, one person in a marriage is reading a book like this, and the other is not. If you are reading this book together, that is wonderful. We have some suggestions for either situation.

If your spouse is not reading the book with you, be encouraged. You will still have many ways to put the ideas, strategies, and principles into action. But you need to give some thought to what you'll try to change on your own, given that your partner is not reading the book. This will mean that you will be changing your actions without your partner trying to change. In fact, your partner may not even know why you are doing some things differently. But very often one partner responds positively to positive changes made by the other. Obviously, it's your call as to whether you want to tell your mate that you are trying some new things based on the book. If you come across an idea you really like, and it's an idea that you both have to try in order to make it happen, we suggest that you ask your partner to breeze through that part of the book so that the two of you can discuss it. Then ask him or her if it's something he or she would try practicing with you. If your partner's answer is no, just keep doing your part in the ways that are making sense to you. Praying for grace and wisdom to do it is always a good idea (James 1:5).

Even if you are reading together, it still doesn't mean that the two of you will be impressed by the same ideas in the same ways. We want people working through this book to be realistic. Each of you may like some of our ideas but disagree about the value of others. Sometimes you may feel like saying to your partner, "We learned a better way to do this. Why won't you try it with me?" Try not to go there. Don't allow the fact that you are learning some new ideas cause you to feel less positive about your marriage. Just keep trying the things that are under your control. Focus on doing your part and not on what you wish your partner would do.

Doing Your Part

1. The first activity is an individual, reflective task. Write down the three keys and put them where you will see them often. You could send them to yourself as a text message or print them on a three-by-five index card to put on the nightstand. Whatever works for you. Here they are again:

   a. Decide don't slide.

   b. Do your part.

   c. Make it safe to connect.

   Take some time to ponder these. What could you do to apply them in your marriage? Does one key have more meaning to you than the others? Why? Think about some specific things you can do with regard to each concept.
   (continued)

Decide exactly what you will do. Smaller is better than bigger here, because you are more likely to be able to make something happen if it is small and in the right direction.

2. If the two of you are working through the book together, talk about the two ground rules we presented. Talk about what you like or don't like about them and exactly what you will do to put them into action.

    If you are working through this book by yourself, consider what you could do to enact these two ground rules on your own. In most relationships, one person can do a lot to create an effective Time Out. Being able to say something like the following does not require your mate to have learned about the idea: "OK, we're getting heated here. How about we give this a break for a couple of hours and try again later when we're not already riled up?" Clearly, Time Outs are going to be more effective when you both agree to use them, but one person can successfully bring them about in many relationships.

5

Talking Without Fighting

Everyone should be quick to listen, slow to speak and
slow to become angry.
JAMES 1:19

Most couples want to communicate well, but many have not
learned to do it when it counts most: when disagreements arise.
There's no danger when the two of you see things the same way.
Conflict arises when you see things differently. Remember, Adam
and Eve covered up the parts of themselves that were most different. Handling conflict well is critical to the success of your
marriage. And communicating well is critical to handling conflict
well. There are two keys to good communication: making it clear
and making it safe.

Making It Clear: The Problem of Filters

Have you ever noticed that what you are trying to say to your
partner is sometimes very different from what your partner hears?
You may say something that you think is harmless, but suddenly
your spouse is mad at you. Or you may ask a question such as "What
do you want for dinner?" and your partner starts complaining
about your not doing your share of the work. She or he obviously
heard something very different from what you meant. We have all
experienced the frustration of being misunderstood. You think
you are being clear, but your partner just doesn't seem to "get it."
Or you are certain you "know" what he said yesterday, and today he
claims he said something completely different.

Like the rest of us, Tanya and Wellington can relate to this common problem. They married five years ago. Their jobs leave them exhausted at the end of each day. There don't have any children yet, so they can usually crash when they get home.

One Thursday night, Wellington got home first and was reading on his iPad while waiting for Tanya to get home. He was thinking, "I'm wiped out. I bet she is too. I'd really like to go out to eat at that crab place and just relax with Tanya tonight." Good idea, right? This is what happened with his idea. (What they are thinking or hearing is in parentheses.)

WELLINGTON: *(Thinking he'd like to go out to dinner with Tanya, as she comes in the door.)* What should we do for dinner tonight?

TANYA: *(Hearing "When will dinner be ready?")* Why is it always my job to make dinner?

WELLINGTON: *(Hears her response as an attack and thinks, "Why is she always so negative?")* It is not always your job to make dinner. I made dinner once last week!

TANYA: *(The negative cycle continues, as Tanya tends to think that she does everything around the house.)* Bringing home pad tai is not making dinner, Wellington.

WELLINGTON: *(With frustration mounting, Wellington gives up.)* Just forget it. I didn't want to go out with you anyway.

TANYA: *(Confused, Tanya can't remember him saying anything about going out.)* You never said anything about wanting to go out.

WELLINGTON: *(feeling really angry)* Yes I did! I asked you where you wanted to go out to dinner, and you got really nasty.

TANYA: I got nasty? You never said anything about going out.

WELLINGTON: Did too!

TANYA: You're never wrong, are you?

You can see where things went wrong for them. Wellington had a positive idea, but conflict blew out the evening. Wellington was not as clear as he could have been in telling Tanya what he was wanting. This left a lot of room for interpretation, and interpret is what Tanya did. She assumed that he was asking her to get dinner on the table.

Many of the biggest arguments you will have may begin with a simple anger-provoking misunderstanding about what your partner is saying. What gets in the way? Communication filters.

Filters change what goes through them. A furnace filter takes dust out of the air. A camera filter alters the properties of light passing through it. A coffee filter lets the flavor through and leaves the ground beans behind. In the same way, what goes through our "communication filters" is different from what comes out.

We all have many kinds of filters packed into our heads. They affect what we say, what we hear, how we interpret things, and how we respond. They are products of how we are feeling; what we think; and what we have experienced in our life, family, and culture. There are three kinds of filters that get in the way of clear communication: inattention, emotional states, and beliefs and expectations.

The Filter of Inattention

A very basic kind of filter has to do with whether you have each other's full attention. Both external and internal factors can affect attention. External factors are such things as noisy kids, a hearing problem, or a bad mobile connection. Internal factors include feeling tired or bored, thinking about something else, feeling irritable, and so forth. To get rid of this filter, you need to make sure you have each other's attention when it really counts most. For important talks, find a quiet place if possible and don't answer the phone or check for text messages. Make it easier to pay attention to one another, and don't assume that your partner is ready to listen right now just because you are ready to talk. Ask, "I'd like to talk about the kids right now. Is this a good time for you?"

The Filter of Emotional States

Moods and emotional states can become filters. Have you noticed that when your spouse is in a bad mood, you get jumped on no matter how nicely you say something? A number of studies demonstrate that we tend to give people more benefit of the doubt when we are in a good mood and less benefit of the doubt when in a bad mood. If you are in a bad mood, you are more likely to perceive whatever your partner says or does as more negative than he or she meant, no matter how positive she or he is trying to be.

One good defense against mood filters is to acknowledge them when you are aware of them. Here is an example. It's dinner time. The kids are hungry and complaining. Melissa just got home and is looking through bills that came in today's mail. Steve is making spaghetti:

MELISSA: This bill from the phone company got missed again. We better get this paid.
STEVE: *(snapping with anger)* I'm not the one who forgot it. Can't you see I have my hands full? Do something helpful.
MELISSA: I'm sorry. I should have seen you were busy. Rough day?
STEVE: Yes. I had a very frustrating day. I don't mean to snap at you, but I've had it up to here. If I'm touchy, it's not really anything you've done.
MELISSA: Maybe we can talk about it some after dinner.
STEVE: Thanks.

Without using the term "filter," Steve and Melissa are acknowledging that one is there. Steve had a bad day at work. He also picked up the kids on the way home, and for whatever reason, both of them were crabby. He's on edge. They could have let this conversation escalate into an argument, but Melissa, who was also on edge because of the unpaid bill, could see that she had raised an issue at the wrong time. She decided not to get defensive and chose to calm her voice. As Solomon said, "A gentle answer turns away wrath, but a harsh word stirs up anger" (Proverbs 15:1). Steve responded by letting Melissa know that he had a filter going on— his bad mood. Being aware of this helped her take control of her own irritation and to be less defensive in reacting to his mood.

The Filter of Beliefs and Expectations

Many filters arise from what you think and expect in your relationship. Research and experience tell us that people tend to see what they expect to see in others, whether it's something they want to see or not. This kind of expectation becomes a filter that colors what we see and distorts communication. Studies also show that our expectations can actually influence the behavior of others. For example, if you believe that your partner is mad at you, she may well sound mad to you, even if she isn't. We tend to "pull" from others the behavior that is consistent with what we expect. Mental filters, especially negative interpretations, can make things seem a lot nastier than they really are.

Alonzo and Heidi were having problems deciding what to do for fun when they had free time. With three kids in elementary school, free time without the kids was very valuable to them. The following conversation was typical. Note how both of them acted as if they could read the other's mind.

ALONZO: *(really wanting to go bowling, but thinking that Heidi was not interested in going out and doing anything fun together)* We have some free time tonight. I wonder if we should try to do something.

HEIDI: *(thinking that she would like to get out, but hearing the tentativeness in his voice, and thinking that he really does not want to go out)* Oh, I don't know. What do you think?

ALONZO: Well, we could go bowling, but it could be league night and we might not get in anyway. Maybe we should just stay in and watch TV.

HEIDI: *(thinking, "That's what he really wants to do")* That sounds good to me. Why don't we make some popcorn and watch some tube?

ALONZO: *(disappointed, thinking "I knew it—she really doesn't like to get out and do things that are fun")* Yeah, OK.

In this conversation, there wasn't any escalation, invalidation, or withdrawal. Nevertheless, the couple did not communicate well due to the belief and expectation filters involved. Alonzo's belief that Heidi did not want to go out colored the entire conversation— so much so that the way he asked her to go out led her to think that he actually wanted to stay in! He "knew" that she really did not want to go (mind reading). In this case, as in most cases where mind reading becomes a problem, it amounts to a negative interpretation.

Alonzo mistakenly concluded that they stayed in once again because that was what Heidi wanted. His mental filter "pulled" the conversation in that direction and became a self-fulfilling expectation. Heidi also did a good deal of mind reading. In this conversation, she assumed that Alonzo was tired and really wanted to stay in. The result was a distorted conversation in which neither said what they wanted. If they had been able to communicate clearly, without these filters, they would have realized that both actually wanted to go out.

Different Planets or Just Different Zip Codes?

You've probably heard the "fact" that women use many more words per day than men—20,000 as compared to 7,000, or thereabouts. It's not true. This is one of the myths addressed by the authors of the book *50 Great Myths of Popular Psychology* (Lilienfeld, Lynn, Ruscio, & Beyerstein, 2009). Serious studies show that there is virtually no difference in the average number of words men and women use per day, though there is a slight nod toward women's using more. Similarly, Lilienfeld and colleagues note that other beliefs about differences in how men and women communicate are also overblown. For example, women are slightly more likely to open up more about themselves to others. Men are slightly more likely to interrupt others. One area where the authors note that there is a larger, reliable difference between men and women is perceptiveness about nonverbal behavior. On average, women read the facial expressions of others more accurately than men.

Men, if you sometimes think that your wife is better at reading your mind than you are at reading hers, it could be that she's just better at reading your face.

Filters and Memory: That's Not What I Said!

Some of the biggest arguments couples have are about what was actually said in the past. How often have you wished you had a tape recording of a previous conversation? Reread the earlier communication between Wellington and Tanya. Notice that they ended up arguing about what was actually said at the start of the conversation. He honestly believed he had asked her out to dinner, but what he actually said was vague. She truly thought he told her to get dinner on the table, which was also not what he said. Without a tape recording, no amount of convincing could get either one to back off from their versions of the story. Some research has revealed that there is no correlation between how strongly someone feels about his or her remembrance and how accurate it is!

We recommend two things you can do to protect your relationship from such fruitless arguments about who said what. First, accept the fact that your memory is sometimes not correct, no matter how strongly you feel that it is. This takes a bit of humility. It's wise to simply agree that the two of you may have differing perceptions about the same interaction. There are countless psychological studies that show how fragile human memory is, and how susceptible it is to motivation and beliefs. Accept that you both have imperfect memory filters and that there is a lot of room for things to be said or heard differently than what was intended.

Second, when you disagree about a memory, don't keep arguing about what was actually said in the past. We don't know of a single case in which that ever helped a couple solve a problem or draw closer together. Don't get stuck in the past, even if it was five minutes ago. Shift the topic to what you each think and feel in the present.

◦ ◦ ◦

We hope you understand how important it is to be aware of filters in your communication. We all have them. Either we can slide into them with little awareness, which can hurt our connection, or we can decide to spot them when conversations are going awry.

Making It Safe: The Value of Structure

There is no fear in love. But perfect love drives out fear, because fear has to do with punishment.
1 John 4:18

This passage makes a powerful point: love is the antidote to fear. Likewise, when you maintain an atmosphere of love and respect in your marriage, you increase the odds of talking without fear of rejection. In contrast, escalation, invalidation, withdrawal, and negative interpretations make it unsafe to express your real heart. You can't be naked and unashamed when you feel as though you'll be put down or hassled for expressing what you honestly think and feel. Filters compound the love-shortage problem, making it a wonder that couples can ever communicate clearly about anything truly important.

Are marriages necessarily safe? No. Although many couples start out with a strong sense of their relationship as a safe haven, many don't stay that way. And some couples don't even start out feeling safe. By "safe" we do not mean that there are no risks. There is a direct relationship between risk and intimacy in relationships. If you are going to share what you are concerned about, hurt by, or hoping for, you are going to take risks. You cannot be accepted deeply without offering something deep for your partner to accept! Conversely, you can take the risk, share deeply, and be rejected. This hurts a lot, because you have chosen to risk a deeper part of yourself in the relationship. But if it goes well, you find a wonderful, soul-satisfying acceptance of who you are, warts and all.

One way to make it safer to draw closer and deal with issues well is to use agreed-on rules to help you stay on track during important conversations. We call this "adding structure" to a conversation. With added structure, you can talk about difficult or important matters with less chance of damage to your relationship. When less is at stake or you are not in conflict, you don't need much structure. Just communicate in whatever way you are most comfortable. But during the tough times, a bit of structure can get you through without damage, and may even lead to greater closeness.

The Speaker-Listener Technique

When it comes to great communication, you can't beat the simple advice of James:

> Everyone should be quick to listen, slow to speak and slow to become angry, for man's anger does not bring about the righteous life that God desires. (James 1:19–20)

Easier said than done, right? Marriage, in fact, may be the hardest place to obey this verse because of our potential to feel hurt by those we are closest to. The Speaker-Listener Technique offers you an alternative way of communicating when issues are hot or sensitive—or likely to get that way. Any conversation in which you want to increase clarity and safety can benefit from this technique. Most couples (although not all) can decide whether to go out for Chinese food without using it, but nearly everyone can benefit from its structure when dealing with sensitive issues like money, sex, and in-laws. It's the structure of the technique that makes it work. The strategy is to use this model to make it possible to talk with more skill and safety. As you'll see, it utilizes taking turns, careful listening, and speaking clearly and frankly about what's on each of your minds. It usually feels artificial and phony at first. But after practicing it for a while, you'll start to pick up its style and use it in your own way. For example, by practicing taking turns—each of you listening carefully to the other—you'll start to have turn-taking show up more naturally in all your talks. Also, as you get comfortable with the whole structure, you can decide to use it when something is really hard to talk about. You can pull out all the stops and follow the full set of rules as we give them here.

Here they are:

Rules for Both of You

1. *The Speaker has the floor.* Use a real object to designate the floor. When giving seminars, we hand out small cards or pieces of linoleum or carpet for couples to use. You can use anything, though: the TV remote, a piece of paper, a paperback book, anything at all. (One couple we worked with used their child's toy rhinoceros.) If you are not holding the floor, you are the Listener. As Speaker and Listener, you follow the rules for each role. Note that the Speaker keeps the floor while the Listener paraphrases, keeping it clear who is in which role all the time.

2. *Share the floor.* You share the floor over the course of a conversation. One has it to start, and may say a number of things. At some point, you switch roles and continue back and forth as the floor changes hands. The Speaker can either offer the floor to the Listener, or the Listener can ask for it.

3. *No problem solving.* When using this technique, you are supposed to focus on having good discussions so that you can really understand each other. Avoid trying to come up with an immediate solution to something important. Quickly formed solutions seldom work well.

Rules for the Speaker

1. *Speak for yourself. Don't mind-read.* Talk about *your* thoughts, feelings, and concerns, not your perceptions or interpretations of the Listener's point of view or motives. Try to use "I" statements, and talk about how you see and feel about things.
2. *Speak in small chunks.* You will have plenty of opportunity to say all you need to say, so you don't have to say it all at once. It is very important to keep what you say in manageable pieces to help the Listener actively listen and be able to accurately reflect your thoughts. A good rule of thumb is to keep your statements to just a sentence or two, especially when first learning the technique.
3. *Stop and let the Listener paraphrase.* After saying a bit, perhaps a sentence or two, stop and allow the Listener to paraphrase what you just said. If the paraphrase was not quite accurate, you should politely restate what was not heard in the way you intended it to be heard. Your goal is to help the Listener clearly understand your point of view.

Rules for the Listener

1. *Paraphrase what you hear.* To paraphrase the Speaker, briefly repeat back what you heard the Speaker say, preferably using your own words. The key is to show your partner that you are listening as you restate what you heard—without any interpretations. If the paraphrase is not quite right (which happens often), the Speaker should gently clarify the point being made. If you truly don't understand some phrase or part of the point your partner is making, ask him or her to clarify or repeat, but try not to ask questions on any other aspect of the issue, unless you have the floor.
2. *Don't rebut. Focus on the Speaker's message.* While in the Listener role, you should try not to offer your own opinion or thoughts.

This is the hardest part, and perhaps the most important part, of being a good Listener. If you are upset by what your partner says, you need to edit out any response you may want to make, so that you can continue to *pay attention* to what your partner is saying. Wait until you get the floor to say what you think or feel.

Here are some ideas about what good paraphrases sound like. Suppose your spouse says to you, "I really had a tough day. Mom got on my case about how I handled the arrangements for Dad's party. Ugh!" Any of the following might be an excellent paraphrase:

"Sounds like you had a really tough day."
"So, your mom was critical of how you handled the party, and
     really got on you about it."
"Bad day, huh?"

Any one of these responses conveys that you have listened and shows that you have understood. A good paraphrase can be short or long, detailed or general. At times, if you are uncertain about how to get a paraphrase started, it can help to begin with the words, "What I hear you saying is . . ." Then you fill in what you just heard your partner say. Another way to begin a paraphrase is with "Sounds like . . ."

When using the Speaker-Listener Technique, the Speaker is always the one who determines if the Listener's paraphrase was on target. Only the Speaker knows what the intended message was. If the paraphrase was not quite on target, it is very important that the Speaker gently clarify by restating the message and not responding angrily or critically. One more key point: when in the Listener role, be sincere in your effort to show you are listening carefully and respectfully. Even when you disagree with what your partner is saying, your goal is to show respect for—and validation of—his or her perspective. That means waiting your turn and not making a face or looking bored. Showing real respect and honor to one another is the goal. You can disagree completely with your mate on a matter and still show respect for how he or she sees it. In fact, we are told in scripture to show respect no matter what

(1 Peter 2:17). Just wait until you have the floor to state your own point of view.

Using the Speaker-Listener Technique

Here is an example of how this technique can transform a conversation that is going nowhere into a great opportunity for connection. Peter and Tessie are in their mid-thirties, with four kids ages two to ten. The couple has struggled for years in dealing with issues. Peter consistently avoids talking about problems. If cornered by Tessie, he withdraws by growing quieter.

In this case, Peter and Tessie have been locked in the pursuer-withdrawer cycle about the issue of preschool for their son Jeremy. However, they have been practicing the Speaker-Listener Technique and are ready to try something different. Let's see what happens.

TESSIE: I'm really getting tired of leaving Jeremy's preschool up in the air. We have got to deal with this, now.   \

PETER: *(not looking up from the TV)* Oh?

TESSIE: *(walking over and standing in front of the TV)* Peter, we can't just leave this decision hanging in the air. I'm getting really angry about you putting it off.

PETER: *(recognizing that this would be a wise time to act constructively and not withdraw)* I've been avoiding it because it seems that talking about it will just lead to fighting. Let's try that technique we've been practicing. I'll give it a go if you will.

The technique is not a normal way to communicate. But it is a relatively safe way to communicate clearly on difficult issues. Each person will get to talk, each will be heard, and both will show commitment to discussing the problem constructively. Peter turned off the TV and picked up the piece of carpet they use for the "floor."

PETER (SPEAKER): I've also been pretty concerned about when and where we send Jeremy to preschool, but I'm not sure this is the year to do it.

TESSIE (LISTENER): You have been concerned too, and you're not sure he's ready.

PETER (SPEAKER): Yeah, that's it. He acts pretty young for his age, and I'm not sure how he would do unless the situation were just right. *(Note how Peter acknowledges that Tessie's summary is on the mark, before moving on to his next point.)*

TESSIE (LISTENER): You're worried that he wouldn't hold his own with older-acting kids, right? *(Tessie is not quite sure she has understood Peter's point, so she makes her paraphrase tentative.)*

PETER (SPEAKER): Well, partly that's it. But I'm also not sure if he's ready to be away from you that much. Of course I don't want him to be too dependent either. *(Note how Peter gently clarifies. He's moving toward Tessie in the conversation, rather than away from her. In general, whenever the Listener feels that clarification is needed, he can use the next statement to restate or expand on what he was trying to get across.)*

TESSIE (LISTENER): So you are feeling torn about him needing me a lot and him needing to be more independent.

PETER (SPEAKER): That's right. Here, you take the floor.

FLOOR SWITCH

TESSIE (NOW THE SPEAKER): Well, I appreciate what you are saying. Actually, I hadn't realized that you had also been thinking about it. I was worried that you didn't care about it. I'm sorry I thought that. *(As the Speaker, Tessie now validates Peter in the comments he has made.)*

PETER (LISTENER): Sounds like you're glad to hear that I'm concerned.

TESSIE (SPEAKER): Yes. I agree that this is not an easy decision. If we did put him in preschool this year, it would have to be just the right place.

PETER (LISTENER): You're saying that it would have to be just the right preschool for it to be worth doing this year.

TESSIE (SPEAKER): Exactly. I think that it might be worth trying if we could find a great environment for him. *(Tessie feels good with Peter listening so carefully, and lets him know it by the way she warms up to him.)*

PETER (LISTENER): So you would try it if we found just the right setting.

TESSIE (SPEAKER): I *might* try it; I'm not sure I'm ready to say I *would* try it.

PETER (LISTENER): You're not ready to say you would definitely want to do it, even with a perfect preschool.

TESSIE (SPEAKER): Right. Here, you take the floor again.

As you can tell, they have been practicing. They are both doing an excellent job following the rules and showing concern and respect for each other's viewpoints. You can have discussions like this on difficult topics, even when you disagree. The key is in using structure to make it safe, and in showing respect for your partner's thoughts, feelings, and opinions. Practice helps you do this well. But the heart of why it can work is that you both want to make it safe to connect, and to keep it safe.

The Advantages of Using the Speaker-Listener Technique

The Speaker-Listener Technique has many advantages over unstructured conversation when discussing difficult issues. Most important, it counteracts the destructive styles of communication described in Chapter Two. This is crucial. It's not that this technique is the be-all and end-all of good communication. It's just one very simple way to be "quick to hear, slow to speak, and slow to become angry," and thereby limit the damage that patterns such as the Communication Danger Signs can cause. In fact, we do meet couples who try the technique and don't like it. We don't get defensive about it or push it. We simply say, "That's fine, as long as you have some other way to have respectful conversations on difficult issues."

You may be thinking, "This sure is artificial." Agreed. In fact, that's the very reason it is so effective. The truth is, what comes naturally to couples when difficult issues arise is often destructive "biting and devouring" and quite the opposite of being "quick to hear, slow to speak, and slow to become angry." Again, the apostle James speaks straightforwardly: "If anyone considers himself religious and yet does not keep a tight rein on his tongue, he deceives himself and his religion is worthless" (James 1:26).

This technique is artificially designed to help couples keep "a tight rein" on their tongues. That's why it works. When you choose to use it, you are making the choice to limit the defensive responses that come naturally and to submit yourself to a more caring, disciplined approach to understanding your mate. You are unleashing your ears and reining in your tongue!

Keep in mind that even though these rules are simple, simple does not always mean easy. Structure can make it easier, but sometimes it takes hard work to implement the structure.

○ ◉ ◎

When you choose to use these skills, you are choosing to protect your relationship from destructive conflict by using more structure. But practice is the key. With regular practice, several positive things can occur. First, the technique will become easier to us and will feel less artificial over time, which means that it will be more readily available when you need it. Second, if you practice this awhile, you'll find yourselves naturally communicating better with each other, even when not using the rules. Just as yeast affects an entire loaf of bread, your new skills will find their ways into all your conversations. You'll be limiting the damaging patterns and fostering great communication at the same time. We see many couples who practice the technique and use it for a time, then hardly ever need it again, although they can always gear down to the more structured style when necessary. That's because the practice has completely changed the way they talk about important matters. They have learned to shift much more naturally into a better, more respectful flow when important topics arise. In our work with thousands of couples, this has been one of the most beautiful transitions we've watched.

If you want to strengthen your marital promise and reduce your chances of divorce, learn to move toward each other and to deal constructively with the issues that have the potential to drive you apart. We will cover many other important principles in this book, but none is more critical. And the Speaker-Listener Technique may be the most useful skill of all.

Doing Your Part

When you are learning a new skill, the goal is to learn it well enough that it becomes a habit—something you can do naturally, almost instinctively. Begin with the basics. When learning to play the piano, you don't start with the most difficult pieces; approach the Speaker-Listener Technique in this way. Talk about easy topics first and then move on to more difficult ones.

1. Practice this technique several times a week for fifteen minutes or so each time (each of you taking a turn as Speaker and as Listener). You'll learn faster by having more frequent, brief sessions than by having fewer and longer sessions. If you set aside the time to practice, you'll find this powerful technique very helpful.
2. During the first week, practice the technique with non-conflict topics only. Talk about anything of interest to either of you: news, sports, your favorite vacation, your dreams for the future, your best friend growing up, concerns you have at work, and so on. Try to stay away from topics that you know will bring up issues. Your goal right now is not to work on problems but to practice new skills.
3. Practice on nonconflict topics five to seven times. After those successful experiences, practice on issues in your relationship that are not likely to spark conflict but that have substance. You can't always tell what might trigger conflict between you, so here's one way to develop a good list of issues that are useful for practicing. Each of you can take out a sheet of paper and write down a list of low-level to high-level issues and concerns you have related to your relationship, home, or family. The higher-level issues are likely to be those more likely to spark conflict, so practice more with the lower-level issues first. By the way, there could even be some high-level issue that you don't write down because you are not ready even to identify it. That's OK. Make your lists. They won't be the same.

   For the sake of practicing, start by talking through issues one or both of you have ranked as low level—and that both of you agree is low level. Save the issues either of you list as higher intensity for later, after you have been practicing awhile. If the discussion gets heated on any issue, when your main goal is to practice, just take a Time Out and drop it. You can come back to it later, when you've had more practice. And you can always go back to practicing on the nonconflict topics if you need to.

Share most of your thoughts and feelings on two or three areas, but don't try to solve problems. Just have good discussions. Your goal is to understand each other's feelings and point of view as completely as possible. In the process, you may actually resolve some problems because all you needed was to understand one another. That's OK, but don't intentionally try to find solutions. Focus on good discussions for now. You'll learn and practice problem solving in the next chapter.

4. When you are doing well with the minor conflict issues, move up to tougher and tougher ones. As you do, remember to stick to the rules. The tougher the topic, the more you need to stay in the structure. The technique will work if you work at it.

6

Finding Solutions to Problems

He who answers before listening—that is his folly and his shame.
PROVERBS 18:13

We have not addressed problem solving until this point because most couples try to solve problems before they have really heard each other's views about them. Lots of problems do not really matter too much for a couple. For the ones that do, it is crucial to understand the problem before attempting solutions. This chapter presents a straightforward approach to problem solving based on understanding and respect. The strategies here are most likely to be useful when you have a significant problem to work through.

Three Key Assumptions

Couples who understand three key assumptions about problems in marriage are more likely, in our view, to do better over time.

All Couples Have Problems

Jesus summed this up quite clearly when he said, "in this world you will have trouble" (John 16:33). He didn't leave anyone out when he said this. Now think about marriage. Have you ever wondered why some couples seem to deal with the challenges of marital life so effectively? This is not because they are problem free. Some couples truly are dealt a worse hand in life than others, but no one gets by with a completely free pass on life's problems. Sometimes you have control over the problems that come your way because your behavior is directly related to those problems. For example, whereas some couples have tremendous financial problems that are not of their own making, other couples create their financial problems, such as by spending too much or taking on too much debt. With many other problems in life, you don't have as much control over the problem itself as you have over the handling of the problem.

It Is Best to Handle Problems as a Team

You have a choice when dealing with a problem. Either you will nurture a sense that you are working as a team against the problem, or you will operate as if you are working against each other. Jeremy and Lisa are a couple who have the sense of teamwork flowing in their marriage. They were talking about how to handle the feeding of their newborn baby (Brent) while Lisa, a nurse, was at work. Jeremy had recently lost his job as a store manager.

LISA: I am worried about breast feeding.

JEREMY: What do you mean? Can't you do that when you're at home, with me giving him a bottle during your shift?

LISA: No. That's not going to work because I'll fill up with milk. I make milk whether he drinks it or not, you know.

JEREMY: I had no idea that would be a problem. You mean you can't go through your shift without him nursing?

LISA: Not without being very uncomfortable.

JEREMY: Oh! What can we do to make this work out?

LISA: Well, either Brent nurses on my break, or I need to pump.

JEREMY: What's better for you? I could help either way.

LISA: Would you be willing to bring him over to work at lunch-time? If he'd nurse well then, that would tide me through the day, and you could give him bottles the rest of the time.

JEREMY: That sounds like something I could do. Obviously, there's at least one benefit to me being out of work right now.

LISA: That would help a lot. I'd also get to see him during the day. It means a lot to me that you'd try to make this work.

JEREMY: I'm super happy to help. Besides, I'd get to see you also.

Jeremy and Lisa approach all sorts of problems like this—as challenges to be faced together. We can't overstate the importance of mutual respect in having this kind of "teamwork" marriage. This is so important that both men and women are specifically called upon in scripture to nurture respect for the other (Ephesians 5:33 and 1 Peter 3:7).

Rushed Solutions Are Poor Solutions

Solomon was one of the wisest persons who ever lived because he asked God specifically for wisdom—something we are all invited to do (see James 1:5). In fact, take a moment and ask God for wisdom in your marriage. Solomon wrote down a couple of points that get to the heart of one of the most important principles for good problem solving.

> He who answers before listening—that is his folly and his shame. (Proverbs 18:13)

> It is not good to have zeal without knowledge, nor to be hasty and miss the way. (Proverbs 19:2)

Many well-intentioned attempts at problem solving fail because couples do not take the time needed to understand the problem together—they get hasty and miss the way. If it is a decision about which movie to see, not much is lost in a hasty solution. That's one of those times when sliding can be no big deal. In contrast, dealing with issues about money or your children, for example, is a whole different deal. Those are times when sliding is unwise and making good decisions together is the path to a better life. Lasting solutions often take some time and attention to find.

Keira and Ryker have been married twenty-four years. They have two children, one in college and one a senior in high school. Ryker sells insurance, and Keira works half-time with a Christian ministry that helps missionaries. Money hadn't been a problem until college bills began accumulating. Ryker's issue is financial, specifically that Keira devotes so much time to a job that doesn't pay very much. The following interchange is typical when this problem area comes up.

RYKER: *(testy)* I noticed that the Visa bill was over $600 again. It worries me that we can't keep up. I'm doing all I can, but . . .

KEIRA: *(gives no indication that she is paying attention to Ryker)*

RYKER: *(frustrated)* Keira, Did you hear me?

KEIRA: Yes. I didn't think we spent that much this time.

RYKER: If we had more income coming in from your work, it would help.

KEIRA: Why don't we just get rid of that credit card? Then you wouldn't have to worry about it anymore.

RYKER: We could do that, and also plan to put aside an extra $150 a month in my retirement plan. What about you asking for a raise?

KEIRA: I don't want to think about that now. For now, let's just try to get rid of the credit card and save more.

RYKER: OK, we can try that and see what happens.

End of discussion. The one good thing about this discussion is that they had it. However, what are the chances that they came to a satisfactory resolution of their money problem? Two months later, nothing was changed. This example illustrates what couples do all the time: make a quick agreement so that they avoid conflict. Solutions arrived at in this manner rarely last, because not all of the important information is "on the table." Ryker and Keira rush to solutions because they hate conflict. For them, this is a relatively big fight. Finding a quick solution can be a relief, but doing so prematurely does not solve anything.

Who Raises Problems More Often—Men or Women?

People often think that men are more oriented toward problem solving than women but that women raise problems more often than men. There really is no good reason to believe the first point. It's not just men who want to fix things; we are a problem-solving-oriented society that rewards people who are good fixers. Both men and women tend to go for the problem-solving jugular, and feel helpless and hopeless when that doesn't work. It's better

(continued)

to resist this urge and listen as a friend might to what is upsetting your partner. And when you know you just want to be heard more than anything else, let your partner know that, so that he or she does not get tempted to start throwing out solutions when all you really want is to share what's on your heart.

Regarding the second point, women may well be more likely to raise concerns in their marriages than men. This is on average, of course. Some research teams, such as Andrew Christiansen and his colleagues at UCLA, have found that men are more prone than women to pull away from conflict in marriage. The reason this is true, they find, is that the one who raises an issue is more likely to keep pursuing it, and the one who didn't raise a particular issue is more likely to be the one to pull away. Christensen and colleagues do not believe that men are more oriented toward withdrawing but that women are more likely to raise issues because they want something to change. The most important point in this is that when either partner has an important concern, it is best if there is enough emotional safety and skill in the marriage for the couple to deal directly with the problem.

Solving Microproblems: Sweating the Smaller Stuff

What are microproblems? They come up in those moments when something happens between the two of you—a misunderstanding, a look, a mistake—and you can either slide right into climbing the crazy ladder or stop, take a moment, and do something effective. Remember from Chapter Two that the problem with climbing up the crazy ladder is that things become less stable and more damage can be done. With many small events and issues in life, you don't need to sit down and do a full-bore problem-solving routine, but you might benefit from quickly and effectively sharing a concern and moving on.

When something frustrating happens, how do you become more real so that you can experience greater closeness? How do you share thoughts and feelings about things that bother you without hurting your partner or stressing the relationship? We're glad you asked. The answer: by using the TIP statement. It can make a huge difference. We call it the TIP statement because it's a great way to tip off your partner about a concern. We want you to TIP each other off rather than just get ticked off!

There are three components to this way of walking in the light and "speaking the truth in love" versus biting and devouring one another.

T is for Trigger. The trigger is what your partner did or failed to do that affected you. We call this the trigger because it starts the ignition on your rocket to nowhere. Many times, triggers are like what we call events (see Chapter Eight). It's the thing that happened that is connected to other stuff that matters.

I is for Impact. The next letter in TIP stands for the impact that the trigger had on you. The impact part of the TIP statement is how you let your partner know how you were affected or how you feel. You can tell your partner about thoughts or feelings, or about how what happened impacted your day ("I ended up being late to my doctor appointment"). Usually, the most important impact to tell your partner about is how you feel or felt when the trigger happened. Telling your partner about the impact can put an immediate stop to mind reading because you are being clear about what happened and how it affected you. Often, this will mean simply saying "I feel that . . ." or "I felt . . ." But watch out: often people mean to express how they feel, but end up saying something negative about the other person instead. "I felt that you were an idiot" does not actually say how you felt.

P is for Preference. As part of making a TIP statement, you state what you would have preferred or would prefer in the future instead of what actually happened. It is best to state your preference specifically and directly, without attacking or stepping on any rung of the crazy ladder. Preferences should never be demands. You are stating what you wish would happen, not demanding that your partner behave a certain way. That also keeps you a few steps away from the ladder. You have to give your partner freedom to decide what he or she will do. You are doing your part by explaining what you'd rather have happen.

Here's an example of how a TIP statement works:

Emiliano and Madeline were hosting their small group Bible study meeting on Wednesday night. Madeline came home early and got the children settled so that she could prepare the house and the snacks for the group. Emiliano not only didn't get home when he usually did; he got home only fifteen minutes before people started to arrive, and he had not called to let Madeline know he was running late. This was not the first time this, or something nearly like it, had happened, and Madeline was very frazzled and frustrated. She decided to let things go during the group and wait to mention anything until afterward. Later, when the children were in bed and everyone was gone, she decided to give Emiliano a very clear TIP.

MADELINE: When you come home late and leave all the preparation for something like our group to me [Trigger], I feel overwhelmed by not being able to get things done [Impact], and I feel mad at you about it [Impact]. When we are having people over, I would prefer it if we'd agree on both getting home early enough to get the house and the kids all settled before people arrive [Preference].

EMILIANO: *(realizing that Madeline was going out of her way to say this carefully and without hostility)* I hear you. I understand what a bad spot that put you in, and I'm sorry. I will work on that with you.

How much better is this than Madeline's blasting him when he walked in the door, their escalating up the crazy ladder, and then having to deal with guests (not to mention the upset children) a few minutes later? Instead of name-calling or hostility, the TIP statement allows Madeline to be effective. Many times in marriage, you can be right (as in self-righteous and angry), or you can be effective. Which do you usually choose?

Part of why this worked well in the example between Madeline and Emiliano is that as soon as she got halfway into her statement, Emiliano recognized that she was giving him a TIP.

She was trying to be constructive, and he responded in kind. Better for everyone. No one is getting wrung out. This example shows you what we mean when we say that there are some situations where you could use some microproblem solving and may not need a big sit-down meeting to figure something out. To be clear, if this type of triggering event kept happening in just this way, then it would become a problem for which the microsolution was not working, and Madeline and Emiliano would be better off using the fuller problem-solving steps we describe in the rest of this chapter.

The TIP statement is a better way to respond when your partner does or says something that affects you in a way that hurts. You can tell them exactly what they did (not what *you* believe they were thinking, intending, or feeling). You can let them know how their actions and your beliefs affect your thoughts and feelings or circumstances. And you can ask them to change their actions to help your relationship become closer—and leave the crazy ladder to others.

Here's another example. Avery and Jackson didn't have any big struggles in their marriage, but one of the persistent issues was their different parenting styles. Avery was tougher on the children in general—firm but tough. Jackson tended to let things go or just make a comment, and Avery would have the children doing consequences for misbehaving. (They loved cleaning things up—not!) One of the children in the home was from a prior relationship Jackson had been in before meeting Avery. Sometimes Jackson felt that Avery was harder on this boy, Bobby, than she was on the other children.

One night, Bobby had given Avery some serious lip about getting after his chores before bedtime. Avery snapped at Bobby and raised her voice, but only a little, telling Bobby he'd lose some TV privileges the next day. Jackson was upset about it, and said to her privately, "I wish you liked my son better." It was a good thing that the children were asleep and that Jackson had the wisdom to wait until later to raise his concern. And it's good that he was raising his concern. But note the type of message he gave Avery. What will happen next? Escalation, of course. There are not a lot of spouses out there who are going to react well to being called a bad or unloving parent. And Avery did love Bobby.

Things would have gone so much better if Jackson had used a TIP statement instead. It could have gone like this.

JACKSON: *(calmly but clearly feeling emotion)* When you told Bobby he'd lose TV time tomorrow [Trigger], it sounded harsh to me, and I got upset [Impact]. I would prefer it if we came up with a plan for me to be more involved in disciplining the children [Preference]. I know I have tended to leave most of that to you, and I think we could figure out some better way to do this together.

AVERY: *(softly and positively)* Wow. I know this has been an issue for us, and I appreciate how you just shared that. I love the idea of coming up with a plan.

JACKSON: I know we can't figure that out right now, tonight, but let's sit down this Saturday after the day goes wild, and start talking out what we could do differently.

AVERY: You got it. I love this.

In this case, the TIP statement is used to give valuable information in a timely manner, from Jackson to Avery. Jackson is using a lot of skill rather than just starting an argument. He wants things to be different, not just stirred up. Notice that in this case, the TIP statement is a microsolution to start a process of a bigger solution. When they sit down on Saturday, that would be a great time for them to use the fuller problem-solving model we present here.

You can vary the way you express the three parts of a TIP statement, but be sure that you use each of them. For example: "I feel confused [Impact] when you become silent like this [Trigger]. I think I must be such a bother to you [another Impact]. Can you tell me more about what your silence means [Preference]?"

When you mean to be more skillful and use a TIP statement, try to figure out what you feel and share it—constructively. Some people have trouble identifying their feelings. Here's a list of feeling words that may help you figure out what feeling you are having when something is up in your relationship.

Feeling Words for Use in TIP Statements

happy	sad	mad	angry	delighted	frustrated
anxious	tense	nervous	joyful	peaceful	content
irritated	annoyed	euphoric	gleeful	disturbed	on edge
warm	depressed	safe	bothered		

Now here's the really good news: you can also use TIP statements to encourage your partner to do more of the things you like: "When you come into the kitchen and give me a hug, I think it means you're really glad to see me. So I feel really loved. We should go for a hug most every night when the second of us gets home. We could do that, and I'd like it a lot."

Simply using a TIP statement can clear the air and move you both forward on a better path. Or it may reveal that you need to talk further about the subject. Use the Speaker-Listener Technique if you need it, to find out what is really going on inside each of you. Sharing your deeper heart with your partner is risky. But it can result in much greater closeness, especially when you use it to replace your negative interpretations.

Problem-Solving Steps for the Bigger Stuff

There are many problems and issues couples have to deal with that they cannot just ignore and hope to have go away. And a lot of issues in life and marriage are not microproblems that you might be able to handle rapidly. Sometimes you have to dig down and work on a lasting solution to something more complex or important.

The approach we teach to solving problems is structured. Although the steps are very straightforward, don't be misled by their simplicity. You must be willing to work together, to be creative and flexible, and to experiment with change. As with the suggestions about the Speaker-Listener Technique in Chapter

Five, what we are recommending here is more structured than most couples are used to when it comes to problem solving. That's why we noted at the start of the chapter that these recommendations can make a huge difference for an important problem you are trying to solve, but that when it comes to lesser issues, you will be fine if you use some of the key principles but not the whole structure of the steps.

Steps to handling problems well include

    I. Problem Discussion
   II. Prayer
 III. Problem Solution
      A. Agenda setting
      B. Brainstorming
      C. Agreement and compromise
      D. Follow-up

As you can see, we are presenting three major steps in handling problems well: Problem Discussion, Prayer, and Problem Solution. Problem Solution has four specific substeps: agenda setting, brainstorming, agreement, and follow-up. We list prayer as the second major step, but when something important is at stake, prayer might be the best place to start, either individually or as a couple if you are comfortable with doing that.

Problem Discussion

When you're dealing with any significant problem, Problem Discussion is the most important step of all. A good discussion lays the foundation for understanding, and it contributes to a sense of teamwork. Although you may not agree about how to solve the problem, a good discussion can lead to a clear sense that you're working together and respecting each other. Whether the problem is large or small, you should not move on to Problem Solution until you both understand and feel understood by each other. We recommend that you use the Speaker-Listener Technique for this Problem Discussion step. We have often seen problem solving go smoothly for couples when the two partners have had a really good talk first.

In many instances, you'll find that after an excellent discussion, there's really no problem solving to be done. Just having a good discussion is enough. That's because, for many issues, what we all really need most is simply to be heard and respected. But when you do need to find a specific solution, the steps we outline here work powerfully.

Prayer

It is wise to invite the Lord to be a participant in finding solutions to important problems. Couples who approach the problem prayerfully as a team of three (God and the couple) instead of just two experience more spiritual intimacy and obtain the Lord's help with the problem. Most of us know the following passage very well:

> Trust in the LORD with all your heart and lean not on your own understanding; in all your ways acknowledge him, and he will make your paths straight. (Proverbs 3:5, 6)

There are many ways to apply this principle. Even if you are sensitive about praying out loud, don't let that stop you. Pray silently, or pray just a sentence out loud. The key is to "acknowledge" the Lord.

Problem Solution

The following steps work very well for couples, provided that the work of Problem Discussion has been done. Prayer can leave you all the more ready to find a solution together. One more thing: as you enter the problem-solving steps here, we do *not* recommend that you use the structure of the Speaker-Listener Technique in these steps. That would be too cumbersome. It serves you best during the discussion phase, but it is not as useful when it comes to moving through these steps.

Agenda Setting

The first step in the Problem Solution phase is to set the agenda. The key here is to make it very clear what you are trying to solve at this time. Your discussion may have taken you through many facets of an issue. Now you need to focus on one facet. The more specific the problem you are tackling, the better your chances of coming to a workable solution. Many problems in marriage seem insurmountable, but they can be cut down in size if you follow these procedures.

For example, you may have had a good Problem Discussion about money, covering a range of issues, such as credit cards, checkbooks, budget, and savings. As you can see, the problem area of "money" can contain many "subproblem" areas to consider. Focus on the more manageable pieces, one at a time. It is also wise to pick an easier piece of a problem to work on first. You might initially decide who should balance the checkbook each month, then deal with budget plans later. Some of the best possible agendas for problem solving answer a time-limited question, such as, "How are we going to handle getting the kitchen cleaned up differently this week?" If you can be this specific, you'll have really homed in on finding a solution to try and then evaluate.

At times, your Problem Discussion will have focused from start to finish on a specific problem. In this case, you won't have to define the agenda for problem solving. For example, you may be working on the problem of where to go for the holidays, your parents' home or your spouse's. There may be no specific smaller piece of such a problem, so you will set the agenda to work on it as a whole.

Brainstorming

There are several rules for effective brainstorming:

- Any idea can be suggested. One of you should write them all down.
- Don't evaluate the ideas during brainstorming, either verbally or nonverbally. (This includes making faces!)
- Be creative. Suggest whatever comes to mind, no matter how ridiculous it might seem.
- Have fun with it if you can. This is a time for a sense of humor; all other feelings should be dealt with in Problem Discussion.

The best thing about this process is that it encourages creativity. Write down all the ideas you can. If you can restrain your tendency to comment critically on the ideas, you will encourage each other to come up with some great suggestions. Wonderful solutions can come from considering some of the wildest ideas that emerge during brainstorming.

Agreement and Compromise

In this step, the goal is to come up with a specific solution or combination of solutions that you both agree to try. Some people have trouble with the idea of compromise. We at PREP have even been criticized for using the term. Obviously, compromise implies giving up something you want for the sake of the relationship. To some, compromise sounds more like "lose-lose" than "win-win." But we believe that compromise is sometimes necessary. Paul tells us to "look not only to your own interests, but also to the interests of others" (Philippians 2:4). Good compromises can allow you each to do this for the other.

Follow-Up

Many couples make agreements to try out a particular solution for a specific period of time, especially when the problem has been an ongoing one. At the end of the "trial period," it is important to follow up about how the agreement is working out. Following up has two key advantages. First, solutions often need to be tweaked a bit to work in the long term. Second, following up builds accountability. Often, we don't get serious about making changes unless we know there is some point of accountability in the future. Sometimes there needs to be a lot of follow-up in the Problem Solution phase. At other times, it's not really necessary. You reach an agreement and it works out, and nothing more needs to be done.

Some couples choose to be less formal about follow-up, but we think that this approach is risky. You are potentially letting an important step slide when you are really trying to make a change last. Most people are so busy that they don't include this step, so the solution just doesn't happen. It is an old but true saying: "If you fail to plan, you plan to fail." Good plans include good follow-up.

Ryker and Keira Work It Out

It did not take Keira and Ryker very long to realize that their problem solving regarding their credit card, her work, and their retirement savings was not working. They decided to try the steps we are suggesting. First, they set aside the time to work through the steps. Let's follow them through the process.

Problem Discussion with the Speaker-Listener Technique

KEIRA (SPEAKER): I can see that we really do have to try something different. We aren't getting anywhere on our retirement savings. .

RYKER (LISTENER): You can see we're stuck, and it sounds like you are also concerned.

KEIRA (SPEAKER): *(letting Ryker know he had accurately heard her)* Yes. We need to come up with a plan for saving more and using credit cards less.

RYKER (LISTENER): You also think it's important to save more, and that we're having trouble with the credit cards.

KEIRA (SPEAKER): I can also see why you are concerned about my part-time job with the ministry, but it is really important to me.

RYKER (LISTENER): Sounds like you can appreciate my concern, but you also want me to hear that the work you are doing is really important to you. I hear that.

KEIRA (SPEAKER): Yeah. That's exactly what I'm feeling. Here, you take the floor. I want to know what you're thinking.

FLOOR SWITCH

RYKER (SPEAKER): I have been anxious about this for some time and worry that without saving more, we won't ever be able to retire. I know that's a long ways off, but we're not saving anything right now.

KEIRA (LISTENER): You're really worried, aren't you?

RYKER (SPEAKER): Yes, I am. You know how things were for Mom and Dad. I don't want to end up living in a one-room · apartment.

KEIRA (LISTENER): You're worried we could end up living that way, too. I didn't know.

RYKER (SPEAKER): I'd feel a lot better if we were regularly saving some money.

KEIRA (LISTENER): I don't see how—*(She catches herself interjecting her own opinion.)* Oh, I should paraphrase. You wish we were putting aside some money.

RYKER (SPEAKER): *(This time, he feels he is really getting her attention.)* I do. I feel pressure about it. I really want to work together on this.

KEIRA (LISTENER): You want us to work together to reduce the pressure, and plan for our future.

RYKER (SPEAKER): *(suggesting some alternatives)* Yes. We'd need to spend less and use the credit cards more wisely. And it would make a big difference if you brought in more income.

KEIRA (LISTENER): So, what you'd like to do is save more and, to do that, get a handle on how we're using credit, right? But it really seems important to you for us to bring in more money.

RYKER (SPEAKER): Yes. I think income is a bigger problem than outgo.

KEIRA (LISTENER): Even if we could spend less, you think we need more income. Can I have the floor?

RYKER (SPEAKER): Exactly! Here's the floor.

FLOOR SWITCH

KEIRA (SPEAKER): *(responding to Ryker's clarification)* Sometimes I think that you think I am the only one who overspends.

RYKER (LISTENER): So you think that I think you are the main one who spends too much. Can I have the floor again?

FLOOR SWITCH

RYKER (SPEAKER): Actually, I don't think that, but I see how I could come across that way *(validating Keira's experience)*. I think I overspend, too. I just spend it in bigger chunks.

KEIRA (LISTENER): It's nice to hear that you agree; we both spend too much, just differently. You may buy some big things we don't need, and I buy more smaller things.

RYKER (SPEAKER): Exactly. We are both to blame, and we can do better.

FLOOR SWITCH

KEIRA (SPEAKER): I agree that we need to deal with our savings. My biggest fear is losing the work I love. It's been the most meaningful thing I've ever done aside from being a mom.

RYKER (LISTENER): It's hard to imagine not having that . . . it's important to you.

KEIRA (SPEAKER): Yes. I can see why more income would make a big difference. But, at the same time, I would hate to lose what I have.

RYKER (LISTENER): You enjoy it, and you are doing something really meaningful. I really get that.

KEIRA (SPEAKER): Exactly. Maybe there is some way to deal with this so that I could do some of what I am doing and help us save what we need for retirement at the same time.

RYKER (LISTENER): You are wondering if there could be a solution that would meet your needs and our needs at the same time.

KEIRA (SPEAKER): Yes. I'm willing to think about solutions with you.

They discontinue the Speaker-Listener Technique.

RYKER: OK.

KEIRA: So are we both feeling understood enough to move on to trying to solve this problem?

RYKER: I am. How about you?

KEIRA: *(She nods her head, yes.)*

Here, they are agreeing together that they have had a good discussion and are ready to try some problem solving. They are consciously turning this corner together.

Prayer

RYKER: Before we try to solve this, I'd like for us to ask God to help us with the solution.

KEIRA: I'd like that also.

Ryker and Keira prayed a moment silently, asking for God's help and wisdom in reaching a solution to their income and spending problems. Neither was all that comfortable with praying out loud, but both believed in prayer, and they prayed together about this problem.

Problem Solution

Agenda Setting

Here, the important thing is for them to choose a specific piece of the whole issue to solve. This increases their chances of finding a solution that will really work this time.

Keira: We should agree on what we want to try to solve. We could talk about the retirement accounts, but that may not be the place to start. I also think we need to discuss spending money and credit cards.

Ryker: You're right. We are going to need several tries at this entire issue. It seems we could break it down into bringing in more and spending less. I'd like to focus on "bringing in more" first, if you don't mind.

Keira: I can handle that. Let's problem-solve on that, then we can talk later this week about spending.

Ryker: So we're going to brainstorm about how to boost the income.

Brainstorming

The key here is to generate ideas freely.

Keira: Let's brainstorm. Why don't you write the ideas down.

Ryker: OK . . . You could get an additional part-time job.

Keira: I could ask the board at work if they could pay me more. I work more, most weeks, than half-time anyway.

Ryker: We could meet with a financial planner to get a better idea of the income we need. I could also get a second job.

Keira: *(Keira didn't like the idea of Ryker's getting another job in addition to the one he already had, but she didn't raise that now, and stuck to brainstorming without critiquing the idea.)* I could look into raising some donation support for the work I do.

Ryker: Jack and Marla do something like that. We could talk to them.

Keira: I feel this list is pretty good. Let's talk about what to try doing.

Agreement and Compromise

Now they sift through the ideas generated during brainstorming. The key is to find an agreement that both can get behind.

RYKER: I like your idea of talking to the board. What could it hurt?

KEIRA: I like that too. I also think your idea of seeing a financial planner is good. But I don't think it is realistic for you to work more.

RYKER: Yeah, I think you're right. What about talking to Marla and Jack?

KEIRA: I'd like to hold off on that until I try first to see if they could pay me more for the work I do.

RYKER: OK.

KEIRA: So how about I talk to the board, you ask Frank about that financial planner they use, and I'll also start looking around at what kinds of part-time jobs there might be. But I'll start with talking to the board at the ministry.

RYKER: Great. Let's schedule some time next week to talk about how we are doing in moving along for the solution we need.

KEIRA: Agreed.

They set a specific time and place to meet.

Follow-Up

At the end of the week, Keira and Ryker met to discuss what they had found out and what to do next. To her surprise, the board member she talked with seemed eager to try to work out something to get her paid more. In the meantime, Ryker had scheduled a meeting with a financial planner for the following week. They also made time on the weekend to start talking about getting spending more under control. They were moving on a set of complex problems that had bothered both of them for a long time.

In many cases like this, the solutions really come out of an ongoing process made up of a series of smaller steps and agreements. The reason this kind of structured model we just presented can work is that it helps you break down a problem so that you can actually make changes. We'd like to tell you that this model always works this well, but there are times when it does not. What do you do then?

When It's Not That Easy

You can get bogged down and frustrated during any segment of the Problem Solution phase. Getting stuck may mean that you have not talked through some key issues or that one or both of you are not feeling validated in the process. If so, it's usually best to cycle back to Problem Discussion. Simply pick up the floor again and resume your discussion. It is better to slow things down than to continue to press for a solution that may not work.

Also keep in mind that the best solution you can reach may not always be the end solution. At times, you should set the agenda just to agree on the next steps needed to get to the best solution. For example, you might brainstorm about the kind of information you need to make your decision.

There are some problems that do not have solutions that work well for both partners. Suppose you've worked together for some time using the structure, and no solution is forthcoming. You can either let this lack of solution damage the rest of your marriage, or you can plan for how to live with the difference until some resolution is found. You can choose to simply live together graciously in the absence of a solution. Paul summarized this idea beautifully in Romans 12:17–18: "If it is possible, as far as it depends on you, live at peace with everyone."

It's not always possible to be at peace with others, but you are called to seek peace as far as it depends on you. In marriage, one of the most powerful ways you can facilitate this is by going back through the problems-solving steps, but this time making the agenda this instead: "How are we going to protect the rest of our marriage from the fallout from this unresolved problem?" This rejoins the two of you in the common goal of protecting your marriage.

○ ○ ○

In this chapter, we have given you ideas for dealing with simpler microproblems and suggested steps for handling larger, more complex issues. In either situation, the goal is for the two of you to preserve and enhance your teamwork. The fuller, more structured model is not something we would expect any couple to use for minor or simple problems. That would be overkill. We do believe that you can benefit from using this model when dealing with more complex matters, especially those that could lead to unproductive conflict and the Communication Danger Signs described in Chapter Two. This is one more way to add structure when you need it most, to preserve the best in your relationship.

Doing Your Part

As an exercise, try the problem-solving steps we have presented here on some issue that you both agree to work on. Pick one that matters but that is not something that causes a lot of conflict between the two of you and that is not one of your more difficult problems. In other words, try out the model on something relatively easy to work on together. For some couples, there are no lower-conflict or easier problems, but usually there are plenty of less-challenging issues you could try this model out on. For example, perhaps you already both agree that you'd like to have the children watch less TV. Or perhaps you have wanted to be more on top of how your children use the Internet. Maybe you both need to make more time for doing fun things together, but you need to do so without spending much money. As long as you both agree to give the steps a try, pick out a topic and just go for it. After you have some confidence in the process, start working on other issues about which you both agree that concentrated problem solving could benefit your marriage.

PART TWO

Complexity

7

Jars of Clay
Why Bodies Matter

But we have this treasure in jars of clay.
2 CORINTHIANS 4:7

In this chapter, we will explore four topics: (1) the chemistry of love, (2) how we respond to threats and how we plan, (3) stress and relaxation, and (4) the importance of sleep. These topics are unified around the theme that your physical being has an impact on your marriage. Each topic also highlights the importance of sliding versus deciding in how you live life together, with each having implications for decisions you can make to protect your marriage.

We chose these four topics in particular because we think they cover a lot of important ground. Before we dig in, let's examine one of the great theological answers to why you even have a body. We think that this creates important context for the rest of what we have to say.

Earthen Vessels and Jars of Clay

In his second letter to the Corinthians, the apostle Paul wrote of the light shining into our hearts from God through Christ. He followed this idea with one of the most fascinating lines in the New Testament:

> But we have this treasure in jars of clay to show that this all-surpassing power is from God and not from us. (2 Corinthians 4:7)

In the King James version of the Bible, the term used is "earthen vessels" rather than "jars of clay." In either case, what the passage clearly says is that human beings are made of dirt. We don't mean to insult you by saying that. It's pretty much what it says in Genesis (2:7). The point is that God was intentional in deciding to give us bodies. One of the chief reasons was so that we would not lose sight of the fact that the real power in life is from Him. The simple fact is that whatever else happens in your life for good or bad or in between, your body will eventually completely humble you. It may do this slowly, it may do this rapidly, and it may do this in any number of ways. But somehow, someway, your body will show you that you are not God. Having a body makes it clear to you that you cannot control everything. It is humbling to have a body.

God doesn't want us to lose sight of the fact that He's the creator and we are the created. He loves us enough to build in this reminder.

The body is a wonderful thing, and you are fearfully and wonderfully made (Psalm 139). However, having a body also presents challenges. Most important for the subject of this book, the vulnerabilities your body brings make your investment in your marriage one of the most important you can make in life. In fact, many people have said a traditional vow on their wedding day that includes the idea of remaining together "in sickness and in health." One of the great promises of a thriving, healthy marriage is your ability to be there for each other through whatever life throws at you—including the wonders and the challenges of being in a physical body.

The Chemistry of Love

No matter how long you have been together, you probably can remember the rush of feelings of first being in love with each other. Although this is an undeniable psychological and even spiritual experience, it is also one based in how you are physically made. When you first become attracted and fall in love, a variety of chemicals in your body are involved in the powerful feelings. And those chemicals will inevitably calm down.

Harry, thirty-one, and Sally, thirty-two, started to get to know one another through the Tuesday-night single adults group at church. Harry had noticed Sally about two months before she noticed him. And by "noticed" we mean that he started to become attracted to her. Both were kept quite busy with their work, friendships, and other interests, but both had made the group a priority. Their interest was motivated in part by spiritual hunger and in part by a desire each had to find a mate who would share their most important beliefs.

Harry thought Sally was gorgeous. He also found her Boston accent irresistible. He liked the way she asked challenging questions during group. She had a somewhat mischievous way of getting her point across. He was hooked pretty early on. Each week, he would sit a little closer to the part of the room where she usually sat. When she would walk into the room, adrenaline would start coursing through his veins. He was aware of his increasing excitement and nervousness. After a number of weeks, he was positively love-struck. The feelings became so strong that he could not keep his mind off Sally.

It frustrated Harry no-end that he acted like a bumbling idiot when around her. It was actually this behavior that caused her to notice him. It was also not hard to notice this handsome man who had trouble putting a sentence together. Sally did not yet know that he was otherwise an excellent communicator. She found the way his words sometimes got twisted up to be kind of endearing. She also noticed that he was looking her way fairly often, and knew what that meant. So she started looking more and more his way, thinking, "He is awfully cute. I hope he's not an idiot." Her chemistry was also starting to kick in.

Pretty soon it was clear that something was going on between them. Sally started to have the same kind of adrenaline rush that Harry was having, as the intensity of the attraction between them grew. After a few more weeks of this, Harry got up his nerve and asked Sally out to get a cup of coffee following the meeting—though neither of them needed any caffeine at this point. Dopamine started to flow, giving them feelings of great pleasure, even euphoria, when in each other's presence.

Limerence: Thoughts on Being Lovesick

The initial rush of falling in love is fueled by all kinds of chemicals. This state has been called everything from being infatuated to being love-struck to being head-over-heels to being madly in love. In her book *Love and Limerence: The Experience of Being in Love* (1979), Dorothy Tennov describes limerence, this stage of intense attraction, as something like being addicted to drugs; the person affected becomes captivated to the point of obsession with having the love of the other.

Helen Fisher, the famous anthropologist and author of *Why We Love: The Nature and Chemistry of Romantic Love* (2005), agrees with Tennov's description of this stage of attraction, though she prefers the term *infatuation*. Fisher described infatuation as including exhilaration, intrusive thinking about the beloved, and the craving for emotional union with the other.

Fisher suggests that intense infatuation can last two, maybe three, years. Following that, it's either curtains for the relationship or deeper attachment and commitment.

The rest is, as they say, history. Harry and Sally started to spend more and more time together. They called each other every night, texted each other often during the day, and spent hours talking together about life, their relationship, their beliefs, and their future. They were married seventeen months after that first cup of coffee.

Along the way, their togetherness included another, increasingly powerful chemical component in addition to dopamine and adrenaline. The deepening love and emotional attachment was propelled at the chemical level by other chemicals such as oxytocin, which is associated with attachment. There is a lot of complex research (and some conflicting findings) related to all this chemistry, though there is no doubt that chemistry—actual chemicals flowing through the body—is deeply involved all the way along.

The downside to all of this initial buzzing, blazing, and, at times, painful chemistry is that infatuation naturally fades over time. You can work to keep the fires crackling and alive, but what is going to take you the distance is the warmth of the coals begun by that fire, coals that need the gentle breath of love and commitment to keep their glow.

People who expect constant, burning passion in their marriage are heading toward a fall—and will miss the wonder of spring, summer, fall, and winter together. This book is full of inspiration and strategies to help you achieve your goal of building and keeping lasting love.

Amy and Flo: Two Key Brain Systems

Another biologically based aspect of who you are is called the fight-or-flight response, which is dominated by a part of your brain called the amygdala. In contrast to the planning and decision-making functions of other parts of your brain (for example, the prefrontal cortex), the amygdala's job is to cause action—and right now. The amygdala acts like radar, detecting threats and setting off instinctual, powerful, automatic reactions. The amygdala is all about action and not much about thought. It is like an action-adventure flick and not like the feelings that go with a warm, deep discussion after a movie.

The amygdala can save your life, and it can get you in trouble. Whatever it does, it does it fast. When someone loses his temper and goes off, the amygdala is running the show. If you come across a mama bear and her cubs in the woods, you want to reach for your amygdala. Actually, it will already have grabbed you. You will be doing something, maybe just freezing and maybe hightailing it toward the nearest tree. Otherwise, you might just be on the bear's menu. If, in contrast, you want to bare your soul to your mate, you are going to want your prefrontal cortex to be involved. Your amygdala? Not so much.

The Amygdala Hijack

In his book *Emotional Intelligence* (1996), Daniel Goleman coined the term "amygdala hijack" on the basis of the research of neuroscientist Joseph LeDoux. Goleman used this term to describe

(continued)

what happens when the hypothalmic-pituitary-adrenal axis (that
will be on the quiz) seizes control from the rational brain. As
Goleman's simple description aptly puts it, the rational brain is
hijacked. One moment you're piloting your life on a steady and
level course toward the horizon of your goals, and the next
moment, you're strapped into a seat in the last row in coach,
back by the bathroom—and maybe needing to use it soon. You
need to get back to the cockpit and take control of the flight.

To get away from jargon about regions of the brain, we'll use
the creative names given to the amygdala and prefrontal cortex
by the team at PREP in their *Anger and Stress* video: Amy (*AMY*g-
dala) and Flo (*F*rontal *LO*be). We've pretty much already intro-
duced Amy to you. She's the wild and crazy one at the party in
your head. She's impulsive, and, at times, she can be unpleasant
to others. Just to protect you, of course. Flo is slower to respond
than Amy, but much more thoughtful and vastly more able to
accomplish a goal.

There are actually two amygdalas and two frontal lobes—one
each on both sides of the brain—but we'll do what others have
done, which is to talk about each as one structure. The frontal
lobe—particularly what is called the prefrontal cortex—is thought
to be the seat of our executive functions and awareness. It also
plays a role in regulating other aspects of the nervous system. For
example, the frontal lobe can inhibit the way you react to signals
from the amygdala.

Imagine that you are waiting in line to see a movie and you
get smacked in the back of the head. Reflexively, your amygdala
interprets this as a threat and begins to mobilize your body for
action. However, as you turn around to confront the threat, you
recognize an old friend you haven't seen in years. You immediately disarm your threat response and hug your friend instead.
Phew—that was close. Good job, Flo!

What Amy and Flo do is related to the structure of your brain
and to brain chemistry. Flo contains the most cells in your brain that
respond to the chemical dopamine. The frontal lobes and the
dopamine system throughout your brain have a lot to do with

planning, motivation, the ability to pay attention, self-control, and the feeling of being rewarded. If you are setting out to accomplish a task or goal, Flo is your go-to system.

How do Amy and Flo affect the dynamics in marriage? There are very many ways we could list, but we will focus on just a couple. In Chapter Two, we described various patterns of negative interaction that have a big-impact on relationships and whether they are going to succeed or fail. Amy can fuel escalation. One way that Amy does this is through the rapid negative interpretations she tends to make. Remember, Amy is primed to detect threat. If you've not been handling conflict very well, Amy will be screaming "warning, warning, warning" when you mostly need to be keeping your cool and doing your part to make it safe to connect.

What can you do when you know that Amy is about to run loose or has already started down the path? This may sound too simple, but when you are riled up, the simplest things are going to be the most powerful things. Simple is all you are going to be able to do when Amy is going wild. Take a breath. Metaphorically, pull your car off the road and park it. Take another breath. The most important thing you need to do when Amy is on a roll is to give yourself a few moments so that Flo can reestablish control. If you practice the relaxation skills we'll describe in a bit, you stand a much better chance of getting yourself back under control when Amy cranks it up.

A Break in the Flo

Many studies have demonstrated that after you have been making a lot of decisions or resisting temptation, your ability shortly thereafter to continue to resist or persist in some other task is weakened. In one classic experiment, Roy Baumeister and colleagues showed that if people forced themselves to resist eating chocolate and ate radishes instead, those people were, in a following task, likely to quit trying to solve a puzzle sooner than those who had given in to the chocolate. In other words, those who had used more mental energy resisting the chocolate had less energy to apply to the next task. They had a letdown. We know what you might be thinking, so just hold on a second. The point of that story is not that eating a lot of chocolate is the secret to success in life. Nice try. The point is that such researchers as Roy Bau-meister, Kathleen Vohs, and others have shown something like this phenomenon in study after study. Unless you are very unusual, your ability to delay gratification, persist in solving a problem, or maintain your goal in various settings will be affected by how hard you have already had to work at something just before.

This means that your "decider" gets tired, and when that happens, your "slider" is ready to rock and roll. As Baumeister has suggested, your executive function is like a muscle. It can get worn out from effort but also strengthened by wise use. How many times have you found it harder to stick with what you thought you should do after you had to do things that required a lot of self-control or making a lot of decisions? The decisions do not have to be very important ones either. When your decider has been working steadily, your slider is going to want you to cut it some slack. If nothing much is at stake, that's just fine. Slide away. In fact, when you've been working hard on something or really pushing your self-control, letting go in some creative or healthy way is a good thing. But the warning in these findings lies more in how it can be hard to stick to something you have decided is important when you are worn down by something else. Those are also times when it is easiest to give into temptations.

Next Frame

Comic strips are built with frames. You follow the story in a comic by going from frame to frame. Life is like that: frame to frame. What the research on the executive functions of the mind shows is that what happens in one frame affects the next frame. Researchers sometimes call this spillover. If you are doing something that takes a lot of mental energy in one frame, you should expect that it will be more difficult not to have a letdown in the next. This is when you will be more prone to do something you may regret—like snapping at your mate.

How can you use this knowledge to protect your marriage? Let's say you've had a difficult day. Perhaps you have an annoying coworker or customer who drives you nuts, and you've had to work hard not to lash out. Or maybe it's just a day when you've had to make a zillion decisions or wrestle with your preschoolers all day. When you reconnect with your mate, Flo will be wiped out. In fact, with stress and low energy, not only is Flo pretty pooped, but Amy is restless and raring to let go. Here's a tip—again, simple stuff. Try to be more mindful of where you are, mentally, so that you can be more careful about how you might react and what you might say. Better still, let your partner know if something has worn out your decider. "Dear, I had to make a gazillion decisions that just wiped me out today. Maybe we could talk about the details of that loan tomorrow night instead? Is that OK by you?"

Josie and Cole live a busy life. He's a deputy sheriff, and she's an ER nurse. If that doesn't make them stressed enough, they have three children between the ages of six and twelve, a grumpy neighbor, and a house where something breaks every other week. Each of them works a job that requires many decisions and loads of self-control. Their family life at home also requires lots of decisions and self-control. Josie and Cole can get out of the Flo pretty easily, and any day can turn into an Amy day. That means they can get snarky and escalate easily.

One thing Josie and Cole can do differently is to work at being more aware of how the work frame becomes a filter that affects the home frame. One of the most important things you can do when you know you are reconnecting after a stressful time is to let your family know you've been having a tough day and may be extra edgy—in other words, announce that filter. That helps your family understand, so they won't take your grumpiness personally. Of course, that does not mean they will enjoy your grouchiness or that you should not work on controlling it better. But it helps.

One of the things that Josie and Cole have also noticed is that talking about anything, important or not, is more difficult in the evenings when either of them has had a tough day. These are not good nights to make decisions. Being mindful of this requires some new habits for Josie and Cole. Think of it this way: you have the ability to strengthen Flo and limit the damage from Amy by developing some simple new habits that take into account the reality of how your brain and body work. For example, you can agree on ways to give each other more grace when either of you is really fried.

You can also try extra hard to give your partner some focused attention before you crash. Here's one idea. Try resetting your awareness of how depleted Flo is *before* you reconnect. Maybe that means putting a sticky note on your dashboard or the bathroom mirror that says something like "How's Flo?" or "Go with the Flo." The idea is to remind yourself to have a "Flo check." Remind yourself that you are not at your best. Take some deep breaths. Pray. Decide whether you need to tell your mate about your mental state. Make an extra effort for the first few minutes of interacting with your spouse. It takes some conscious effort, but you can build new habits by taking the time to handle those first minutes well.

We'll say a lot more about habits in the next section.

Stress and Relaxation

What causes you stress? Are there parts of your life that are chronically stressful? How about work? Do you have many days when it's difficult just to get through? Or maybe you have been dealing with the stress of finding work. Maybe you struggle with anxiety every month when the money runs out before the month does. Some families have one or more members with a chronic illness. Almost everybody has stress of some kind.

Life can be hard. Jesus said that in this world we will have trouble (John 16:33). The apostle Paul said not to be anxious about anything (Philippians 4:6), but he would not have written that if we didn't struggle with anxiety. God doesn't want us to be anxious, but wants us instead to hold tight to the fact that he cares deeply about every aspect of our lives. For some people, life is almost always hard. One of the most powerful ways for spouses to stay connected is to join together as a team to alleviate each other's stress, whenever they can. That's a powerful way for the two of you to be like Christ in serving others in love.

Chronic stress affects a person mentally, spiritually, and physically. Stress researchers have long observed that chronic stress wears the body down, increasing the risk for serious illnesses. Such stress causes problems with sleep, headaches, back pain, and blood pressure. It even raises the risk of heart disease and stroke. Stress not only can break your body down but also increases your risk for depression and anxiety. When we're in survival mode, Amy stays on a hair trigger, and Flo gives up trying to cope. Chronic stress leads to trouble with concentration, irritability, and an increase in angry outbursts.

Young and old alike are affected by stress. Worry about money and keeping a job is something that affects all ages. It is true that the same amount of stress may adversely affect the body of an older person more than the body a younger person. That's because older bodies do not regulate as well as younger bodies. But whether one is young or old, it's never too late to start managing stress better.

Chronic stress drains strength from your relationship. Over time, trust can be damaged as it becomes harder to give your partner the benefit of the doubt. Conflicts and distance increase, and both partners can move deeper into protecting themselves. If you have significant stress in your life, it will damage your marriage unless you take action to fight it. Obviously, that would include many of the strategies we describe throughout this book.

Much of life is habit. Some brain scientists believe that 40 percent of our behavior is made up of automatic habits. This allows more brain energy to be used for other functions. If you have driven a car for long, you know about the gas pedal, brake, steering wheel, gauges, street signs, stoplights, other cars, and police cars. You know all that, but how much of it did you think about the last time you drove somewhere? We bet none of it. Your driving skills are automatic. Your brain is doing the processing for you so that you can drive safely without really thinking a whole lot about it.

The brain marvelously automatizes all of these kinds of functions in life. Once you acquire the habit, the habit just works. Stress is automatic, too. In fact, most people don't really have to learn how to be stressed out. When you're worried about something or your health is suffering or some important project is becoming difficult, you're not going to have to work at feeling stress. Worry and fear and anxiety come naturally. What does not come as naturally are behaviors that allow you to cope more effectively with the thoughts, feelings, and sensations you experience when stressed. It takes some effort to establish habits that fight stress and protect your body, spirit, and mind from its harmful effects.

There is no more powerful way to stop a negative response or habit than to put something in its place, like a positive habit. If you can increase certain positive habits, you are likely to experience better health, more enjoyment in life, and a better marriage. Here, we will focus on two specific strategies for dealing with stress—strategies that can help you protect your marriage. One involves prayer and meditation, and the other involves physical relaxation. These habits are powerful, once developed.

Prayer and Meditation

Scripture encourages prayer and meditation as powerful practices for coping with the stress, anxiety, and worry of this world. Let's add another passage to the ones we've already mentioned:

> Humble yourselves, therefore, under God's mighty hand, that he may lift you up in due time. Cast all your anxiety on him because he cares for you. (1 Peter 5:6, 7)

God invites you to throw all your worries onto His shoulders. Meditation on God's care for you is one of the most powerful things you can do, especially when you couple it with prayer. For example, take a moment and think about the picture implied in the phrase "casting all your anxiety on Him." Really, just slow down a moment, stop reading, and think about that. Imagine lifting the heavy weight that is on your shoulders and throwing it over to Jesus, who stands there waiting to catch it for you. Also meditate on the Lord's motive: "because he cares for you." Imagine seeing the concern and expectation in His eyes. His heart for us seems too good to be true, and people have trouble believing this it at times. Yet it is a valuable truth for comforting our anxieties.

There are many books written about prayerful contemplation. Here we are just lightly touching on the subject to encourage you to pursue this to fortify yourself in dealing with stress. We want you to take seriously that you have a body and mind that are affected by the stress of the world but also that there are things you can do that will make a difference.

Physical Relaxation

There are many ways to boost your relaxation response, including exercise and physical touch, such as massage. Something as simple as giving each other a back rub or a foot massage can put a big dent in your stress. If either or both of you are under a lot of stress, talk about strategies you can pursue to reduce its impacts in your life.

Intentional relaxation is one of the best ways to do this. Research consistently shows that the practice of physical relaxation counters the negative impacts of stress on your body and mind. We will present just one specific, proven relaxation strategy.

This specific technique goes by various names, but it is most often called progressive muscle relaxation. If you practice this a few times a week, you are not only putting your body in a more relaxed mode as you practice but also developing your body's ability to respond to your conscious intention to relax when you become aware of stress. You can practice it on your own or together.

Here are some steps to help get you started. Begin by getting comfortable, whether you are lying down, sitting up, or reclining. The key is to put yourself in whatever position is comfortable for you. If you like, turn the lights down. Make the room quiet, or play music that relaxes you.

- Close your eyes and focus on your breathing as a way to tune in to your body and start the relaxation response. Take a deep breath or two, and then settle into just noticing your breathing for a couple of minutes. You might try resting your hand on your stomach to feel your body respond to the breath going in and out. Slow your breathing down a bit, and purposefully relax the muscles that seem to be tense.
- Now work your way through the rest of your body, tensing and relaxing muscle groups as you go. Start with your toes and work your way up through the top of your head. You can focus on small groups (like your toes and then your feet) or larger groups, like your legs, then pelvic area, and on up. It's

your call. Tighten each set of muscles for a few seconds and then let go. Repeat this two or three times for each muscle group before you move to the next.

What follows is the text from the *Calming Skills* CD developed by PREP. It shows you more fully what we mean by working your way through your body as you continue to breathe in a relaxed way.

Clench your toes, hold them tight for a second and then, as you breathe out, let go of the tension and relax your feet. Next tighten your calf muscles, and as you breathe out, let out the tension. Do the same with your thigh muscles. Now tighten the muscles in your stomach and chest. Hold it for a second, and the next time you breathe out, relax those muscles and let the tension flow away. Next, tighten your shoulder muscles and the muscles in your upper arms. As you breathe out, relax and let the tightness flow down your arms like warm water. Next clench your fists and your forearms, and, as you breathe out, relax those muscles. Finally, the muscles in your neck and upper shoulders: do the same thing. And very last, clench and release the muscles in your face and head. Now let your awareness go over your body and see if there are any tight places remaining. If there are, go ahead and tighten and relax those muscles again. Each time you breathe out let your muscles relax. Continue breathing gently, and let a feeling of warmth and relaxation settle over your whole body.

This is simple, and it works. If you practice it regularly, you will be more relaxed and you'll handle stress more effectively when it comes. It will have a beneficial impact on your body, mind, and soul. You will also be better able to respond calmly and lovingly with your mate when tension and stress are knocking on your door.

Josie and Cole, whom we mentioned earlier, were being eaten alive by stress. They were drifting further apart, and their children were suffering along with them. The couple had a choice: they could allow the pattern to destroy their marriage, or they could take action to move things in a better direction. It was slide-or-decide time. One night, Cole looked into Josie's eyes and said, "How about we change this?" gesturing with his hands as if to say, "all this we are dealing with." When Josie replied, "Change what?" he clarified: "How we're dealing with all of this crud that is smothering our life together." She liked that he used the word "life," not "lives." Both realized that it was their life *together* that was being threatened.

That was the start, and it was a good one. Everything we've learned about how couples change, from both our counseling and research, confirms that the start—the turning point—is a good 80 percent of how change happens. Someone has to start the effort to stop the current slide that threatens the marriage. Then the two can decide together how to make things better. That is not always possible, by the way. Sometimes one spouse is just not ready to move things in a different direction. Sure, change is more potent when both partners are ready to move, but that is not always how it works. One partner can bring a lot change and blessing to the relationship, especially by praying for his or her mate and marriage (Chapter Three). But if you are able to work together to fight the stress, you should go for it.

Josie and Cole started talking about what they could change. The mass of things seemed unchangeable. Touch is a powerful way to provide emotional support. It releases the stress-busting effect of oxytocin in our bodies. Josie and Cole began by touching more, giving hugs and other little things like back rubs. They also started sharing encouraging biblical passages and texted little reminders through the day that they were thinking of each other. They did a lot of small things that added up to a big change in the direction of their marriage. They were taking control and developing new habits. It can be done. It has been done.

Depression and Marriage

There is a strong association between the state of a marriage and depression. A happy, thriving marriage is one of the best protections against depression. But it is equally true that difficulties in marriage are one of the most common causes of depression. There are many other causes of depression, including such biological factors as low thyroid, genetic tendencies,

(continued)

and childhood abuse. Circumstances such as unemployment and other kinds of chronic stress can also increase one's risk for depression.

Once depression really takes hold and becomes serious, it involves your body as well as your mind. That is why the most effective treatments for some people will include both medication and counseling. There are effective treatments for depression, and if you or your mate is seriously depressed, it is very important to seek help.

Experts who study depression and marriage, such as Steven Beach at the University of Georgia and Mark Whisman at the University of Colorado, say that the link between depression and marriage goes both ways: distress in marriage greatly increases the odds of becoming depressed, and serious depression in one or both partners increases the likelihood of marital distress. Therefore, if marital problems are clearly the cause of the depression, treatment that includes counseling focused on marital problems can be particularly beneficial. When the depression is not caused primarily by marital problems, beefing up the emotional support between the partners can play an important role in treatment. Counseling can be one way to strengthen the way a couple copes together. That includes helping the nondepressed partner be more supportive and helping the couple fight the depression as a team.

Our point is that there are a number of effective ways to fight depression. You do not have to be in the battle on your own—as an individual or as a couple.

Sleep and Your Marriage

The answer to the question of why human beings sleep has been elusive. One of the more compelling theories is that the brain needs downtime for maintenance every night, kind of like some Internet servers. If you've tried to do Internet banking late at night, you've probably received the message that the server is down for maintenance. Some speculate that the brain needs the time in the night to process and package the experiences of the day. Whatever the reason for sleep, it's clear that almost all people need about eight hours of sleep each night.

If you struggle with sleeping well, you are not alone. The Centers for Disease Control and Prevention (CDC) estimate that about seventy million Americans have chronic sleep problems.[1] They also note that sleep deprivation is associated with "injuries, chronic diseases, mental illnesses, poor quality of life and well-being, increased health care costs, and lost work productivity." Couples increasingly tell us that sleep has become a major issue for one or both partners. When you are not sleeping well, everything else suffers. You become tired, less focused, more irritable, more prone to depression, and less able to cope with challenges. There is a lot at stake with sleep problems.

Some couples get trapped in a vicious cycle in which sleep problems lead to an increase in marital problems, which lead in turn to an increase in sleep problems. Research shows that couples are more likely to be negative with each other the day after sleeping poorly. Then, the night after a day of being more negative, most people sleep more poorly still. Once you are in the vicious cycle, it doesn't really matter whether the sleep problem led to the marriage problems or vice versa. You're health and your marriage are going to suffer.

If you're one of those fortunate couples in which both of you sleep easily and well, you probably can skip the rest of this section.

Sleeping Together, for Better or for Worse?

An English sleep researcher, Dr. Neil Stanley (no relation to coauthor Scott), caused quite a stir in 2009 by recommending that people would sleep a lot better if they slept alone—as in, not with their mates.* Stanley's main point is that all kinds of sleep problems are compounded by sleeping together. He's not just making this up; research proves him right. Why, you wonder? The behaviors of one partner, especially snoring and tossing and turning, often negatively impact the other's sleep.

*"Bed Sharing 'Bad for Your Health,'" *BBC News*, September 9, 2009, http:// news.bbc.co.uk/2/hi/8245578.stm.

(*continued*)

Studies also suggest that women pay the bigger price because men are more often the ones who seriously snore. Keep in mind that this is research—it's all about averages. Your marriage could be one of the exceptions. What matters is what happens in your own relationship.

Most people aren't going to follow Stanley's advice to sleep apart, because they want to be together through the night. In the same excellent article on the BBC website that mentioned Stanley's work, another sleep researcher, Robert Meadows, noted that "people actually feel that they sleep better when they are with a partner but the evidence suggests otherwise." In spite of what the research shows, if you ask people whether they sleep better with or apart from their mate, they will say "with." Sleeping together is important for all kinds of reasons, including increased emotional connection.

If one or both of you have developed a serious sleeping problem, see your doctor for advice and a checkup of all systems. If you've ruled out treatable medical causes, it could be time to consider the benefits of sleeping in separate rooms—at least for a while. You can always double up on your other efforts to connect!

There are a few common problems—snoring, motion, tension, and schedules—for which *planning* together can make a big difference.

If you or your mate sounds anything like a freight train at night, get checked out by your doctor. There are sleep studies and treatments for sleep apnea. Many people go a long time before getting it checked, and many other aspects of your quality of life will suffer for years if you let it go. Snoring can also be a sign of a serious health problem, so check with your doctor if you snore. If snoring is a problem and there are no medical issues, make it OK for the one who doesn't snore to poke, prod, or give other some kind of signal for the other to move or turn to a new position to stop the snoring. Some people, especially women, don't feel comfortable asking their partner to do this. Talk about it together to work out a signal you both feel comfortable using.

Tension in the bedroom affects the sleep of many couples. We mean tension between the two of you. Our advice in other chapters for dealing with issues more effectively can come in very handy in reducing sleep-busting tension. For instance, you can agree not to talk about issues, conflicts, or problems within two hours of the time you should be falling asleep. Simply don't let stuff come up at those times. And when it does, get the issues and events back on the shelf quickly. This means you need to find other times to have these talks, when you are at your best and can work together as well as possible. This reduces tension and will pay off in a better bedtime routine, better sleep, and a happier marriage.

Finally, consider your bedtime routine in terms of what you each need in order to fall asleep and stay asleep for at least eight hours. How compatible are the two of you with regard to what time you get into bed, what time you turn out the lights, when you need to have it all quiet, and so on? When partners travel, the issue of differences can be more significant because you experience enough nights apart to know what your individual preferences are, and switching back and forth from your own preferences to what you need to do with each other can be difficult.

Some sleep experts recommend not having a television in the bedroom. In fact, for people who are having significant sleep problems, specialists almost always recommend removing the television from the bedroom or not using it at all. These professionals believe that you have the best chance of sleeping well if you keep your bedroom devoted exclusively to sleep or making love.

Ernesto and Gloria slept well through the first nine years of their marriage, including the early years with their children, who were now five and seven years old. Like many couples, they watch television in their bedroom. For years, their routine has been to turn off the TV at 10:30 after the end of a sitcom they both like. All was fine until another sitcom that Gloria really loved began being shown at 10:30. Gloria started watching TV later and later.

It had been Ernesto's habit for years to put his head on the pillow and be asleep within minutes, snoozing away by 10:50 most nights. With the TV on later, he started to miss this window to fall asleep and would then be awake until 1:00 or 2:00 in the morning. He started to get more and more tired and to have difficulty falling asleep. That made it harder to get up for work. Gloria's sleep pattern had also changed, but it didn't seem to be affecting her negatively the way it was affecting Ernesto. He was fast becoming more and more irritable and cranky. Each of them felt they were arguing a lot more than ever before, but neither really had any idea why.

One evening, during the news show they both watched before the first sitcom began, there was a brief story about sleep. An expert from a medical school in their city was talking about sleep problems couples had when sleeping together. One of the problems she described was exactly what Ernesto and Gloria were going through. They quickly figured out what had been happening, and took control over their bedtime routine. They didn't remove the TV from the bedroom, but they both agreed to an ironclad rule that it would go off at 10:30, no matter what. They decided and didn't let the pattern slide back into their lives. That was all they needed to get back on track with sleep and to restore peace in their marriage.

The bottom line: you need to take seriously the reality that you have a physical body. That means working together to get the sleep you need.

Is Your iPad Ruining Your Crash Pad?

Sleep experts have caught on to the fact that a lot of people are using their tablet computers through the evening. One of the problems with using bright, backlit screens right up to bedtime is that your body is very responsive to light in determining when you should be asleep and when you should be awake. A number of sleep experts believe (and some research shows this) that light streaming into your eyes suppresses melatonin, a chemical that helps regulate your sleep. Essentially, you are giving your body cues that it should be waking up, not shutting down.

As we noted earlier, sleep experts say TVs are a problem in the bedroom, but laptops and tablets are considered a greater problem because the light source is closer to your eyes and more intense. If you're having any trouble falling asleep and your habit is to read on a backlit device later into the evening, consider changing this pattern for a few weeks and see what happens. What do you have to lose? If you love to read at night, remember that there are still things called magazines, books, unlit e-readers, and even some Bibles that are still printed on paper. Imagine that!

⊙ ○ ⊙

In this chapter we have highlighted the importance of habits. Habits are crucial in managing the fact that you have a body and that you are married to someone who also has one. In each of the areas covered, you already have habits or automatic patterns that direct your behavior. Remember that to make changes, you have to replace old habits with new habits. That means becoming intentional in making smart and reasonable decisions about what you want to do differently and then acting to make that change happen.

Doing Your Part

1. Practice the relaxation exercise we gave you. It would be best of all for your health to practice it regularly, indefinitely. But, at the least, practice the progressive muscle relaxation routine several times a week for a month. With that level of practice—and continuing with occasional tune-ups—you will find you are able to make your body more relaxed when stress and anxiety rear up. You will have been building the relaxation response into the repertoire of your coping systems. Practice it together, if you like, taking turns guiding each other through the various muscle groups.

    There are many audio programs you can use to practice relaxation. Given your faith, you may want to be somewhat careful about what is taught in different approaches. PREP sells an inexpensive CD called *Calming Skills*.

    (continued)

2. Whether or not you and your mate are working though the book together—if your mate is up for this—find twenty minutes to talk together about your sleep patterns. Are you both sleeping well? Are there some simple changes you could make to improve sleep for both of you? Don't let sleep problems slide. Sit down together and decide what you can do to make them better.

3. Pray for wisdom about any ongoing stress you are facing. Ask God to give you new ideas for relieving and coping with stress. Pray for peace and the ability to face this enemy of intimacy as life partners who also happen to be living together in "earthen vessels."

8

Handling Events, Understanding Issues

Accept one another, then, just as Christ accepted you,
in order to bring praise to God.
ROMANS 15:7

All couples experience frustrating events, and all couples have difficult issues. In this chapter, we'll help you understand how issues and events are connected and how important it is to deal with them separately. Then we'll discuss the deeper, often hidden issues that affect relationships.

Issues Versus Events

There are many problems that couples encounter in marriage. These can be sources of conflict between partners or stresses that impact the whole marriage. There are many types of problems that couples struggle with, some of the most common being money, communication, and children. Other problems include struggles over in-laws, recreation, alcohol and drugs, religion, sex, careers, faith practices, and housework. We call all these things *issues.* Issues are not necessarily the things that couples argue about most frequently. What they do most often argue about are the small, day-to-day happenings of life. We call these things *events.* We want to help you handle events and issues separately and then separate the issues that are more apparent—like money, communication, and sex—from the deeper, often hidden, issues that impact your relationship. An example will help you see what we mean.

Ellen and Gregg have big money issues. One day, Ellen came home from work and put the checkbook down on the kitchen counter as she went to the bedroom to change. Gregg became livid when he took a look at the checkbook and saw an entry for $150 made out to a department store. When Ellen walked back into the kitchen, tired after a long day at work, she was looking for a hug or a "How was your day?" Instead, the conversation went like this:

GREGG: What did you spend this $150 on?

ELLEN: *(very defensive)* None of your business.

GREGG: Of course it's my business! We just decided on a budget, and here you go blowing it.

All of a sudden they were off into a huge argument about the issue of money. But it happened in the context of an event—Gregg's discovering that Ellen had spent $150. (It was actually for a new sweater for Gregg to celebrate his new job offer! But that never came up.)

Arguments about events like this are common. Issues and events work like the geysers in Yellowstone National Park. Underneath the park are caverns of hot water under pressure. The unresolved issues in your relationship are like these cauldrons of pressure. The issues that give you the most trouble contain the greatest amount of heat. The pressure keeps building up when you aren't talking about them in constructive ways. Then events trigger the messy eruption.

Many couples deal with important issues only in the context of triggering events. For Ellen and Gregg, there is so much negative energy stored up around the issue of money that it's easily triggered. They never sit down and talk about money in a constructive way, as a separate issue, but instead argue like this when checks bounce, bills come, and so on. They never get anywhere on the big issue because they spend their energy just dealing with the crises of the events. What about you? Do you set aside time to deal with issues ahead of time? Or do you wait until events trigger them?

Another couple, Tom and Samantha, had avoided talking about the intrusion of relatives on their time together. One evening, they went to a baseball game—the first time they'd been out for three or four weeks. On the way, Tom got a call on their cell phone from his mother. When the phone call ended, Samantha confronted him:

SAMANTHA: Why do you always let her interfere with our relationship? This is *our* evening out.

TOM: *(flaring up instantly)* Why do you always blast me when we're going out to have fun?

SAMANTHA: *(sounding indignant)* Well, I didn't know you were planning to bring your mother along!

TOM: *(dripping with sarcasm)* Ha, ha. Real funny, Sam.

Their evening was destroyed. They never even made it to the ballpark. They spent the night arguing about his mother calling and whether or not she was too involved in their lives.

Events tend to come up at the most inopportune times—you're ready to leave for work, you're coming home from work, you're trying to get everyone ready for church, you're going to bed, you're out to relax, the kids are fighting, friends have come over, and so forth. Events come up at times like these, but these are usually the worst times to deal with the issues.

What Are You Fussin' About?

There have been numerous studies of the top problem areas for couples. For example, in 1990, Ragnar Storaasli and Howard Markman at the University of Denver published a study examining the top-rated problem areas from before marriage to early into marriage. They found that before marriage, the top-rated problem areas were money, jealousy, relatives, and friends; but early in marriage, the list shifted to money, communication, and sex. Money was number one both before and after marriage. But notice the changes in the rest of the list: the problems shift from those related to defining the boundaries around the relationship (jealousy, friends, and relatives) to those related to how the two partners deal with each other (communication and sex). That makes sense, developmentally.

(continued)

In another study from the University of Denver, published in 2002, coauthor Scott Stanley, along with Howard Markman and Sarah Whitton, found in a national sample that money was the top-rated argument starter for first-time married couples, with problems about children being number two. However, for marriages other than first marriages, children were the number-one argument starter, followed by money. In both first and other marriages, chores were rated as the third most common source of conflicts, but at a rate far below the issues of money and children.

The reasons people give for divorcing are different from what they report as causing arguments. In one large random survey conducted in 2000–01 by a team of scholars for the state of Oklahoma, the top three reasons people gave for divorcing were a lack of commitment, too much conflict and arguing, and infidelity. The same reasons for divorcing, in a slightly different order of importance, were given by individuals interviewed about their divorces by Shelby Scott and colleagues at the University of Denver in a study published in 2013. Using a large national sample, Paul Amato at Penn State University and Denise Previti published a paper in 2003 showing that people were most likely to report infidelity, incompatibility, and drug use as reasons they divorced.

What do all these findings mean? The daily stresses and strains in marriage tend to be things like money, children, and chores, but the factors that really tear a marriage down over time are problems with commitment; chronic, poorly handled conflict; and substance abuse. You are normal if there are issues you struggle with in your relationship, but your commitment and how you treat each other will tell the most important story for your marriage over time.

How to Deal with Triggering Events

We suggest that you edit out the tendency to argue about the issue *right then*, when an event triggers it. Don't try to deal with important issues only in the context of triggering events. There are times when simply dropping the matter for the moment is the wise strategy. As Solomon in all his wisdom tells us, "There is a time for everything, and a season for every activity under heaven: . . . a time to be silent and a time to speak" (Ecclesiastes 3:1, 7). In the argument just described, Samantha could have said, "That phone call from your mother really set off an issue for me. We need to have a talk about it later." In this way, the event is acknowledged, but the issue is left for a time when the two of you can deal with it more effectively. Likewise, Tom could have said, "Listen, let's take a Time Out. I can see you are feeling hurt, but let's wait for a better time to talk about the issue. How about tomorrow after dinner?" If they've been practicing the skills we've presented so far, they could have saved their evening by containing the event so that it didn't trigger the explosive unresolved issues about Tom's mother and their time together. That's what we mean by separating issues from events. It's a very wise thing to do.

When an event does occur, you could also try to have a brief but effective talk about the issue for just a few minutes—agreeing to have a more thorough discussion later. You might say, "Let's talk about what just happened for a few moments and then try to move on and have a nice evening together." You can use the Speaker-Listener Technique so that you are sure you both are heard. Then let it go until later.

One reason people focus on events and let them turn into issue discussions is that "later" never happens (avoidance). So the person who is most bothered by the issue doesn't feel that he or she can wait. When this happens a lot, you can feel as though you're living in a marital minefield, with the issues being the explosives and the events being the triggers. You never know when you're going to step on another mine. One effect of living in a minefield is that you feel tense around one another most of the time, rather than open and relaxed. What you want most is simply to enjoy each other as best friends. But instead you end up feeling uptight around each other a lot of the time. The effect on your marriage can be devastating. The goal is to control where, when, and how you will deal with the issues in your relationship.

Hidden Issues

It's often easy to recognize the issues being triggered by events because they are pretty closely connected to one another. With

Ellen and Gregg, his looking at the checkbook started the event, and the issue was money. That's not hard to figure out. But sometimes couples get into fights about trivial events—like the toilet seat being left up—that don't seem to be attached to any particular issue.

Arguments about these kinds of things are signs that you aren't getting at the real issues. It's not about money, it's not about careers, it's not about housework, it's not really about his leaving the toilet seat up; the real issues are deeper and more elusive. We call these *hidden issues*. Hidden issues often drive couples' most frustrating and destructive arguments. For example, Samantha and Tom ended up arguing about his mother and his taking calls from her at any time. But the real issue is probably that Samantha feels that she is not as important to him as his relatives.

When we say these issues are often "hidden," we mean they are usually not the things being talked about openly, even though they are the really important issues. But they get lost in the flow of the argument. For instance, you may be very aware of feeling uncared for, but when certain events come up, that's not what you talk about.

To summarize, events are everyday happenings such as dirty dishes or a check bouncing. Issues are those larger topics, like money, sex, and in-laws, that all couples must deal with. Hidden issues are the deeper, fundamental issues that usually lie underneath the arguments about issues and events. We will discuss five hidden issues that come up frequently in our work with couples: *power, caring, recognition, commitment,* and *acceptance.* There are surely others, but these five capture a lot of what goes on in relationships. As you will see, because these issues are the things closest to our hearts, they often have a deeper spiritual significance.

Hidden Issues of Control and Power

With control issues, the question is one of power and status. For instance: Who decides who does the chores? Are your needs and desires just as important as your partner's, or is there an inequality? Is your input important, or are major decisions made without you? Who's in charge? If you deal with these kinds of issues a lot, you may be dealing with the hidden issue of control.

This hidden issue tends to come into play when decisions come up—even small ones. For example, what happens if one of you really wants to order pizza and the other really feels like having Chinese food? This is an event without a lot of long-term significance. Nevertheless, if either of you is unyielding in what you want, you can have a lot of conflict about something as simple as what's for dinner. Whatever the topic or disagreement, control issues are least likely to come up when there's a good sense of being a team and each partner's needs and desires are considered in your decisions. Such teamwork reflects love and humility. Control and power arguments reflect selfishness. James really nailed it when he wrote,

> What causes fights and quarrels among you? Don't they come from your desires that battle within you? You want something but don't get it. You kill and covet, but you cannot have what you want. You quarrel and fight. You do not have, because you do not ask God. When you ask, you do not receive, because you ask with wrong motives, that you may spend what you get on your pleasures. (James 4:1–3)

As James says, a lot of power battles arise from selfish motives, as we struggle to get *our* way, to have what *we* want. It's no accident that money is rated the number-one problem area in our studies at the University of Denver. So many decisions in our lives revolve around money. If you have significant power or control issues in your marriage, it's likely that you struggle a lot with money, as well as with any number of other things. Money in and of itself isn't the deeper issue, but it's an issue that provides many events for triggering the deeper issue of control and power.

Also, anytime you must make a decision together, especially if it's an important one, the control issue can be triggered. Working together as a team is the best antidote to battles for control. Letting things just slide is not the answer.

Hidden Issues of Needing and Caring

A second major arena where we see hidden issues emerge involves caring. Here, the main theme is the extent to which you feel loved and cared for by your partner.

Jill and Mitch repeatedly fought over who should refill the orange juice pitcher. But OJ wasn't the real issue. As it turned out, Mitch had always seen his mother refilling the OJ as a demonstration of her love for him. Because Jill wouldn't do it, he felt that it meant she didn't love him—a hidden caring issue. So he was always pushing her to refill the OJ. He was very aware of feeling uncared for, but in their arguments about orange juice, he didn't talk about it. Instead, he focused on what he saw as Jill's stubbornness.

For her part, Jill was thinking, "Who's he to tell me to make the orange juice? Where does he get off saying I have to do it?" Jill had a hidden control issue, thinking he was trying to force her to live a certain way. That really wasn't his motive, but she was very sensitive about control because she'd previously been married to a domineering man. Their individual hidden issues were underlying their arguments. For Mitch and Jill, a good discussion about what was happening around this seemingly simple event of making OJ finally touched on the hidden issues. As a result, they ended up feeling much closer, and OJ no longer seemed all that important.

MITCH (SPEAKER): So for me, it's really not about wanting to control you. I've been so primed by my upbringing to connect refilling the OJ with love that I've put this pressure on you to do it to be sure that you love me.

JILL (LISTENER): *(She summarizes in her own words.)* So for you, the key issue is wanting to know I care, not wanting to control me?

MITCH (SPEAKER): *(He goes on to validate her as well.)* Exactly, and I can see how you'd be feeling controlled without knowing that.

FLOOR SWITCH

JILL (SPEAKER): You're right. I've really felt you wanted to control me, and that's a real hot button, given what I went through with Joe.

MITCH (LISTENER): So it really did seem to you that I just wanted to control you, and that's an especially sensitive area given what you went through with Joe.

JILL (SPEAKER): You got it. I want to be your partner, not your hired hand.

MITCH (LISTENER): *(He captures what she's saying in his own words.)*
 Sounds like you just want us to work as a team.
JILL (SPEAKER): Yeah! That's really important to me.

As you can see from the tail end of their conversation, talking about the deeper concerns paved the way for greater connection instead of alienation over an empty OJ container. This is another example where it would be very hard to solve the problem about the event (refilling the orange juice) unless they were communicating well enough to get the hidden issues out in the open. But it's hard to talk about such vulnerable stuff if you can't talk safely! The key is to be able to talk about these kinds of deeper issues in a safe way, rather than letting them operate as powerful pressure points in arguments.

Hidden Issues of Recognition

The third type of hidden issue involves recognition. Are your activities and accomplishments appreciated by your partner? Whereas caring issues involve concerns about being cared for or loved, recognition issues are more about feeling *valued* by your partner for who you are and what you do.

 For example, many people tell us that they do not feel that their partners appreciate what they do for the marriage or family. For example, many people work hard to bring in income but feel taken for granted by their mate. For others, it is not so much work outside the home that raises feelings of being unappreciated but work inside and around the home. Overall, married women still do more housework than married men, but men, on average, do more than they used to do. Many women who work full-time outside the home feel that their husbands do not recognize how hard they also work within the home. Many men feel that they do more around the house than they ever saw their fathers do, and feel unrecognized by their wives for their efforts at home. And we've mentioned only household tasks and responsibilities. Life is full of opportunities for partners in a marriage to feel that the other does not recognize something important about who they are or what they do.

Even the apostles seem to have struggled with the recognition issue. Even after years of walking with Christ, Jesus' most trusted companions got into an argument about who deserved the highest place in His kingdom (Matthew 20:17–28). Jesus rebuked them, linking this desire for recognition with the desire to have power over others, and admonished them to focus instead on serving one another (Matthew 20:26, 27). Such advice couldn't be more apt in marriage. This may seem like a paradox, but one of the best ways to serve your mate is to recognize his or her contributions to your marriage. That's a gift you can give to your mate that will return to you in kind. How long has it been since you told your partner how much you appreciate the things he or she does?

Hidden Issues of Commitment

The focus of this fourth hidden issue is on the long-term security of the relationship—"Are you going to stay with me?" One couple we worked with, Alice and Chuck, had huge arguments about separate checking accounts. He would complain bitterly about her having a separate account whenever the bank statement arrived and he saw her balance.

For Chuck, the hidden issue was commitment. When he was a child, his mother had taken him and left his father. He knew prior to leaving that his mother had begun to put money in her own bank account, which he was instructed not to tell Daddy about. His mother left his father after she'd saved up several thousand dollars in her account. Now, when the statement for Alice's account would arrive, Chuck associated it with his childhood experience and would think that Alice could be planning to leave him. That was not at all her plan. But because he had never talked openly about his fear, she wasn't given the opportunity to alleviate his anxiety by affirming her commitment. The issue kept fueling explosive conflict in events connected to it.

When your commitment to one another feels secure, it brings a deep kind of safety to your relationship—safety based in a confidence in your mate's promise to always be there for you, to lift you up in tough times, to cherish you for a lifetime, no matter what. As we said in the first chapter, the oneness that God planned for marriage is a oneness of permanence—not because God loves restrictions, but because he cares about our need to have a relationship that we can count on.

Many people who have experienced divorce (their own or their parents') or forms of abandonment as children (such as their father disappearing from their lives) struggle with fears related to commitment. In this day when more people than ever before have grown up with fragmented families, the hidden issue is not all that hidden for many couples. It is more important than ever before to protect and reinforce the commitment in your marriage so that you both can feel the security that comes from trusting that you will be there for each other through life.

Acceptance: The Bottom Line

There seems to be one primary issue that can underlie all the others we've discussed: the need for acceptance. Sometimes this is felt more as a fear of rejection, but the fundamental issue is the same. At the deepest level, people are motivated to find acceptance and to avoid rejection in their relationships. This reflects the deep need we all have to be both respected and connected. Consider again the foundational teaching we looked at in the first chapter. Adam and Eve did not know fear, only openness and no shame, until they sinned. The fall brought fear of rejection and barriers they had not known before:

> Then the eyes of both of them were opened, and they realized they were naked; so they sewed fig leaves together and made coverings for themselves. Then the man and his wife heard the sound of the LORD God as he was walking in the garden in the cool of the day, and they hid from the LORD God among the trees of the garden. But the LORD God called to the man, "Where are you?" He answered, "I heard you in the garden, and I was afraid because I was naked; so I hid." (Genesis 3:7–10)

This fundamental fear of rejection drives so many other hidden issues. And the fear is real. Marriage involves imperfect people who can deeply hurt and even reject each other at times. You can see this fear of rejection come up in many ways. For example, some people are afraid that if they make their real desires known, their partner will reject them. Perhaps one partner asks for what he wants indirectly rather than directly. For example, "Wouldn't you like to make love tonight?" rather than "I would like to make love with you tonight." Many people are indirect about what they ask of their partners. Their desires are not stated clearly because of a fear of rejection.

The issue of acceptance is so critical that we are specifically called on in scripture to accept one another:

> Accept one another, then, just as Christ accepted you, in order to bring praise to God. (Romans 15:7)

Passages like these are not specific to marriage, but we can think of no other relationship in which acting on what we are called to do matters so much. No matter what our differences or problems, we are called to accept our mates with a richness that frees them to feel safer in the relationship. What is even more important, as we accept one another in this way, the result is that God's acceptance of us is modeled to the world in perhaps the fullest expression of grace that can be known. And—when His marvelous grace is seen in human relationships—He gets the praise.

Recognizing the Signs of Hidden Issues

You can't handle hidden issues unless you can identify them. There are four key ways to tell when hidden issues may be affecting your interaction.

Wheel Spinning

One sign of hidden issues is finding each other talking about some problem over and over again but getting nowhere. It's as if you're spinning your wheels. These repeated struggles can be very discouraging. If an argument starts with you thinking, "Here we go again," you should suspect a hidden issue. You aren't getting anywhere on the problem because you probably aren't talking about what really matters—the hidden issue. So you go around and around in a hopeless circle.

Trivial Triggers

A second way to identify hidden issues is to notice when minor things blow up out of all proportion. The earlier argument between Jill and Mitch is a great example. The refilling of the OJ container seems like a trivial event, but it triggers horrendous arguments driven by the issues of power and caring.

Avoidance

You can suspect that hidden issues are in play when one or both of you are avoiding certain topics or levels of intimacy. It could be that some walls have gone up between you. This often means that there are important, unexpressed issues affecting the relationship. Perhaps it seems too risky to talk directly about feeling unloved or insecure. Trouble is, those concerns have a way of coming up anyway.

There are many topics that couples avoid, reflecting hidden issues in their relationship. For example, we have talked with many couples from different cultural or religious backgrounds who strongly avoid talking about these differences. We think this usually reflects concerns about acceptance—"Will you accept me fully if we really explore our differences here?" Avoiding such topics not only allows hidden issues to remain hidden but also puts the relationship at greater risk, as these are often important differences that can have great impact on the marriage.

Other common but taboo topics in marriage include issues of sex, weight, and money. There are many such sensitive topics that people avoid dealing with in their relationships out of fear of rejection. What issues do you avoid talking about?

Scorekeeping

When one or both or you start keeping score, there are probably hidden issues in your relationship. Scorekeeping reflects some problem that needs attention. It could mean that you are not feeling recognized for what you put into the marriage. It could mean that you are less committed, as we'll explain later. It could mean that you are feeling controlled, so you're keeping track of the times you think your partner has taken advantage of you. Whatever the issue, scorekeeping can be a sign that there are important things not being talked about—just documented.

Handling Hidden Issues

Recognizing the signs that hidden issues are operating is an important first step. But what can you do once you realize that one is affecting your relationship? The most important thing you can do is simply to talk about these hidden issues constructively, perhaps at a time set aside just for this purpose. This will be easier if you are cultivating an atmosphere of teamwork using the techniques we've presented thus far. We strongly recommend using the Speaker-Listener Technique when you are trying to explore such sensitive areas. Make it safe to connect!

One other important strategy is to deal with the issue in terms of Problem Discussion, not Problem Solution (see Chapter Six). Try not to jump to shallow solutions. The deeper the issue, the less likely it is that problem solving will be the answer. What you need first and foremost is to hear each other and understand the feelings and concerns. Such validating discussions have the greatest impact on hidden issues because they work directly against the fear of rejection. If you haven't been talking about the real issue, how could your solution address what's really at stake? There is no more powerful form of acceptance than really listening in an understanding way to the thoughts and feelings of your mate. Safe, open, "no-fig-leaf" talks have real power to overcome fear of rejection and to heal the wounds of the past.

A Detailed Example

We round out this chapter with a detailed example of how the really important deeper issues will come out if you are communicating clearly and safely. Simon and Rachel were newlyweds but struggling. Both were working long hours to make ends meet. When they did have time together, they'd frequently run into difficulties with TV, especially because Simon would watch a great deal of sports. Rachel was very upset about this. Many events arose around the TV, but much more important hidden issues were involved. As you will clearly see, Rachel was really concerned about caring and Simon about acceptance.

They could have argued forever on the level of the *events*—for example, who would control the TV. They made much greater progress when talking about the *issues* within the safety of the Speaker-Listener Technique. This was one of the first times they used the technique, so you'll see that their skills were a little rough around the edges at this point, with some mind reading and less than ideal paraphrasing. Yet they ended up talking about the real issues.

We hadn't told Simon and Rachel to focus on hidden issues, but they came out anyway. We find that this happens regularly when couples are doing a good job with the Speaker-Listener Technique.

RACHEL (SPEAKER): It seems like you spend more time with the television than conversing with me. There are times when you can stay up late to watch television, but if it comes down to spending time with me, you're tired. You can go to bed and fall right to sleep.

SIMON (LISTENER): So you are saying it's more comfortable for me to watch television than it is to be with you?

RACHEL (SPEAKER): *(with a clear sigh of relief at being heard)* Yeah.

Rachel is not feeling accepted or cared for by Simon. This comes out clearly here, yet in the past when they'd argued about the TV, they never got to what was really going on. When he paraphrases that it seems to her that he's more comfortable watching TV than spending time with her, he really hits home. In one sense, his paraphrase goes way beyond her words, but it seems to reflect exactly what the matter seems like to her. She can tell from the quality of his paraphrase that he's really listening to her. This does more to address her hidden issue of wanting to know he cares than all the problem solving in the world could do.

It's not clear whether he agrees that he's more comfortable watching TV, but it is clear that he heard her. If he is uncomfortable with her, it may be the result of how they've been mishandling the hidden issues around the TV events. They go on:

SIMON (LISTENER): Can I have the floor?

FLOOR SWITCH

SIMON (SPEAKER): Before we were married, you never had any gripes about me watching sports.

RACHEL (LISTENER): So what you are saying is that in the beginning I didn't mind the fact that you watched sports so much. We did spend a lot of time together, and that seemed to satisfy me.

SIMON (SPEAKER): Right, and also before we were married, even though we spent time together, you never really had the opportunity to see that I did watch football as much as possible.

RACHEL (LISTENER): So what you are saying is that I didn't get to see this part of you watching football as much as I do now.

SIMON (SPEAKER): Right. But you did know about me playing sports, that I was actively involved in sports—not just football.

RACHEL (LISTENER): So what you're saying is that because you played sports in your previous time of knowing me, I should have known that you would really be sports oriented as far as watching it all the time.

SIMON (SPEAKER): Yes and no. I'm not saying that you should have known, but you saw that was a part of me, whether you want to accept it or not.

RACHEL (LISTENER): OK, so what you are saying is that I saw this part of you being involved in sports, so this is something that I should have known was going to come up throughout the relationship. Is that what you're saying?

SIMON (SPEAKER): More or less.

When Rachel complained about Simon watching so much football, he felt that she was attacking a core part of his identity. So for him, the fundamental hidden issue revolves around acceptance of who he is and recognition of this part of him. He really gets this out in the open in his statement that "you saw that was a part of me, whether you want to accept it or not."

After enough discussion on these deeper levels, they went on to engage in some very effective problem solving about time together and time watching TV. But we believe that they could not have done this if they had not dealt more directly with the hidden issues first.

Going Deeper with Christ

Hidden issues are complicated, mostly because they involve fear about the deeper issues of one's soul. Most deeper desires and fears are legitimate; some are not and are more based in self-protection. In either case, we believe that people are less prone to be triggered by hidden issues if they have no hidden issues with the Lord. For example, when you know at a deep level that you are perfectly cared for and accepted in Christ, you're a lot less likely to be triggered about acceptance and commitment in your relationships with others—especially your mate. After all, there is such a deep security that comes from knowing who you are in Christ that there's much less to be threatened by with other people. As we end this chapter, we present a meditation on the person and character of Jesus Christ as we think about the deeper issues we have considered here.

Jesus has no hidden issues, so He is completely open with us. He cannot be triggered by hidden issues because He has a totally secure identity. Because we are forgiven in Christ, the father can pour out His love on us. Experiencing this love can drive out the fear that causes us to be defensive about hidden issues (1 John 4:18). If we deeply believe in His love for us, we may well have fewer hidden issues with Him and with others as well. The following passages are merely a few examples of the things we know about the Lord, which should challenge our own defenses and deepest fears about our relationship with Him. As we continue to grow in the experience of His wonderful and absolutely perfect acceptance and love for us, we can become less defensive and be released to express the same radical love that He showed to others. Expressing that love in your marriage would have a powerful effect.

POWER: Contrast Jesus' model of power with the world's. What do we have to fear from someone who has given His very life for us?

Jesus called them together and said, "You know that the rulers of the Gentiles lord it over them, and their high officials exercise authority over them. Not so with you. Instead, whoever wants to become great among you must be your servant, and whoever wants to be first must be your slave—just as the Son of Man did not come to be served, but to serve, and to give his life as a ransom for many." (Matthew 20:25–28)

CARING: Jesus' care for us is indisputable, but do we really believe it?

As the Father has loved me, so have I loved you. Now remain in my love. (John 15:9)

Greater love has no one than this, that he lay down his life for his friends. (John 15:13)

RECOGNITION: What more recognition could we expect than to realize that the Lord of the universe has valued us to the point of making us coworkers with Him in His labors?

As you sent me into the world, I have sent them into the world. (John 17:18)

COMMITMENT: Want someone you can depend on forever and completely?

Keep your lives free from the love of money and be content with what you have, because God has said, "Never will I leave you; never will I forsake you." (Hebrews 13:5)

ACCEPTANCE: Meditate on the profound acceptance of being called Jesus' friend.

I no longer call you servants, because a servant does not know his master's business. Instead, I have called you friends, for everything that I learned from my Father I have made known to you. (John 15:15)

o o o

Our goal in this chapter has been to give you a way to explore and understand some of the most frustrating aspects of intimate relationships. You can prevent a lot of damage by learning to handle events and issues with the time and skill they require. Using the concepts we have presented in this chapter, along with all the skills and techniques presented in the first part of the book, will help you do just that.

For all too many couples, the hidden issues never come out. They fester and produce fear, sadness, and resentment that erode and eventually destroy the marriage. It just doesn't have to be that way. When you learn to discuss deeper issues openly and with emphasis on validating each other, the issues that had been generating the greatest conflicts can actually become means of deepening your oneness and drawing you closer together.

Doing Your Part

To help you look at your own relationship, we recommend that you first pray for your relationship and for your mate. Hidden issues are hidden because they are difficult to think and talk about. Instead of allowing anxiety or fear to build barriers, ask God to help you build and maintain a deeper connection. God is eager to hear your requests about everything (Philippians 4:6)—including your marriage.

Work through the following questions on your own, then plan a time to talk together about your impressions.

1. Take some time to reflect more on why there is no need for hidden issues with the Lord. Meditating more deeply on who Christ is and what He has done for you is the most powerful basis we can imagine for breaking down barriers in relationships.
2. Think about the signs of hidden issues. Do you notice that one or more of these come up in your relationship? What do you notice happening most often: Wheel spinning? Trivial triggers? Avoidance? Scorekeeping?
3. Consider which hidden issues might be triggered most often in your relationship. Note if there are certain events that have triggered or keep triggering the issues. Make a list of the common triggering events for the issues of power and control, caring, recognition, commitment, and acceptance.
4. Set aside time to talk together about your observations and thoughts. Most couples have certain hidden issues that come up repeatedly. Identifying these can help you draw together as you each learn to handle those issues with care. Also, as you discuss these matters, you have an excellent opportunity to get in some more practice with the Speaker-Listener Technique.

9

Unraveling the Mysteries of Expectations

Hope deferred makes the heart sick, but a longing fulfilled is a tree of life.
PROVERBS 13:12

In the previous chapter, we described hidden issues. Hidden issues can act like deep unmet expectations and can fuel conflict and create distance between partners. Now we're ready to build on those concepts by focusing on expectations: what they are, where they come from, and whether or not they are reasonable or "doable." This chapter includes a very important exercise that will help you explore and share your expectations for your relationship. In fact, this entire chapter is designed to prepare you for the exercise—it's that important.

The Power of Expectations

Expectations reflect what we long for and how we wish things would be. When they are fulfilled, they are a "tree of life." But when what we expect does not happen, the hope deferred makes our hearts sick. To a large degree, we are disappointed or satisfied in life based on how well what is happening matches what we expect. Therefore, expectations play a crucial role in determining our level of satisfaction in marriage.

We want you to think about expectations more as the ways you think things are *supposed* to be in your relationship. For example, you have specific expectations for such minor things as who will refill the orange juice pitcher or who will balance the checkbook—the stuff of events. You also have expectations about such common issues as money, housework, in-laws, and sex. In addition, you have expectations about hidden issues—what it means to be cared for and loved, how power will be shared (or not shared), and what commitment means in your relationship. Because expectations touch on such important matters in life, many also have direct spiritual overtones.

Bumping into Walls

Imagine moving into a new house. This house looks wonderful from the outside, but you soon discover that it has a feature you may not have counted on—many of the key interior walls are invisible. Although you cannot see all the walls clearly, you still bump into them and find that you have to move slowly to keep from smashing your head. Over time, you learn to mark these invisible walls as your awareness of their presence grows. But for some time, it can look like marriage in mime, as you feel for the invisible walls you now know are there.

Unmet expectations carry great potential for conflict because they so clearly highlight that you and your mate are, in fact, different people with differing needs and desires and views about marriage. On the positive side, working together to clarify the expectations in your marriage can really help you move from "me-ness" to "we-ness."

Expectations and Conflict

Sue and Mike have been married about a year, and things have gone pretty well. Sue, however, is upset about the way Mike goes out once or twice a week with his longtime guy friends, sometimes to movies and sometimes to sporting events and sometimes just to hang out together to watch TV or play video games. This drives Sue nuts. During their premarital counseling at church, this type of thing was discussed as an example of issues around the meaning of "leaving and cleaving." There was not really anything wrong with what Mike was doing with his friends except that he was doing so much of it. He was gone several evenings a week.

In some ways, Mike has remained stuck to elements of the single lifestyle. Sue, in contrast, has expectations of spending more time together now that they are married. Sometimes the event of his going out triggers huge arguments between them, like this one.

SUE: *(feeling frustrated and lonely)* I don't see why you have to go out again tonight. You've been out a lot lately.

MIKE: *(obviously irritated, and rolling his eyes)* How many times do we have to argue about this? I go out just a few times a week. I don't see any problem with that.

SUE: Well, I do. All of your guy friends are single, but you are not.

MIKE: So?

SUE: So, they are doing what single guys do, not what married *men* do. Plus, how are those guys not also talking and thinking about girls a lot? What's that like for you? You found one, remember?

MIKE: *(angered, feeling attacked)* We don't go out hunting for girls. I don't like it that you don't trust me.

SUE: I just don't think a married man needs to be out so often with his single friends. It's not what marriage is about.

MIKE: *(turning away and walking out)* You sound jealous. I have to leave now; I'll be back by ten.

Sue and Mike are arguing about an expectation. She didn't expect that he'd still go out with his friends so often after they got married. She associates their "going out" with being single, not being married. Mike expected to cut back time with friends, but not to stop seeing them altogether. He was used to hanging out with them several nights a week for years. Further, these nights do mean a lot to him. He sees nothing wrong, except that Sue isn't handling it very well.

When important expectations don't match, there will be pain and conflict. You can easily imagine that hidden issues of caring and control are at work in Sue's heart. Mike is feeling controlled by her expectations about marriage. They each think that the other's expectations are unfair and unrealistic.

Men, Women, and Thoughts of Divorcing

In 2002, Scott Stanley, Howard Markman, and Sarah Whitton published findings from a national survey wherein participants rated their marriages on several measures: divorce potential, overall positive connection, and negative interaction (in other words, the Communication Danger Signs described in Chapter Two). Divorce potential was measured by asking people if they had thought about divorce or talked about getting a divorce with friends or an attorney in the past year. Positive connection was measured by asking about overall marital satisfaction, the ability to talk as friends, satisfaction with the sensual connection, and whether they have "a lot of fun together" with their mates.

Popular writers have overblown the degree of difference between men and women in marriage. Differences do exist, but they are, on average, far smaller than is usually claimed. Of course your marriage could strongly fit the stereotypes—or be just the opposite from them. Stanley, Markman, and Whitton found that for both men and women, less positive connection and more negative interaction were associated with higher divorce potential. No surprise there. However, the researchers did find a difference between men and women. For women, lack of positive connection was more strongly associated with divorce potential than negative interaction, whereas the pattern was just the opposite for men: negative interaction was more strongly associated with divorce potential. In other words, women are more likely to be thinking about leaving a marriage when there is not enough positive connection, and men are more likely to be thinking about leaving a marriage when there is too much conflict.

We think these findings could mean that women strongly expect their marriages to have intimacy and positive connection, whereas men strongly expect their marriages to have peace. Both expectations are reasonable and achievable. What matters the most to you?

Where Expectations Come From

Expectations build up over a lifetime of experiences. Most expectations are based in the past, but still operate in the present. There are three primary sources for our expectations: our family of origin, our previous relationships, and the culture we live in.

Family of Origin

You picked up many expectations unconsciously as you grew up. Your family experiences laid down many patterns—good and bad—that became the models for how you think things should or will be. Expectations were transmitted both directly by what your parents said and indirectly by what you observed. They are expressed in your relationship clearly or unclearly. No one comes to marriage with a blank slate.

Let's look at several examples. If you observed your parents avoiding all manner of conflict, you may have developed the expectation that couples should seek peace at any price. So if there's disagreement and conflict in your marriage, it may seem to you as though the world is going to end. Or if you observed your parents being very affectionate, you may have come to expect that in your marriage. If your parents divorced, you may have some expectation in the back of your mind that marriages don't really last. If you observed your parents having personal devotions, you may have arrived at the belief that this expression of personal spiritual intimacy is vital for a healthy Christian marriage. You get the idea.

Nancy and John had terrible conflicts about parenting their five-year-old son, Joey. Nancy came from a Christian home, but her mother and stepfather were extremely harsh in their discipline. Her stepfather would actually chase the kids around the house when he was angry. If you were caught, you were spanked, sometimes very hard. Worse, almost, was that both parents were perfectionists who screamed or nagged about the slightest mistakes. John came from a family where the kids could pretty much do whatever they wanted. There were limits, but they were pretty loose or vague. Whenever Joey acted up, John responded by raising his voice and adding his middle name. There were no real consequences. So Joey had learned to all but ignore John's raised voice and only stirred when his middle name was used.

With her background, Nancy expected that someone was about to get spanked when John raised his voice. Her expectation was based in the past, but still had real power. She'd even get sick to her stomach from the tension when Joey was about to get in trouble. It was as if her stepfather were chasing her all over again.

At times, she saw John as being abusive, even though he wasn't. Her expectations became powerful filters, distorting her perception of what was really going on. Actually, John, like his parents, was quite lenient. Sure, he could lose his temper and yell from time to time, but he was really a softy.

As a consequence of their expectations, neither of them provided consistent discipline for Joey, who suffered from their inconsistency. His teacher reported that he was one of the most difficult kids in the school. We could give thousands more examples like this. The point is, you each have many powerful expectations that come from your families of origin. Understanding this can be an important first step in dealing more effectively with those expectations and in reducing the conflict that arises as a result of them.

Previous Relationships

You have also developed expectations from the other important relationships in your life, such as previous dating relationships or marriages. You have expectations about how to kiss, what is romantic, how to communicate about problems, how recreational time should be spent, what church to go to and how often to attend, who should take responsibility for the first move to make up after a fight, and so on.

Suppose, for example, that you got dumped in a previous dating relationship when you began to open up about painful childhood events. Logically, you might have developed the expectation that people can't be trusted to accept the deepest parts of who you are. If you have, you'll pull back and withhold this kind of information, and this could reduce the potential intimacy in your present relationship.

Studies show that people who have come to expect that others can't be trusted have more difficulty feeling securely attached to another person. The mistrust can lead to trouble if it is so intense that you can't allow someone you really love to get close. This would be all the greater reason to keep it safe to connect in your relationship. It's also a reason why we believe that maintaining clear and strong commitment in marriage is both more challenging and harder to do than ever before. There are more people all the time who have had serious experiences of insecurity in family or prior relationships.

At the other end of the spectrum, many expectations are about such minor things that it's hard to imagine they could become so important. It all depends on what meanings are attached to the expectations. Paul, for example, told us that his past girlfriend had drilled it into him that she didn't want him opening doors for her. He thought, "OK, no big deal." Now, with his wife, Janet, he was finding quite the opposite. She liked men to hold doors, and she'd get upset with him if he forgot. He had to work to unlearn the expectation he'd finally learned so well.

Door-opening events happen pretty often in life. For Paul and Janet, they triggered conflict because she'd interpret his trouble remembering as a sign that he didn't care about her. This is another example of a negative interpretation causing more damage than the actual event. Believing that his devotion was being challenged, he'd get angry at her. This just confirmed what she already believed—"I knew he didn't care."

Are you aware of the expectations you have for your partner that are really based in your experiences with others? It's worth thinking about, as your partner isn't the same person as those you've known from the past.

Cultural Influences and Background

There are a variety of powerful cultural factors that influence your expectations: books, television, movies, and so forth. What expectations would you have about marriage, for example, based on watching thousands of hours of TV in America? For most of us, this is not a hypothetical question. Popular shows send very powerful messages about what is expected or "normal." Some of the expectations from television are reasonable; many more are not. What expectations do people learn from reality shows?

What about your cultural background? Did you both grow up in the same country and in the same culture, or do you have very different backgrounds? When couples come from different cultures (even different parts of the same country), they have learned different rules, values, and expectations for all kinds of things. These expectations cover areas as wide ranging as child discipline, sexuality, money management, and roles in marriage. It's very important to understand these differences and how they affect your relationship, rather than to assume that you both see things from the same vantage point. You may not be on the same page as much as you believe.

Core Beliefs

In addition to all the general expectations you have for marriage and your relationship, you also have core beliefs about life, God, and how it all fits together. Even if you do not see yourself as being religious or spiritual, you have a core belief system. For many, that belief system is reflected most clearly in spiritual beliefs and religious practices. What was the spiritual or religious tradition of your upbringing? How is that similar or different from where you are now? Did you grow up in a "Christian" home? What kind? What if you and your partner are from entirely different spiritual backgrounds? How will you, or are you, handling that?

Studies have consistently shown that greater differences in religious background translate to greater risk for a marriage. It's not that a marriage is somehow doomed to fail when there are significant differences in this area, but there usually is more to work out and more room for conflict. In contrast, it's probably easier for couples to construct a shared "vision" for their future when the two partners have a clearer, shared core belief system. This makes it easier to see why Paul warned about couples unequally yoked in marriage (2 Corinthians 6:14). Sometimes couples from different backgrounds marry believing that the differences will not matter. But many people return to their roots when they have children or as they age. What does not seem very important now may become much more important later.

One more point of caution. Don't be misled into thinking that just because you may both have a "Christian" background, you automatically see all spiritual issues similarly. We know many couples in which both partners come from seemingly very similar backgrounds but still get into intense conflicts over many areas touching on core beliefs. For example, say you both believe strongly in giving to the Lord's work, but for one of you, that means tithing your gross income, and for the other it means giving twenty bucks when the plate is passed on Sunday morning. How are you handling that? You can see how in this case, the spiritual belief combines with what is already a major conflict area for many couples, leaving room for real fireworks. What about prayer together, or how often you attend church together? These issues are associated with very real expectations in marriage— expectations that too many couples do not directly discuss.

What to Do About Expectations

Expectations can lead either to massive disappointment and frustration or to deeper connection. There are four keys to handling expectations well:

1. Be *aware* of what you expect.
2. Be *reasonable* in what you expect.
3. Be *clear* about what you expect.
4. Be *willing* to listen to the Lord.

Be Aware of What You Expect

Even when you are not fully aware of them, unmet expectations can lead to great disappointment and frustration. These feelings are your most important clue that some expectation is unmet. It's a good habit to take a moment when you are disappointed, sad, or angry about something in your marriage and ask yourself what you expected. Doing this can help you become more aware of important expectations that otherwise may be unconsciously affecting your relationship. Part of the discipline of doing this is your recognizing that disappointment doesn't necessarily mean that your partner is doing something wrong. It means that you hold an expectation and that you can start by being more aware of it as an expectation.

Jim, for instance, would feel very sad when he'd ask his wife, Dawn, to go boating with him and she'd say, "That's OK. Go ahead without me and have a great time." She'd rather stay home and garden. He worked very hard during the week as an appliance repairman for a major department store chain, and boating was the greatest relaxation for him. Dawn didn't care for boating, but really wanted him to feel OK about having a nice time without her.

Jim's sadness was a clue that there was some important expectation at work. In thinking about it, he realized that he had expected that they'd share this very important interest of his. If she didn't, what did that mean? Although she loved him dearly, the hope that she'd become interested in his hobby stirred sadness about the hidden issue of wanting to feel cared for. Once he was aware of his expectation and the reasons for his sadness, he was able to express what boating with her meant to him. She had had no idea. Although she didn't love boating, she was glad to join him more often, once she knew it meant so much to him.

After becoming aware of an expectation, the next step is to consider whether your expectation is really reasonable.

Be Reasonable in What You Expect

As we noted earlier, many important expectations people have just aren't reasonable or realistic. Some unreasonable expectations are very specific. For example, is it reasonable to expect that your partner will never seriously disagree with you? Of course not. Some Christians expect that they shouldn't have conflict, simply because they are Christians. That's just a crazy belief.

When expectations are unreasonable or unrealistic, relationships are more likely to be distressed. For example, Barb and Mike have been married for eleven years. He's a contractor, and she does bookkeeping for several small businesses. Sex has become a huge issue for them. If he had his way, they'd make love every night of the week, and most mornings, too. He not only has a strong sex drive but also believes that there is something wrong with a marriage if a couple doesn't make love at least five or more times a week. The average is a lot lower than that, by the way, but what matters most is what you each expect and desire. Because Barb seems interested only once or twice a week, Mike believes that something is wrong with her, and he tells her so. As you can imagine, that really helps put her in the mood. Mike has an expectation that is just not very reasonable. Unless they can negotiate some way through this problem, it may threaten their future.

Some couples that progress well with the material we are presenting here develop unreasonable expectations about what they are learning. That can take a couple of forms. Some people expect that if they work on making some small changes in their marriage for a week or two, everything will be fine. For some couples, that's true; for others, it's not reasonable to expect that. Some people expect that they, as a couple, will enact every idea we recommend in this book and stay at it until death do they part. That's not very realistic, either. We do hope that couples who consistently apply our principles will have fewer negative events. But events will always happen, and it's very easy to fall back into old patterns. There's a difference between being perfect and handling issues well. The former is impossible, and the latter is the key to a great marriage.

Be Clear About What You Expect

Bill and Natalie, a couple who were beginning to enjoy retirement, were pretty stressed out when they attended one of our workshops. They decided to follow up on the workshop with a few counseling sessions to fine-tune some of the things they had learned. In the course of our work, we discovered that they loved to travel together, but many of their excursions ended up in periods of cold silence in the car.

An exploration of their expectations revealed that Bill had been an Air Force wing commander before he had retired. He took his driving seriously, and drove with the dedication of a fighter pilot determined to keep the two of them safe on the mission. What Natalie hadn't realized was that he expected a copilot's dedication from her and that this included navigation and situational awareness. She didn't want to be totally aware of the situation while he was driving. She didn't see too many targets out there, and she wanted to read on her e-book. When she failed to "do her part," he would become upset and would silently stew for days. When his expectation was clarified, the whole travel experience was transformed for them. The starting point for their figuring out how to handle this difference was to recognize that they had different expectations. Neither was failing the other, and neither intended to be mean. They simply did not expect the same things.

Expectations are, by definition, unreasonable when you expect your partner to read your mind and "just know." Your partner can't do anything about something he or she doesn't know about. So it's crucial to tell your partner about your important expectations. We all tend to assume that our partner's model of the ideal marriage is the same as ours. If it is, then why should we have to tell them what we expect?

Unless you make your expectations clear, you'll have trouble working as a team. You simply can't work from any kind of shared perspective if you don't share your perspective! You need to be aware of your expectations, willing to evaluate them, and willing to share them with your partner. Otherwise, expectations have the power to trigger meltdowns over some of the hottest issues and hidden issues in your relationship.

Meeting Your Partner's Expectations

It is not as crucial for the two of you to hold all the same expectations as it is for each of you to do your best to try to meet the important (and realistic) desires of the other. For example, many people expect that their partner will share their views on how to demonstrate love. But that's often not true. Some people expect gifts as signs of love, and some prefer hugs and kisses (to name only two ways of showing love). As Gary Chapman (the author of *The 5 Love Languages*) suggests, people have different expectations about giving and receiving love. It's normal that you will each want different things from the other, in all sorts of aspects of your life together. What's most important is that each partner in a marriage try to meet the reasonable and important expectations of the other.

Be Willing to Listen to the Lord

Agreement is essential to walking together in oneness. Being aware, being reasonable, and being clear are central to reaching a deeper agreement. There's one more level here that we'd like you to consider. As the creator of life and designer of marriage, God has a critical part to play in how your life unfolds. God has expectations, too! Couples who learn about His expectations and take them into account are much more likely to have a lasting marriage. Fortunately, God's expectations are not hidden. Nor are they unclear or unreasonable. Consider a little background from history here. Amos the prophet was called by God to preach to the Israelites about their unfaithfulness to Him. God spoke to them through Amos, including this often quoted line:

> Can two walk together, except they be agreed? (Amos 3:3, KJV)

Matthew Henry, the Bible commentator, summed up the simple point of the message this way: "they could not expect any comfortable communion with God unless they first made their peace with him" (Matthew Henry's Commentary, Amos 3:3). Unless we are each willing to listen to the Lord's direction in our lives, we cannot have the deeper fellowship implied by the metaphor of walking with Him.

Although there are many traditions within Christianity about what and how God has revealed Himself, there is wide agreement that God both designed and has expectations for marriage and relationships in general. Do you take God into account when thinking about what your marriage should be like or about how you should treat your mate? We believe that there are particular blessings in life that come from being on the path God wants you to be on. We are not suggesting that we know exactly what that means for the two of you. But we think you might know someone who does know—God. You can ask for insight and wisdom at any moment.

○ ○ ○

The exercise we are about to present is as important as any in this book. It will take time and perseverance to do it well. We hope you will find the time and be motivated to complete the task. Combining the insights you will gain with the other skills you are learning can have a major impact on the depth and strength of your relationship, both now and into the future.

Doing Your Part

The following exercises are designed to help you explore some of your expectations. Plan to spend time thinking carefully about each area. Both of you should write your thoughts down on a separate pad of paper, then share what you have come up with. Each point here is meant to stimulate your own thinking. There may be numerous other areas where you have expectations. Please consider every expectation you can think of that seems significant to you, whether or not it is listed here. Remember, you won't get much out of this exercise unless you are willing and able to really put time into it. Many couples have found this to be extremely beneficial for their relationship. It does not matter how much you write, by the way. But do take down some notes for talking together. Thinking trumps writing, but writing helps you remember your thinking.

This work on expectations can be very valuable whether you have been married for decades or have not gotten married yet and are closer to starting out—and anywhere in between. We think this exercise is one of the most valuable things a couple can do as part of premarital preparation.

General Relationship Expectations

In this first section, we ask you to consider all manner of expectations about marriage in general. The goal is to clarify your expectations for how you want your marriage to be or how you think it should be. You are not to evaluate how it is or how you guess it will be. Write down what you expect, whether or not you think the expectation is realistic. (The expectation will affect your relationship whether it's realistic or not, so you need to be aware of it.) It's essential that you write down what you really think, not what sounds like the "correct" or least embarrassing answer.

(continued)

It can also be valuable to think on what you observed about each of these areas in your family growing up. This is probably where many of your beliefs about what you want or don't want come from. With many areas of expectations, we have provided some references to key passages of scripture that deal with that area, in case you want to look some things up.

1. Write about what you want (or how you think things should be) regarding each of the areas that seems significant to you:
   a. What do you expect in the area of loyalty? What does "leave and cleave" mean to you? (Genesis 2:18–24; Ruth 1:16–17)
   b. What are your expectations and concerns about the longevity of this relationship? "Till death do us part"? (Mark 10:7–9)
   c. "Marriage should be honored by all, and the marriage bed kept pure" (Hebrews 13:4a). What does this say about God's expectation for marriage? What do you expect about fidelity, including whether your partner should have friends of the opposite sex, and so on?
   d. What does being loving and caring mean to you? Do you expect that you should always have loving feelings? Do you expect this to change over time? (1 Corinthians 13)
   e. What about your sexual relationship? Frequency? Practices? Taboos? Who should initiate lovemaking?
   f. What are your expectations about romance in your marriage? What is your particular "love language"?
   g. How about having children (or having more children)? Who should discipline the kids? How? What about spanking?
   h. Were you married before? What about children from a previous marriage? Where do they live, or where will they live? How do expect discipline to be handled with these children?
   i. Think about work, careers, and the provision of income. Who should work in the future? Whose career or job is more important? If there are or will be

children, should either partner reduce the time spent working outside the home to take care of them? What about work after your nest is empty? Retirement?

j. What are your expectations and concerns about the degree of emotional dependency on the other? Do you want to feel taken care of? In what ways? How much do you expect to rely on each other to get through the tough times? What about depending on family and friends for emotional support? In what areas would you expect to be more emotionally independent?

k. What should be your basic approach to marriage? As a team or more as two independent individuals? What about the implications of the roles described in scripture? (Ephesians 5:20–31)

l. How should you work out problems? Do you want to talk these out, and if so, how? What about the expression of strong emotions like anger?

m. Think about power and control: Who do you expect will have more power in what kinds of decisions? For example, who will control the money, and who will discipline the kids? Who should make the final decision when you disagree about a key area? Who seems to have more power in your relationship now, and how do you feel about that? (Ephesians 5:20–31; Colossians 3:18–21; 1 Peter 3:1–7)

n. Consider household tasks. Who should do what? How does the current breakdown match up with what you ideally expect?

o. What are your expectations, desires, and concerns about time together? How much time do you want to spend together (versus time alone, with friends, at work, with family, and so on)?

p. What do you expect about sharing all of your thoughts and feelings? Are there feelings that shouldn't be shared?

q. How do you envision friendship with your partner? What is a friend? Should your partner always be your best friend?

(*continued*)

r. Think about some of the "little things" in life. Where should you squeeze the toothpaste? Should the toilet seat be left up or down? Who sends greeting cards? Think about the little things that have irritated you in the past. What do you want or expect in each area?

s. How do you believe technology should be handled? What about how much you contact each other through the day? Does one of you believe in messaging or sharing a lot more often than the other? Is that OK with both of you? How about time spent with devices on a daily basis? Video games?

t. Should you remain connected, through social media services and the like, to people with whom you had a romantic relationship prior to being with your mate? Should you unfriend and discontinue all contact with prior partners?

u. Now, with your mind primed from all the work you've done so far, consider again the hidden issues we described in the previous chapter. Do you see any ways now that some of these deeper issues of yours might influence your expectations? What do you expect, want, or fear in the areas of power, caring, recognition, commitment, and acceptance?

v. Write about any other expectations that come to mind for you. Some other areas might include money (saving, spending); free time, recreation, and TV; use of alcohol and drugs; your interactions in public; and relatives.

2. Next, go back to each of the listed areas and rate each of your expectations in terms of how reasonable you think it is. Use a scale of 1 to 10 where 10 = completely reasonable ("I really think it is OK to expect this in this relationship.") and 1 = completely unreasonable ("I can honestly say that even though I expect or want this, it is just not a reasonable expectation for me to have in our relationship."). For example, suppose you grew up in a family where problems were not discussed, and you are aware that you honestly expect or prefer to avoid such discus-

sions. You might now rate that expectation as really not very reasonable.

3. Place a big check mark by each expectation that you feel you have not clearly discussed with your partner.

4. Share your expectations. After you and your partner have finished the entire written exercise, schedule times together to discuss each of the areas either of you thinks is important. Please don't try to do this all at once. You should plan on a number of discussions, each covering only one or two expectations. Discuss the degree to which you each feel that the expectation being discussed has been shared clearly in the past, and how the expectation may have affected your relationship. Talk about the degree to which you both feel that your expectations are reasonable or unreasonable, and discuss what you will agree to do about differences that you identify as you talk.

As you talk through your expectations, consider using the Speaker-Listener Technique if you would like some additional structure to help you communicate clearly and openly about what you are discovering. You might also find it useful to go through the problem-solving steps we taught you earlier as you work through some of the areas where you need to do something different from what you are now doing.

Religious and Spiritual Beliefs and Expectations

The goal in this section is to help you both identify what you believe, where those beliefs came from, and how they affect or will affect your relationship in the future. As we said earlier, these kinds of expectations are very critical because they are associated with your ability to construct a shared vision together. Even where you do not share a similar view on such important matters, it's still much better to handle these differences openly and with respect than to ignore them. In fact, for many couples, talking together about what each believes and why can be a key element of the mutual friendship, even when you don't see eye to eye at this point in life.

(continued)

The following questions are designed to get you thinking about a broad range of issues related to your beliefs. There may be other important questions that we've left out, so feel free to answer questions we don't ask as well as those asked.

1. Write down an answer to each question as it applies to you. This will help you think more clearly about the issues and will also help you when it comes time to talk with your partner about them. As you think about and answer each question, it can be especially valuable to note what you were taught as a child versus what you believe or expect now as an adult.

   a. What is your faith (core belief system or worldview)? What do you believe in?

   b. How did you come to believe in this viewpoint?

   c. What is the meaning or purpose of life according to your belief system?

   d. What was your religious affiliation growing up? How were the key beliefs practiced in your family of origin? Religious practices? Other?

   e. What is the meaning of marriage in your belief system?

   f. What vows will you say, or what vows did you say? How do these tie in to your belief system?

   g. What are your beliefs about divorce? How does this fit with your faith or belief system?

   h. How do you practice—or expect to practice—your faith in your relationship? This could mean church attendance, prayer, scripture reading or sharing, discussions of spiritual matters as you go through life, and so on.

   i. What is your understanding of sexuality? Are there specific beliefs about sexuality or family planning in your faith?

   j. Do you give, or expect to give, financial support to a church or other ministry? How much? How will this be determined? Do you both agree?

   k. Do you see potential areas of conflict regarding your beliefs? What are they?

l. What about observance of major religious holidays? What did you do growing up? What do you like to do now?

m. Can you think of any other questions to consider in this area?

2. After you and your partner have finished the entire exercise, plan to begin spending time together discussing these expectations. You should plan on a number of discussions. Discuss the degree to which you each feel that the expectation being discussed has been shared clearly in the past. Use the Speaker-Listener Technique if you would like some additional structure to help you communicate clearly and openly about what you are discovering.

The key in all these questions is to get you thinking and talking together. This takes real time and effort to do well. But when you do that work, it can go a long way toward helping you develop and express your overall, long-term vision for your unique expression of oneness.

10

Protecting "Us" in iWorld

Marriage and Technology

Above all else, guard your heart, for it is the
wellspring of life.
PROVERBS 4:23

When the first edition of *A Lasting Promise* was published in 1998, the cyber-revolution had not yet had the impact on everyone's life that it does today. This brave new world now touches nearly everything people do. The impact on marriages has been profound. We acknowledge that some of our thoughts about the use of technology may be obsolete by the time you read this, but the issues are important and can't be ignored.

The focus of this chapter is on helping you become aware of the impact technology is having on your marriage. With that goal in mind, we will cover four general themes: distraction, social networking, temptation, and ways technology can be used to enhance your marriage. Throughout all we say here, our overarching goal is expressed in the opening verse from Proverbs: guard your hearts, for in doing that, you guard the essence of your life together.

Distraction in an "Always-On" World

Jody and Tristan were newlyweds with trouble brewing. Although they had been together only a couple of years, their marriage was marked by growing distance. Jody was becoming upset about it. She felt that Tristan had little time for her. It was not that he worked so many hours. It was that, home or not, Tristan was constantly glued to his computer, his smartphone, or the gaming system. He was always plugged in electronically, but increasingly disconnected from her.

Jody told her friend Carol, "Tristan plays games on his phone, texts his buddies, plays games with scads of other guys on the Internet, and I think he texts one woman from work pretty often, too. He says it's about work, but I think it isn't right for him to be in touch with her so much outside of work. We don't get time to do anything. I don't have any time with him." Earlier in their relationship, they had spent a lot more time doing things together as well as staying connected electronically. Tristan used to call or text her a lot. And when they talked or did something else together, they spent less time checking and returning calls and texts from others. Life was more about the two of them then, but now it seemed as though life was about staying connected to the whole world.

As a result of the massive changes in technology, millions of people are literally plugged in and connected to others from moment to moment. Yet we are much less connected in our most important relationships. And computers, phones, tablets, and whatever may come next will consume greater and greater amounts of our time.

More people than ever relate to the sense of being "on call" 24/7. For many, there is no longer a boundary between work and personal time. Work is not left at work but brought home on laptops, phones, or tablets. Although many jobs still allow one to walk away and leave it all at the end of the day, fewer people than ever before have jobs where there is *not* a need to bring work home. An ever-increasing number of jobs include tasks that can be performed around the clock and from virtually anywhere. Work is calling us at all hours, and we can be called by others in all moments. The benefits of technology come with costs, and one of the greatest is distraction that cuts into marriage and family life.

Scarlett and Xavier were both busy professionals who worked for companies that placed constant demands on their time. Evenings would often be interrupted by phone calls or texts from colleagues. It was not unusual for them to be expected to bring laptops home and work through the evenings, especially when critical projects were approaching deadlines. Their solution was to set aside chunks of time with their cell phones and computers turned off and totally out of sight. They scheduled time each evening to catch up on their day, plan the next day, and simply chat with each other. If they received a call, text, or email, they knew they could always handle it later. That may be one of the better things about the nature of devices and services these days—although it's tempting to respond instantly to others, you usually do not actually have to. So unplug! We know that more and more people are living as though they have to respond immediately to every contact coming in from the outside world. If you work in some type of crisis management field, that is probably true. But most of us just become conditioned to acting as if this were true when it really isn't. We just slide into doing what our culture expects.

Scarlett and Xavier had decided to stop being plugged in all the time. They could have easily let this slide and found their distracted relationship growing more distant over time, but they set boundaries so that they could have time to nourish their togetherness. Both felt more loved because their time was protected from interference. It was not easy to make the change at first. They each had some difficulty leaving their phones in the next room with ringers off. For many people, it feels strange after years of being constantly connected with the world to start carving out times when the world is completely shut off. How will the world keep spinning without our being connected to it?

The Rapid Response Trap

There are many things that reinforce behavior, including positive feedback, money, and food. Another source of reinforcement is immediacy. If we reach out to another with a concern or question or just to connect and that person responds immediately, it is very reinforcing. Likewise, when we attempt to respond to others electronically and as rapidly as possible, we reinforce their contacting us. We're not suggesting that you not be available to your friends and coworkers. But it may be smart to respond a little less rapidly to others. We suggest that you try to be more immediately available to your spouse relative to the rest of the world.

Unless managed, this instant availability by cyber-device can control your lives, bringing the world into your private time with each other. One of the major themes in this book is to make it safe for couples to connect. You also have to make it *possible* to connect. Find ways to unplug so that you can be together and keep your channels open for your marriage.

Social Networking and Social Media

It's hard to keep a current list of all the networking and media services available. By the time you read this, there may be new and amazing ways to stay in touch with others and to keep up with what is happening in the world. At the time of this writing, there are at least a half dozen hugely popular ways of staying connected online through computers and mobile devices, including Facebook, Twitter, Tumblr, Line, and many others. Some of these are oriented toward networking and some toward sharing information about yourself in tiny bits or large chunks at a time.

These cyber-tools, and services like them, are captivating and can be hugely distracting. They provide ever-increasing opportunities for learning and for connecting with others. Perhaps it is the very sense of their endlessness that is so intriguing to many. For some, these opportunities to connect with others immediately and at any time have replaced their focus on connecting with God. By the way, God was the original "always-on" connection people could have! When a person's connection to God is affected so fundamentally, his or her perspective and priorities will get out of balance.

Perhaps you are the kind of person who posts an update to your networking page about having lunch with your spouse while having lunch with your spouse. Some people seem to post most of the events of their lives on their Facebook page. We do not intend to be judgmental about this, but we do want to note that many people are constantly hovering near some device and posting or consuming some content. It's worthwhile for all of us to ask ourselves if the time spent is taking too much time from things that matter more.

Social networking sites can bring blessings to marriage and family life. These services have opened up accessibility to old friends, schoolmates, and other acquaintances. They provide easy ways to immediately update friends and family members about our personal experiences. The ease of connecting via social networking also brings some dangers to marriage.

Jayden and Makayla have been married for eleven years, and their marriage has become ever better. They have supported each other through a lot of challenges, truly having each other's backs. Like many couples, they've had some difficulty keeping credit card spending under control, but it is not a source of conflict between them. They both agree that they want to manage this better and have even set out specific goals for how and when they will use credit. It's important to both of them because they are committed givers and because they're saving for a house.

Makayla is an avid poster of updates on Facebook. She and several friends of hers update their Facebook pages several times a day and follow each other's updates pretty closely. Both she and Jayden have a lot of friends at church, which has led to their having a lot of friends on Facebook. One evening, Jayden became emotional as he told Makayla that he had bought a new smartphone even though he had known it was outside their spending plan. They had worked so well together at trying to keep their spending under control that he was truly embarrassed. It was a sign of the quality of their relationship and their emotional connection and safety that he could tell her in the way he did. She was going to find out anyway, of course, but by telling her about it first, he revealed his trust in her as well as his feelings of vulnerability about having blown it. As a matter of fact, their talking about it the way they did led to an incredibly good evening.

The next evening, Jayden was playing a video game while Makayla was watching TV in the next room. Jayden heard his phone vibrate and checked the incoming text message from his friend Charles. The message said, "Way2go high roller. How's the new $$$$ phone u spent all ur $$$$ on? lol." Even though he was alone in the room, he turned bright red. He didn't need a Facebook update to know that Makayla had shared something with the world about him buying the new phone. He was totally embarrassed. He didn't even feel angry, or if he did, it was anger at himself. But he felt very hurt that Makayla had shared with everyone else what he had done. This kind of careless sharing is not an uncommon problem. These days, information spreads at the speed of light. Type something or take a picture and press "send," and it's no longer under your control. Whatever you've shared might be immediately seen and passed on by scores of people whom you never meant to read or see what you shared.

It's no fun when we embarrass ourselves, but it's worse when we embarrass our mates in this way. Makayla and Jayden had never really talked about what was OK and not OK to share; not many couples do. But they were going to have that talk now. To their credit, they handled this awkward talk as well as they had handled other difficulties when they came up. Makayla felt bad that she had embarrassed Jayden. That was not her intention. She was simply used to sharing just about anything and everything with her Facebook friends.

Honor each other's privacy and the privacy of your relationship so that you can prevent a problem like the one Makayla and Jayden experienced. Have a talk about where you want the lines to be. But also recognize that things happen fast, and try to move on and forward when something happens that is damaging but where no harm was intended. Make some decisions ahead of time about sharing. Don't try to guess or just thoughtlessly slide into whatever you might do.

Temptations

Innumerable temptations have resulted from the steady stream of new devices, software, and services continually emerging on the electronic frontier. And the new opportunities for sin have only begun. It seems a certainty that today's temptations to misuse technology—especially the temptations to reconnect with old flames and use pornography—are only the tip of the iceberg. These, more than any others, are the ways technology is seriously damaging many marriages.

We see two categories of temptation: temptations about real relationships and temptations about unreal relationships. By real relationships, we mean marriage-damaging relationships with real people. By unreal relationships, we are referring to fantasy relationships in the burgeoning world of pornography. We'll start by getting real before getting into the unreal.

Real Relationships That Are a Problem

Calvin and Vanessa celebrated their twenty-fifth anniversary in the same year that Calvin turned fifty and Vanessa turned forty-seven. They have done well, building a good life together and raising a wonderful daughter, who was just starting out in college. Calvin had never expected to have negative feelings about turning fifty, but he did. He felt older. Although fifty is pretty young these days, Calvin suddenly became aware that he was packing on the years. This got him thinking about his younger days, and that led him to wondering about a girl he had dated in high school, Karla. As is not unusual, he occasionally wondered where she was and what she was doing in life.

In the "old days," you could wonder all you wanted to about an old love interest, and—unless you came from a small town that you occasionally returned to, or you never left the area where you grew up—you had no easy way to find out about people you once dated (or wanted to). It's far easier now to locate someone from the past. Many people do this—we have no idea how many. There are all kinds of Internet services that help people find others.

Calvin was minding his own business one day at work, collecting some stats for his boss from some Internet sites. He noticed an ad for a person-finder service that said it would cost only $25 to find out about someone. As his mind drifted away from work, he paid the $25 and found a great deal of information about Karla. He immediately knew where she lived, that she had three kids, and that four years ago she had divorced a guy from high school—a guy he had never liked. He even discovered where she worked and went to that company's website to see if he could find a current picture of her. He could. She looked different, but it was Karla.

Calvin slid right into all of this, in the course of twenty-three minutes. He hadn't planned to, but he was into it before he really recognized what he was doing. Over the coming days, he became obsessed with Karla and began to think about all the "what ifs." He convinced himself that what he was doing was not being unfaithful. But it was starting to feel creepy, and he didn't think it was exactly a very good idea, spiritually. The more he thought about it, the more he wondered if he had gone way beyond being curious. In fact, he knew Vanessa would be pretty hurt if she knew he'd spent as much time as he had finding out and wondering about Karla. Was he lusting for her or just curious? Was this a real relationship? It had been real in the past, and some of his current feelings were certainly painful. He decided he needed to back away from whatever he was messing with. He wished it had not been so easy to find out more about Karla.

Calvin experienced something many believers go through. Some of the new possibilities are so tempting that many people wish they could wave a magic wand and make the options go away. If you have had this wish about some of your own electronic activities, it might be evidence of temptation toward something that is not good for you or your marriage. Temptation itself is not sin, but it's the on-ramp to it (see James 1:13–18). There is no magic wand, so you have to be careful about what happens in the first place.

Couples today are likely to struggle with problems like this more than in the past because of changes in our culture. First of all, people are more likely to have had a larger number of serious relationships before marriage than in the past. It's become OK to shop around a lot and even to have had several intense and sexual relationships before marriage. Christians have been somewhat less subject to these trends, but not all that less.

A second change is that social networking services make it easy to reconnect with past partners. This is just not something that most married couples used to have to cope with. It's not always been that convenient to have a lot of "friends."

Everyone considered Paige and Sanford a beautiful couple. Both were very attractive and very outgoing. They married in their early thirties; both had been involved in several different large-church singles groups through their twenties. Both had been looking seriously for a good match for life, and both wanted their mate to be a solid believer. They were also both involved in projects to help others, organized by one of the churches.

They had each dated more than twenty people before they met and fell in love. They both had long been involved in social networking—Paige somewhat more than Sanford, but he also was pretty active in maintaining his Facebook page. Now that they were married, they discovered that it was a little too complicated to be around so many people they had dated.

But what should they do about all these past "friends" in "iWorld" now that they had moved into "usWorld"? Sanford thought that they should simply unfriend all their prior partners. Paige had a lot of trouble with that idea. She was in love with Sanford and didn't feel in any way tempted by her lingering connections with the guys she used to date, but Sanford seemed to be almost jealous. What should they do? Was there any threat to their marriage in all this? If not now, would there be in the future?

These questions are important, and two partners can have very different expectations about how to resolve them. In general, we think that many people put too little weight on the potential threat in maintaining contacts with past romantic partners. We get it that this is far more complex than it used to be, so it takes some real skill for a couple to come to a solid agreement that works for both partners. In addition to the issue of maintaining friends through online services like Facebook, it is important for couples to work through what level of privacy they both feel comfortable with when it comes to sharing about their relationship and family online.

Many couples need to make clear decisions about each of these questions rather than letting them slide. But these can be awkward conversations. Just to start such a conversation requires some vulnerability, because by starting the talk, you are acknowledging that you could at least imagine some uncomfortable or risky situations coming in the future. We recommend that you take time to talk about things like this, which will be a lot easier for you if you are both doing your part and keeping it safe to connect.

Clearly, many affairs begin or are partly sustained by electronic contact. Although the percentages are probably very small, there are some relationships that exist entirely electronically and become sexualized without the two people ever engaging in physical contact. These constitute affairs of the heart in all ways except that they lack the risk of contracting a sexually transmitted disease. Otherwise, such relationships are clearly incidents of infidelity and can destroy a marriage. For a greater number of people, the relationship becomes face-to-face, and ongoing electronic contact remains a part of the relationship.

This is not a book on infidelity, though we give an extensive example in Chapter Fifteen, "Forgiveness and Restoration." What we want to do here is raise the issues clearly enough that everyone reading this will recognize that they are not immune to similar situations. Before you know it, what seems to be a harmless contact can morph into something that threatens all you have invested in your marriage.

Unreal Relationships That Are a Problem

Lauren and Mark had been in marital therapy for some time when Lauren came for an appointment by herself. She looked distraught. She had grabbed Mark's tablet a couple of days ago to look something up. What she found when she began typing her search term into Google was very upsetting—all kinds of recent searches appeared in the search field. She was shocked and wanted to stop looking further, but couldn't help herself. Becoming both more curious and more upset, she used the browser's history and discovered more websites that Mark had apparently been visiting.

Forty-five minutes later, Lauren was fully aware that Mark had been looking at porn, and she was really upset by the nature of the pornography she saw. She had always felt that she and Mark had a healthy sexual relationship and that they were, to her way of thinking, pretty creative. But she was disgusted to see some of the things that Mark must have been interested in. When she sat down with the therapist, she stated, "I am so sickened by what I saw. I can't stand for him to touch me now. What do I do?"

This is a significant and growing problem in our society. It is unclear just how many people regularly use or have used pornography at some point. Although the secular culture in many industrial nations is increasingly accepting of pornography, and some say that it's no big deal, pornography remains something that most users are not eager to acknowledge, at least to their mates.

This era of electronic media has made it very easy for people to use pornography, probably including many people who otherwise never would have become involved, or so deeply involved. Some people go looking for pornography on the Internet, but others find it accidentally. Although the spiritual implications are obvious, there are also physical implications that make it all the more difficult to cope with the temptation.

We have not seen reliable estimates of the percentage of people who regularly use or have been affected by addiction to pornography—it's not something people are overwhelmingly open about. Nevertheless, there have to be an increasingly large number of people who are struggling in this area and who may need outside help to break the cycle. There are continuing professional and scientific arguments about the nature of addiction to pornography and other hypersexual behavior. But, in brief, pornography can become addictive because the experience is associated with the release of powerful chemicals in the brain. Most behaviors and substances that are addictive meet some psychological need and cause a potent neurochemical response in the brain. In the case of addictions, a substance or behavior initially causes pleasure by being associated with releasing dopamine in what experts call the pleasure centers of the brain. Experts who study the brain believe that addictions become very hard to stop because the brain actually changes over time with repeated use of whatever is addictive. The brain's receptivity to chemicals like dopamine is altered so that more is needed—more of a drug or more of a behavior like using pornography. Some people become totally drawn in and obsessive because they become desperate to keep the positive feelings going, but it becomes more and more difficult to do so.

The following facts are supported by solid research studies. (We do not provide endnotes for most of the research underlying the topics in this book; instead, we have included a robust reference section [Appendix C] that lists many of the studies that back up what we say. For this section, however, we do supply endnotes at the end of this book for specific references to the points made here.)

- Pornography use is greatest among men between the ages of eighteen and twenty-five who are sexually active and have had numerous sexual partners.[1]

- Men tend to find their partners less attractive after viewing sexually explicit photos of other women.[2]
- Although women are increasingly using pornography, men are far more likely to become involved. One set of careful estimates suggests that around 34 percent of all adult men in the United States use pornography within a given year, which could mean rarely or frequently.[3] This same study, with a large national sample, also found that
  - Being more religious is associated with a somewhat lower likelihood of use.
  - Use of pornography is associated with having more accepting attitudes about premarital sex, teenage sex, and extramarital sex.
  - Use of pornography is associated with having a greater number of lifetime sexual partners and a small but greater likelihood of infidelity.
- In another national sample, unmarried individuals ages eighteen to thirty-four were asked if they viewed pornography on their own, viewed it with their partner, or not at all.[4]
  - Seventy-seven percent of the men and 32 percent of the women reported that they viewed pornography on their own, sometimes or often; 45 percent reported that they sometimes viewed pornography with their partner.
  - Those who reported never viewing pornography reported higher relationship quality than those who used pornography.
  - In their review of the literature, the authors of this study noted that no studies have shown that the use of pornography has a positive impact on relationships and that numerous studies have documented negative impacts, though some less so than others.

The existing studies suggest that most *unmarried* men in the United States have viewed pornography, and many use it regularly. The estimate in the previous list (77 percent) is from a sample of people in serious but unmarried relationships. Therefore, the sample is tilted toward those who are less religious, as people who are more religious are more likely to marry, and to marry sooner in life. Nevertheless, what is striking in that study is that 45 percent of younger unmarried people reported that they have sometimes watched pornography with their partner. Pornography now affects many relationships, unmarried and married.

One of the big questions researchers argue about has to do with causality. That is, does using pornography lead to changes in attitudes and behaviors, or are people who already hold more liberal attitudes about sexuality also more likely to use pornography? The answer to such questions for researchers is almost always, "both." There is, however, emerging evidence that regularly viewing pornography can lead to changes in attitudes and behavior.[5] That research is mostly on adolescents, but the trend in the findings is clear: pornography can affect what people believe is OK to do.

That using pornography can lead to changes in attitudes and behavior should not be too surprising. What experts in this area believe is that people are influenced by what they take in through the media, learning new "scripts" for how things should be in their relationships. Also, because pornography is associated with powerful chemical and sexual release, people who use it regularly are retraining their brain in terms of what they find exciting[6] and what they believe is OK. What we put into our mind can transform us in one way or another. As the apostle Paul wrote, "Do not conform any longer to the pattern of this world, but be transformed by the renewing of your mind" (Romans 12:2).

◦ ◦ ◦

If you or someone you love has a problem with pornography, consider getting help. The Internet has a lot of information about where to find services and support. Some churches have ministries for those who want to overcome the grip of porn, and there are many ministries on the Web built for guiding people in how to overcome temptation, involvement, and addiction to it. People are imperfect. As it says in scripture, everyone falls short of the glory of God (Romans 3:23). The difference among people lies not so much in whether they struggle and sin but in whether they are moving toward God and greater connection with others or moving away from these most important connections.

Using Technology to Benefit Your Marriage

Technology can be a friend to your marriage. It offers wonderful opportunities for you to enhance your life together. By the time you are reading this, things may be so different that our recommendations will give you a good chuckle. But probably not. You'll most likely think of a lot of ways to create variations on our suggestions, and at the time you read this, there may be some pretty amazing new things to try out. For example, we know there is an ever greater number of mobile apps to help people with their relationships.

Stay Connected

There are many ways technology can enable you to connect with your mate. We suggest that you use it to up your connecting game a bit. When couples first fall in love, they tend to send reminders that they are thinking about each other all the time. It's very normal for this tendency to lessen over time, but it does not have to disappear! When was the last time you messaged your mate with some small, thoughtful comment? You could do that right now. Why not?

"Just thinking of you."
"Luv U2."
"I'm happy about us."
"You are wonderful."
"Praying for you and your meeting today. You can do it."

You can think of better ideas than these, because you can say the things from your own heart that will remind your mate that you love and are thinking of him or her. A lot of the ways to make your marriage a priority do require significant time and energy. But some of the ways are very brief and can be very powerful. The big meaning from a small message is that your mate is in your heart and mind throughout the day.

Play Games

Many couples play video games together. If you are older, you might find this hard to fathom (there are huge generational differences when it comes to gaming), but maybe not. We know plenty of aging gamers. We're not endorsing every game that's out there, but we know that there are plenty of games that couples enjoy playing together, including full-fledged video games.

Some couples have found that games can be a fun way to stay connected. Some of the most popular ones are played using apps on tablets or smartphones. For instance, one of the games that has gained great popularity is Words with Friends. It's a lot like Scrabble, and it is optimized for two players. There are many games like this that you can play together, usually with turn taking so that you don't have to both be free at the same time. Finding a game or two that you both like can give you another small way of staying connected in this crazy, busy world. Try it! You have nothing to lose. In fact, just trying out various games and critiquing them can be something fun to do.

Send Pictures

Sending a picture to a loved one has become easy to do with smartphones and tablets. Although there are a lot of ways people have gotten themselves in trouble with variations of this idea, photos can also let you share a moment when you are not together.

One couple, Brenda and Mac, travel a lot for business, so they are apart more than they would like to be. They stay connected by sending a photo or two on the days they are away from each other, such as a picture of a special sunset. For those of you who have never learned how to do this, it's really easy. Some couples do this during the day even if they don't travel anywhere. Send a picture of a rose. Real ones are good too, but a picture can also be a little reminder of love. Think of sending photos here and there as sending a little picture of your life in order to keep sharing the life you have together.

What does this idea require? Only a moment of thoughtfulness.

Use Skype or FaceTime

These kinds of services only keep getting better. They allow families and couples to stay connected during the day, especially when traveling or far away. You can use these services to stay more connected, partner to partner, or to stay more connected as two parents raising the next generation together.

Read a Book and Share Some Highlights

Tablets and cell phones are great ways to read books. Downloading books and magazines is economical and a more convenient way to stay up on what's new. Consider sharing the highlights of what you are reading. When you come across a nugget, send it by text or email to your partner. It's a way to keep your mate up-to-date on what you're thinking about. And if you like reading the same things, it's an even better way to stay connected.

Create Play(ful)lists

You can share music with each other in any number of ways. You can message your partner to say, "Love this song, check it out" and provide the title and artist. Or you can set up a whole playlist on your partner's device when he or she is not looking.

YouTube is made for sharing. Its fare ranges from stupid to profound to hysterical. Some of the best Bible teaching and discussions of spiritual issues can be found on it. It's easy to send a link to your partner. Sharing a laugh nearly always draws people closer, and your mate will like knowing you wanted to share something that's meaningful to you or that cracked you up. It's another way to say, "Just want you to know I am thinking about you."

Connect with Facebook

Post messages on each other's wall. By writing "sweet nothings" on your mate's wall, you are letting the world know that you treasure him or her. Post photos. Check out what your partner has posted during the day. You might learn something interesting that you wouldn't have known otherwise. You didn't know that she was having a cheeseburger and fries for lunch at your favorite burger spot? Now you do. Does that change the world? No, but you are sharing a little more of it with him or her.

Serious point: if you are into posting pictures on a sharing site, be sure to post current pictures of yourselves together. It sends a positive message about who you are and how you see yourselves as a team. It's a great way to broadcast your ongoing commitment to each other. And it tells others that you are both "off the market."

Remember Stuff That Matters

OK, we shouldn't have to say this, but some of you need to hear it, so we will. Put reminders on your phone or whatever electronic calendar you might be using to help you keep track of special dates such as birthdays and anniversaries. It's easy to set a reminder to come up every month or year. If you tend to forget important dates, schedule your reminders to go off in plenty of time for you to take action for that special day. No excuses. You don't have to do something huge or expensive to "score points," but you can lose a ton of points if you forget.

You can also use reminder functions to help you pray for your mate and marriage. It's easy to forget prayer in the crush of your life and to forget that God is central to what your life with your mate is all about.

Moving Forward

We conclude this chapter with a summary of the most important points we've made. Before we list those, take to heart the fact that you are the one who controls your use of cell phones, email, computers, tablets, wrist transporters (who knows what will be available by the time you're reading this!), and the myriads of services, hardware, and applications available. You, and no one else, make the decision about whether (and when) to answer the phone or return a text message. You decide which email messages you will read and which ones you will respond to. Some people are living so automatically (sliding) that they lose track of this very simple point: tech can work for you. You don't have to be a slave to it. Decide to use it responsibly and wisely. It will be of great benefit if you do. But don't let others' expectations about how you should use it cause you to slide into its control. Here are some ways to take control of protecting "us" in iWorld:

- Unplug sometimes.
- Pay more attention to your mate than to your media.
- Talk together about how you use social media and whether either of you has concerns about what is shared.
- If you think you might be tempted by something you are doing with technology, you are already over—or just about to go over—the line. Be honest with yourself.
- If you are already having trouble with technology in a way that will harm your marriage, get help now, before it gets a lot harder. Talk to a trusted friend. (Choose wisely, because the person you choose will determine a lot.) Talk to your pastor. Find a group that helps people gain victory over the particular issue you are struggling with.
- Use technology to strengthen your connection. Try some things you think might be fun. Stay creative while technology is creating new opportunities.

Doing Your Part

1. Send some positive and encouraging messages to your mate—with whatever system you are using now. Do something you haven't done before, like sharing a Bible text that has meant something to you. Just try it and see what happens.

2. Sit down and talk about some things to try together, perhaps a game or sharing something you read in a book or heard in a streaming video. You don't have keep doing anything forever. Experiment. Try out some new things. Maybe you'll discover some ways that technology can help you stay connected, in positive ways, in this very busy world.

3. Regarding social networking: Set aside times together when neither of you has access to your communication devices. Talk with your mate about any postings that you

(continued)

are not sure are OK—before you post them. Decide to set boundaries on the amount of time you spend on the Internet or with your tablet device, even when not at home.

4. Regarding pornography: if you have any struggle at all in this area, find and read some of the Christian books about pornography. Many are written by men who have struggled with the problem and gained victory over it. There are also numerous online ministries for helping those struggling with pornography. You might have to research a number of them to find one that seems right for you. You could also acknowledge your problem to a wise friend whom you trust who can give you advice and who could be an accountability partner.

Seek out wisdom from those in ministry about what other steps you can take to be free. Use software provided by Christian ministries to keep you from accessing porn sites. There are various services available to help you turn off the switch without completely unplugging from the Internet. If you have a more serious struggle in this area, search for a therapist who is knowledgeable about sex and porn addiction.

Last, we list a few well-regarded resources here. There are many other resources that you could look into; if these do not seem helpful or right for you, keep searching for what is.

http://www.xxxchurch.com/
http://www.faithfulandtrue.com/
http://www.stonegateresources.org/
Schaumburg, Harry. (1997). *False Intimacy: Understanding the Struggle of Sexual Addiction.* Colorado Springs, CO: NavPress.

Remember, in all these areas, to "guard your heart, for it is the wellspring of life" (Proverbs 4:23).

PART THREE

Deeper Connection

11

Positive Bonding

Keeping Fun and Friendship Alive

God, who gives us richly all things to enjoy.
1 TIMOTHY 6:17B (NKJV)

What people seem to want most of all in a mate is to be connected—to have a best friend for life. To be enjoying one another and enjoying life together is fully consistent with the character of God and the spirit of scripture. It is what we are made for and something in which God delights. But this great connection can fade after years of marriage if it is not protected.

Fun plays a vital role in keeping a relationship intimate. Knowing that fun times are coming can rejuvenate your connection and refresh your daily routines by giving you something to look forward to. Your shared memories of fun can also be important investments in your relationship's emotional bank account. And friendship works hand in hand with fun to maintain the closeness in a marriage. Friends are people with whom we have fun, share things in common, and open up, and whom we count on to remain companions for life. A friend is someone who supports you and is always there to strengthen you during the tougher times of life. Research confirms that people who have friends (especially at least one really good friend) do better in almost every conceivable way—especially in terms of physical and mental health.

Friendship means that you can share your weaknesses, hopes, fears, dreams, and burdens. Active friendship can be a path to deeper intimacy, which some define as being able to share what's really in your heart and have it richly heard and uncritically accepted by another. Friendship means that you can be truly authentic, warts and all, and the relationship won't be threatened by it. Friendships usually grow closer, not more distant, when vulnerabilities are shared. We will focus on the importance of this dynamic of sharing and supporting in Chapter Thirteen.

Such acceptance is a crucial part of Christian unity:

> May the God who gives endurance and encouragement give you a spirit of unity among yourselves as you follow Christ Jesus, so that with one heart and mouth you may glorify the God and Father of our Lord Jesus Christ. Accept one another, then, just as Christ accepted you, in order to bring praise to God. (Romans 15:5–7)

We are to strive to accept one another as Christ has accepted us. He accepted us by grace. Accepting one another is one of the most remarkable ways to be like Christ. As we make clear in the chapter on forgiveness (Chapter Fifteen), that does not mean accepting unacceptable behavior in marriage or other relationships, but a growing, thriving marriage will have a friendship that is alive and that is based on genuine acceptance and interest between partners.

Barriers to Fun and Friendship

Here are some of the reasons couples have shared with us about why fun, friendship, and feelings of connection erode over time in their relationships.

"We Don't Have Time"

We all lead busy lives. Between work, the needs of the children, personal interests (for example, hobbies and sports), the upkeep of the home, involvement at church, and staying in touch electronically, who's got time for fun and the leisure of friendship? All too often, couples fail to take the time to simply chat as friends or do something fun together. Early in relationships, couples usually put a high priority on playing and talking. But all too often, fun and friendship take a backseat to the needs as well as the distractions of our lives. But these great ways of connecting don't have to slip away—and they can be resurrected if they have slipped.

Karen and Frank are a good example of a couple who have refused to let the demands of life come between them and their connection with each other. They've been married for twenty years, and every Friday night for most of those years, they've gone out together to do something fun or meaningful. They vary what they do when they go out—swimming, taking bridge lessons, walking in the park, watching the sun set, enjoying dinner and a movie, attending an interesting talk at church, or babysitting for the younger, worn-out couple next door. These experiences have built a positive storehouse of many pleasant memories that help offset the draining effects of the tougher times that they experience, as most couples do.

"We Get into Conflict, and It Spoils Our Good Times"

Conflict is a real killer of a couple's best times together. We're pretty sure that you didn't get married to argue with each other—who does? For too many couples, issues come up during times for connection, and that special time, along with any feelings of closeness, is damaged by the negative feelings. When you're feeling hurt or angry about something that's been said, you're not going to feel much like having a good time together. We believe this is the chief reason that some couples date less and talk less as friends over the years—they aren't keeping their issues from damaging the good things in their lives. After a while they even start unconsciously avoiding what had been the best times they had together. You cannot relax with someone if you aren't sure whether or not an argument is going to erupt at any moment. Fun and friendship thrive when there is emotional safety between two partners.

Brooke and Zack were in their mid-thirties and had been married for eight years. They had a good track record of making time for fun, but they started to let it slip away, allowing pleasant moments to turn into opportunities for conflict. Increasingly, they'd be out to have time to connect, and some event would trigger an issue that would kill the lightness of the moment. One night, they'd arranged for a sitter for their two young children and went out to take a class in couple's massage. They thought, "This will push us a bit to have some fun in a new way." Great idea! The instructor was making a point to the class about paying attention to your partner's reactions. Zack whispered to Brooke, "That's a great point." She whispered back, "I've been trying to tell you that for years." It was all downhill from there. They didn't even stay to finish the class, and spent the rest of the evening stewing in silence.

Remember the second ground rule from Chapter Four: "We will make time for the blessings of marriage: fun, friendship, physical connection, and spiritual connection. We will agree to protect these times from conflict and the need to deal with issues." You have to decide to protect this kind of positive connection time from conflict, not let it slide away into poorly handled conflict. Deal with issues, but agree to separate that time from time you've protected to be friends and have fun together. You can do this if you are both resolved to make it happen.

"We Don't Expect Friendship to Be a Part of Our Marriage"

One of the expectations some people hold about marriage is that it's not supposed to be a friendship. Many people have told us that they were friends with their spouses to begin with, but not anymore. Now they're just married, which is pretty different from JUST MARRIED! So they don't feel like friends in the way they did before. It's as if once you're married, you can't enjoy each other. Don't get us wrong: marriage is a serious calling in life. As we tried to make clear in Chapter One, your marriage matters to God, and marriage plays an important role in what God means to convey about Himself to the world. A happy, joy-filled marriage is one of the most amazing things you can build to live out this purpose. Don't buy into the misbelief which says that because you're married—or planning to be—you can't have fun and be connected as friends over the long haul. You can.

Think about what Solomon said:

> Enjoy life with your wife, whom you love, all the days of this meaningless life that God has given you under the sun—all your

meaningless days. For this is your lot in life and in your toilsome labor under the sun. (Ecclesiastes 9:9)

As Solomon pondered the meaning of life, he concluded that it was too full of toilsome work. Life can be a drudge. Solomon realized that even though this is true, it is still possible to enjoy life with your mate for all your days. At the end of their lives, when people are asked what they wish they'd done differently, hardly anyone says, "I wish I'd worked harder, finished my to-do list, made more money, and completed more projects." People usually wish they had played more with the kids or spent more time connecting with their spouse and others in their families. Life slides away if you are not deciding to make time for the great things.

"We Only Talk About Problems"

What do friends talk about? Ideas, feelings, current events, politics, spiritual questions, funny stories from the day, and so forth. What do couples tend to talk about after they've been married for years? Problems with the kids, problems with work, disagreements about money, problems with getting the car fixed, concerns about who's got time to do some project around the house, hassles with in-laws, problems with the neighbor's dog, concerns about each other's health . . . The list goes on and on. Sure, some of those things are important for friends to talk about, especially if you are able to provide emotional support for one another. But is that the type of talking that builds connection in the first place? Not for most couples.

If you aren't careful, most of your talks in your marriage will end up being about problems and concerns—not points of view, what's going on in your lives, and shared interests and dreams about the future. You do have to talk about the unpleasant stuff, but too many couples let the problem discussions of life crowd out the kind of relaxed times they enjoyed at first. And because problems and concerns can easily become events that trigger issues, there's much more potential for conflict than there is for having fun together or just hanging out as friends.

If you've been married for some time, think for a moment about a friendship you enjoy with someone other than your mate.

How often do you have to talk with that person about problems between the two of you? Not often, we'd bet. Friends aren't people with whom we often argue. In fact, one of the nicest things about friendships is that you don't usually have to work out a lot of issues. Instead, friends focus on positive mutual interests—fun things they've done or will do, spirituality, sports, the news, and so on. Or they spend time sharing their burdens with each other. But they seldom focus on problems *between* each other. In marriage, you have to do both—but you have to work at the positive stuff to keep it alive. Make it safe to connect as friends, not just as teammates dealing with the icky stuff of life.

Guidelines for Connecting Through Fun and Friendship

Although you were effortlessly spontaneous earlier in your relationship, once you're married, having fun and talking as friends have to become intentional. Both sources of connection take some thought and planning, or else they will slide away. Here are some pointers that can help you stay on track in both realms. We will follow these general pointers with specific strategies for both fun and friendship. You will note that the major suggestions that follow are amplifications of Ground Rule 2, which we covered in Chapter Four.

Set Aside the Time

> *There is a time for everything, and a season for every activity under heaven: . . . a time to weep and a time to laugh, a time to mourn and a time to dance.*
> —Ecclesiastes 3:1, 4

It's unlikely that you'll have special times together without setting aside the time to make them happen. Sure, you can and should have spontaneous moments of playfulness and meaningful chats just about anywhere, anytime. Even a quick joke together, gentle teasing, or talking about something funny on TV can add to your closeness. But to get the full benefit of quality time together, you have to make it a priority, or it just won't happen. *This means you need to be serious about carving out time to be less serious.* It means you'll need to set some limits on many of the other things you do in life—such as the amount of time you devote to work or to making sure your kids have every opportunity for enrichment, or perhaps even the amount of time you devote to ministry. It will probably mean cutting down on some of your other expenses so that you can set aside a few dollars just for doing something fun. It may even mean that you keep that old car a little longer or buy a less costly house the next time you move so that you don't have to work as hard to keep up the payments. Lots of couples are house rich and connection poor.

You will probably need to schedule fun and friendship times together, as artificial as this might seem. People talk a lot about quality time versus quantity time. The truth is that many of the best-quality times come from having set aside a quantity of time. Sometimes the most magical moments arise naturally from having a block of time together to relax. When you have set aside time to be close, try to eliminate distractions. It's not very relaxing to know that you could get a call at any moment, and nowadays people have their mobile devices instantly within reach most of the time. Protect the time. Ignore all your texts and calls that are not emergencies so that they can't interrupt your enjoyment of each other.

Protect Connection Time from Conflict

This one is crucial. Many couples try to multitask during the time they've set aside. They try to combine quality time *and* resolve difficult issues "while we have this chance for some time together." Avoid this. If something should come up during friendship time, call a Time Out and decide when you will talk about the issue later. That's why setting aside time to talk (safely) about problems is so important, as we discussed in a number of earlier chapters. Doing so takes the pressure off your connecting times together. The good news about problems is that they don't go away! They'll still be there to work on after your special times.

Taking the Risk

James Cordova conducts research on intimacy at Clark University. He suggests that the deepest kind of intimacy develops when one partner shares something he or she feels vulnerable about, and the other partner responds in a positive and accepting manner. That response of warm acceptance does something very powerful that transforms a relationship: it makes it more likely that each partner will continue to risk being emotionally vulnerable in the future, in large part because they share a growing expectation that it is safe to do so. This is also one of the defining features of really great friendships. Most of the time, you talk about fun stuff, meaningless stuff, and just whatever stuff is happening. But sometimes, you share more deeply about something that is affecting one of you profoundly. That is where the risk comes in, and that is where the blessing of emotional safety makes all the difference. Remember, make it safe to connect. That's what friends do.

Have you grown to fear taking this kind of risk in your relationship? That's a worrisome sign of distance creeping in. To stay deeply attached, you need to nurture the ability and confidence to share meaningful thoughts and feelings as you walk through life together.

Frank and Karen learned this lesson the hard way before they got into the groove of doing it right. Earlier in their marriage, they went through a period when they were so busy that they'd try to schedule everything into the few times they had together. They'd get a sitter, go out for fun, and mess up the evening with issues. For example, one night they went out to an ice skating show. While they were seated and waiting for the show to start, Frank said, "We haven't had time to talk out how to pay for that basement renovation. Let's see if we can get a little headway on that while we're waiting." That started off an argument, ruining the special time together.

When you feel confident that issues won't come up because you've decided to deal with them at their own time and place, you'll find it much easier to relax and enjoy being together. You can even decide that *all your time* will be in the "friendship mode," except for those times you have decided to set aside for work on problems. Some couples find it very helpful to agree on specific times when issues will *never* be brought up, such as when they are getting ready for church, reconnecting at the end of the workday, having meals together, and being around the kids. These times need to be protected. Some couples decide that their bedroom will be one place where they will try not to talk about problems. Both partners have to work hard to make something like this happen. If you agree to try it, you have to do your part, even when your partner slips up. The key is to realize together that *you are not at the mercy of your issues.* You can take charge of them. They no longer have to be in charge of you.

Strategies for Fun

Let's look at some specific ways to make fun happen. It's often not hard to keep fun alive, but you have to decide to make it happen. If you are not having as much fun now as you could, sliding will just get you more of the same.

Brainstorm About Ways to Have Fun

For many couples, coming up with ideas about fun things to do together is difficult. What do you do? Have you fallen into the common dinner-and-a-movie rut? Have you ever had this conversation: "What would you like to do tonight?" "Oh, I don't know. What would you like to do?" "Well, let's just go to a movie." Last-minute choices are choices to stay in the same ruts. Instead, sit down together and think about what you will do—*before* the time to do it comes up. You can repeat the most enjoyable, interesting, and fun things you've done before, or you can try new things you would like to do together. Brainstorm to make a list of all ideas that come to mind, no matter how foolish or outrageous they may seem. Part of the fun in brainstorming is throwing out the wackiest ideas you can. It can be one way to have fun together all in itself.

Don't get stuck on activities that are too expensive or time consuming. Little things like watching the sunset or taking a walk in the rain at the spur of the moment may become some of your most memorable moments. The important thing is that you be intentional about having fun together.

Over the years, we've noticed that when we have couples brainstorm about enjoyable things to do, sex usually isn't mentioned until many other things have been listed. Couples tend to forget that sexual connection is one of the most enjoyable things they can do together. God created sex as a fundamental part of your joy and oneness. How about setting aside an evening without the kids to make love in front of the fireplace? If you don't have a fireplace, be creative about something else a little out of the ordinary—if you both want to. All too often, the sensual-sexual area also falls victim to the barriers against fun that we discussed earlier. Many professionals believe that sexual chemistry inevitably decreases over time, yet many couples are able to sustain and even improve their sex lives as they mature together.

We don't believe that couples fall out of attraction the way people fall out of trees. Instead, attraction gradually fades away because couples neglect the very things that started it in the first place, fun being one of the most important.

Power Up Your Fun Time

Here are some things that make fun time especially effective:

1. Do active rather than passive activities. By this we don't mean you have to climb Pike's Peak together. Just do things that involve your body—for example, hiking, window shopping downtown, playing a board game, or working in the garden.
2. Try novel experiences. Sometimes the most enjoyable times come from doing something new. The newness of the activity becomes a big part of the fun. You'll be surprised what you'll discover about each other when you're doing something neither of you has done before. You can start with some of the suggestions we've listed at the end of this chapter, simple ideas like getting a massage together or feeding the ducks at the park. The possibilities are endless. You can climb a mountain or collect sea shells, do research at the library about your next vacation or wash the car together. You get the idea.

3. Choose to do some things that are cheap. We've noticed that lots of couples get focused on fun activities that cost a lot of money. Although some couples can afford to do that routinely, most really cannot, and they are creating other problems by focusing their fun on expensive activities. For instance, it does not cost very much to buy and prepare totally different foods for dinner. This can be more fun and a lot cheaper than taking in some off-Broadway play or a hockey game.

Share in the Preparation for Fun Time

A lot of time together for fun and friendship is not really going to be thought of so much as a date as just hanging out, relaxing. But a real date out together can be fun to plan and fun to do. There are two parts to planning a great date: deciding what to do and making the arrangements to do it. Rather than deciding what to do at the last minute, create a fun-time idea bank. Write down some of your best brainstorming ideas on index cards. Be sure to include some of your personal favorites. Then, using your stockpile of ideas, you can take turns with the two parts of fun-time planning.

Here's how it works. A few days before your date night, give your mate three cards with your chosen ideas on them. Your mate's job is to select one of the ideas. This way, you will be doing something that at least one of you will like, and with your mate having a choice among the three options, probably it will be something you both like. If you want, you can both agree that one of you—for example, the one choosing among the three options—will take charge of making that date happen. Then, next time, reverse roles. This keeps some balance in the types of things you do together during time you've set aside for connection.

Strategies for Friendship

Now we'll go through some ideas for protecting and deepening friendship in your relationship. Remember, friendship is something that most people want more than anything else in their relationship with their mate, so choose some strategies and make them happen.

Begin Again to Talk as Friends

To do this, you have to listen as friends listen. Good friends listen with little defensiveness. So when you're sharing, you don't worry whether your friend's feelings are getting hurt or whether he or she is being offended. That's because a friend cares about what you think and feel, and relationship issues are rarely at stake. Friends accept you as you are. A friend of ours, Bill Coffin, once said, "A friend is someone whose face lights up when they see you and doesn't have any immediate plans for your improvement." When you're talking as friends, you aren't trying to change one another or solve problems. In fact, try to make sure that these times to talk are not about anything that causes tension or conflict between the two of you so that you can both relax and just enjoy the conversation. Even when we let our hair down and talk about something really serious, we don't want our friends to tell us what to do—we just want them to listen. Friends don't give advice unless they are asked for it. It helps a lot just to know someone cares. Friends often provide that kind of support, and you can do this for each other in your marriage relationship.

Talk About Things You May Have Never Discussed Before

At first it may be difficult to find something to talk about, especially if most of your talk has been about the day-to-day things of life. When you're having fun, just talk about the here and now. During your time set aside to talk more as friends, share your hopes and dreams, your spiritual struggles, what you'd like to accomplish during the next year, or even your bucket list. Or just talk about something funny you read that week or something that interested you about world news. We have provided a list of great ideas to talk about at the end of this chapter; use that to start your own list!

Talk from Your Heart

This means sharing not only your opinions but your convictions, desires, and feelings. You can deepen intimacy by sharing feelings.

Being truly heard at this level of the soul is one of the most intimate experiences you can have. Jean-Philippe Laurenceau at the University of Delaware has found that people feel the greatest intimacy when they are able to self-disclose to another who is responsive to them about what has been shared.

○ ◎ ◉

Like so many other things you've learned in this book, having fun and building greater closeness need to involve intentionality and planning. They don't just happen magically, as they may have seemed to at first. We hope you'll use some of our ideas to bring freshness and greater joy into your relationship.

Doing Your Part

Fun-Time Exercises

We encourage you to do some of the things we discussed in this chapter. Here they are again:

1. Brainstorm and make a list of fun activities. Be creative. Have a good time coming up with ideas. We've listed a few below to help you get started.
2. Write these ideas out on index cards to build your own fun-time stack. It will come in handy when you don't have much time to decide what to do but you're ready for some fun.
3. Set aside a regular time for fun. Include a default time in case your schedule gets interrupted.
4. Pick out three cards describing some of your favorite ideas and hand them to your partner. Make that idea happen. Next time, reverse roles and do it again.

Fun-Time Ideas

• Rent a romantic movie and cuddle on the sofa with a bowl of popcorn.
• Share a Starbucks drink with two straws. Or with one straw if you like.

(continued)

- Go to a restaurant that serves some type of food you've never eaten before. Pretend you are restaurant critics and talk about what you'd write up about the restaurant. (And if you really want to do so, write a little review and post it on one of the many apps or websites for restaurants!)
- Build a snowman together. Or a sand castle.
- Attend or audit a free adult education class.
- Go to the mall and spend the evening just watching people.
- Read a short story together on a blanket at your favorite spot.
- Take a walk in the rain under one umbrella.
- Check out the neighborhood Christmas lights on a snowy night.
- Prepare a meal together, then feed it to each other.
- Put a kite together and fly it on a breezy day.
- Cook breakfast together and eat it together in bed.
- Take a candlelight bubble bath.
- Take $5.00 and shop at the mall, buying each other the craziest thing you can find.
- Watch the sunrise together in your warm car, then go out for a hearty breakfast.
- Go to a park and play at the playground before a picnic.
- Visit an art gallery and talk about what you like and don't like.
- Go bowling or miniature golfing.
- Take a walk in a summer rain *without an umbrella!* When you get home, take a warm shower and dry each other off. Who knows what might happen next!
- Take a walk through your neighborhood and pray for your neighbors.

Friendship-Time Exercises
Plan some time for these exercises. Have fun, relax, and enjoy your friendship.

1. Plan a quiet, uninterrupted time. Take turns picking topics of interest for each of you. Ban relationship conflict issues and problem talk. Then consider some of the topics we've listed here.

2. Talk together about how you can build time for friendship into your weekly routine. If you both believe it should be a priority, how do you want to make sure it is?

Things to Talk About as Friends

- My idea of a perfect day [from sunup to bedtime] is . . . (Share details about getting up, breakfast and other mealtimes, activities during the day, and so on.)
- My favorite memory between ages six and twelve is . . . What made it meaningful was . . .
- If I had a thousand dollars to give, the ministry I would give to is . . . (Give your reasons why.)
- The most challenging thing [or thing I enjoy most] in my life right now is . . .
- The three [five? ten?] most important things I'd like to do or see happen before I die are . . .
- The thing in my future I am most looking forward to [or dreading most] is . . .
- If I had unlimited funds and time and could take a vacation to anywhere, I would . . .
- The most painful experience for me when I was growing up was when . . . To think about it now makes me feel . . .
- "Struggle and pain are required for spiritual growth." I [agree or disagree] with this statement because . . . When I hear statements like this, I feel . . .
- My most treasured memory of our life together is . . . When I think about it, I feel . . .
- I feel that our relationship is unique in the following special way(s):
- If God could use us together in a mighty way, this is what I dream it might look like:
- My biggest problem outside our family right now is . . .
- My closest same-sex friend these days is . . . What I like most about [him or her] is . . .
- My [most embarrassing, most fun, craziest, saddest, most scary] memory from my teenage years is . . .
- The thing I tend to be most fearful about is . . .

(continued)

- The person in my life who helped me most to grow spiritually was . . . What I liked most about [him or her] was . . .
- The thing that comes to me "as natural as breathing" is . . . I would like to develop this by . . .
- The way I most want to grow personally in the next year is . . .
- When I pray, the mental picture I have of God is . . .

12

Touch and Sexual Oneness

*Until the day breaks, and the shadows flee, I will go
to the mountain of myrrh and to the hill of incense.*
SONG OF SONGS 4:6

God, who "richly provides us with everything for our enjoyment"
(1 Timothy 6:17), created marriage for physical oneness as well
as for all the other kinds of oneness we have covered in this book.
As a matter of fact, the foundational picture of oneness in scripture is a picture of two coming together in "one flesh" (Genesis
2:24). Scripture clearly honors the importance of sexuality in marriage. But sensuality, too, is portrayed very positively. In this
chapter, we'll look at these two wonderful aspects of marital
oneness and discuss some of the common pitfalls couples fall into
that deprive them of some of the blessings God had in mind at
creation.

We realize that some couples who read this are in a very good
place in terms of their total connection. Their marriages are
delightful and alive, and their main goal in this chapter may be
to enhance further what is already working very well. For other
couples, problems have crept in, and they need to renew their
physical union, not merely make a good thing better.

Sensuality in Marriage

We live in a culture that glorifies sex. In fact, it may glorify sex
outside of marriage more than *in* marriage, through various

207

images, story lines, and reality TV shows that undermine the importance and beauty of sensual and sexual connection in marriage. One clearly gets the impression that marital sex—especially in Christian marriages—is boring. The Bible speaks to love, sensuality, and physical pleasure in marriage, especially in the Song of Songs, written by Solomon. Although many have viewed Solomon as depicting either God's love for Israel or Christ's love for the church (or both), the Song of Songs is also one of the most magnificent descriptions of love, devotion, and passion ever penned. Consider just a few passages:

Beloved

While the king was at his table, my perfume spread its fragrance.

My lover is to me a sachet of myrrh resting between my breasts.

My lover is to me a cluster of henna blossoms from the vineyards of En Gedi.

Lover

How beautiful you are, my darling! Oh, how beautiful! Your eyes are doves.

Beloved

How handsome you are, my lover! Oh, how charming!

And our bed is verdant. (Song of Songs 1:12–16)

Awake, north wind, and come, south wind! Blow on my garden, that its fragrance may spread abroad. Let my lover come into his garden and taste its choice fruits. (Song of Songs 4:16)

I am my lover's and my lover is mine; he browses among the lilies. (Song of Songs 6:3)

Many couples struggle with their sexual relationship, and others, struggling or not, hardly know how to be intimate other than sexually. Sexuality without a broader connection (including sensuality) spells trouble for a marriage. Couples who enjoy the most rewarding physical unions realize that in a sense, all of marriage is foreplay. Emotional, intellectual, and spiritual closeness, along with nonsexual sensuality, serve as the foundation for great experiences of love in sexual union. You can enjoy more of the blessings of physical oneness as God created it when you nurture the other kinds of oneness we've discussed in this book so far. Now let's now look at sexuality and sensuality in a bit more detail.

Emotional Safety Begets Physical Intimacy

A number of studies have shown that sexual self-disclosure in marriage promotes sexual satisfaction. By self-disclosure, researchers mean the sharing of desires, likes, and dislikes with each other. One reason why self-disclosure is associated with a better sexual relationship is simply that each partner gains a better understanding of what is pleasing to the other. And, within the bounds of what each is comfortable with, being aware of and trying to meet your partner's sexual desires is one of the surest ways to create a deeper, more satisfying marriage.

The less obvious reason why sexual self-disclosure is associated with a better sexual connection in marriage is that, for most couples, being able to share in an open way reflects emotional safety in the marriage. Many, but not all, people feel somewhat vulnerable about sharing directly what they like and do not like sexually. Anytime you are sharing about something you deeply desire, you are revealing more of who you are—which can open you up for rejection at a deeper level. It also opens you up for deeper acceptance. Do you want to have a wonderful sexual oneness together? Make it safe to share.

Sensuality and Sexuality Are Different

Think about the word *sexuality* for a moment. What comes to mind? For many, the first thought is of sexual intercourse or other specific acts of sex. Or perhaps you think of the things that are arousing to you or your partner, or the feelings you have when you want to make love.

Now think about *sensuality*. What comes to mind? People usually think of some pleasant experience that involves touching, seeing, smelling, or tasting—like walking on the beach or being massaged with sweet-smelling oil. How about the roughness of a beard or the silkiness of hair? The smell of your partner after a shower or a bath? Chocolate? You get the idea. These are sensual experiences that are not necessarily connected with sexuality. The Song of Songs is full of sensuality.

Sensuality includes physical touch, but it is not always associated with making love. We'd include hugging, affectionate cuddling, nonsexual massages—all the experiences that provide physical pleasure in nonsexual ways. All involve the senses. This distinction between sensuality and sexuality is important—you likely want your relationship to be alive in both areas. However, in order for there to be growth, there needs to be a willingness to explore, discover, listen, laugh, compromise, change, and practice.

In the early stages of relationships, touching, holding hands, hugging, and caressing are natural. Over time, many couples tend to bypass the sensual and move directly to goal-oriented sexual behavior. Less time is spent on the kinds of touching that had been so delightful before. The focus is more on the end product of sex than on the process of expressing love. This leads to problems, because nonsexual touching is an important part of your overall physical intimacy.

Kristen and Andrew have been married for eight years. They used to spend a lot of time just cuddling and caressing. As time went by, they got busier with kids, work, and other duties—as most of us do. After a year or two of marriage, they had settled into a pattern of having sex about once a week. It was OK, but less and less time was devoted to sensuality. One or the other would initiate sex after they went to bed, and they'd quickly have intercourse, usually finishing in about ten minutes.

The couple had become quite efficient at making love or, more accurately, at having intercourse. They didn't make extra time, so they simply made do. In fact, they were "making do" rather than "making love." Their focus on sexual intercourse without much sensuality led to their dissatisfaction. "What happened to all those times we'd just lie around for hours together?" Kristen wondered. "It seems like Kristen used to be a lot more responsive when we made love," Andrew mused. We'll come back to them in a bit.

Keeping the Sensual Alive and Well

It's important to make sensual experiences a regular part of your relationship, apart from sexuality. Sensual experiences set the stage for better sexual experiences. The whole climate for physical intimacy is better when you have preserved the sensual. It's also important to keep sensuality as a regular part of your lovemaking. When you focus on touching in a variety of ways, you elevate the pleasure of the whole experience. Most couples prefer this broader sensual focus to a narrow focus on sex. It provides a much richer expression of intimacy in your physical relationship.

Protecting Physical Intimacy from Anxiety

Arousal is the natural process by which we are stimulated to sensual or sexual pleasure. It's a state of pleasurable excitement. Although just about everyone is capable of being aroused, this pleasurable feeling can be short-circuited by anxiety. Numerous studies suggest that anxiety inhibits sexual arousal. There are two key kinds of anxiety that we'd like to discuss in this context: performance anxiety and the tension from conflict in your marriage.

The Barrier of Performance Anxiety

Performance anxiety arises when you have too much concern about how well you are "doing" when you make love. Frequently asking yourself such questions as "How am I doing?" or "Is my partner enjoying this?" reflects performance anxiety. To be clear, noticing what is pleasurable to your mate and trying to adjust to improve the experience for him or her is not a problem. But when you're keeping an eye on your performance, you put distance between you and your partner. You're focused on how you are doing rather than on being in the experience with your mate.

The focus on performance interferes with arousal because you are distracted from your own sensations of pleasure. This distraction leads to many of the most common sexual problems people experience—premature ejaculation, problems keeping erections, and difficulty lubricating or reaching orgasm. You simply can't be tense and pleasantly aroused at the same time. You can't relax and enjoy being with your partner if your focus is on not making mistakes.

Let's think about Andrew and Kristen again. Andrew became aware that Kristen was becoming less and less pleased with their lovemaking. Without a focus on sensuality and touching through-out their relationship, Kristen began to feel as though Andrew was just using her sexually. That's kind of harsh, because he didn't think this way at all. But it felt like that to her. This feeling was intensified because he'd have an orgasm every time they made love, but her climaxes were less and less frequent. As dissatisfying as their lovemaking was for both of them, it seemed to Kristen that it was still better for Andrew. So her resent-ment grew.

Andrew wanted to make things better. But instead of talking it out and working on the problem together, he decided he'd just do a better job of making love to Kristen. He'd go into superman-lover mode. This wasn't all bad as ideas go. The cape was a little much, though. (Kidding.) Where things went wrong was that he became focused on performing, which led to increased anxiety. "How's Kristen doing? Is she getting excited? How am I doing? Does she like this? I wonder if she thinks I'm doing this right. Man, I'd better try more of this for a while; I'm not sure she's ready."

Andrew wasn't feeling at all connected with Kristen when they made love. He was performing, not being with her. Kristen knew there was some change in Andrew's attention to her arousal, which did please her to some degree, but she had a growing sense that Andrew was somewhere else when they made love. She was reaching orgasm more often, but she didn't feel that they were close while they made love.

The key for Kristen and Andrew was to rediscover the sensual side of their relationship. They had to begin talking openly about what was going on. You can prevent a lot of problems from devel-oping in the first place if you work to keep the sensual connection alive. And if you have lost it, the strategies described here can help you get it back.

The Barrier of Conflict and Anxiety

Mishandled conflicts can destroy your physical relationship by adding tension, both in and out of the bedroom. Let's face it: when you've been arguing and you're angry with each other, you don't feel like being sensual or making love. For some, the sexual relationship is temporarily enhanced by conflict followed by makeup sex. That's one way to go, but how many arguments do you want to have in the effort to boost your sex lives? (And we covered how bad open conflict is for children in Chapter Two.) Makeup sex notwithstanding, poorly handled conflict adds a layer of tension to a relationship. Your physical relationship is probably more vulnerable to the effects of conflict and resentment than any other area. If you are experiencing unresolved conflict in other areas of your relationship, you'll probably find it difficult to feel safe or excited about making love. It's even worse when conflicts erupt in the context of lovemaking.

Earlier, we described how the Song of Songs portrays wonderful images of sensual and loving connection in marriage. In the midst of this Hebrew poetry of love and passion is a verse that people often overlook. A friend of ours, Tim Doyle, brought this to our attention in a conversation about oneness in marriage.

> Catch for us the foxes, the little foxes that ruin the vineyards, our vineyards that are in bloom. (Song of Songs 2:15)

To sense the full impact of this verse, you need to realize just how much of the imagery in the Song of Songs is about a garden and the fruit in it (2:1–3; 4:13, 14; 4:16–5:1; 6:2, 3). For example:

> Beloved
>
> Awake, north wind, and come, south wind! Blow on my garden, that its fragrance may spread abroad. Let my lover come into his garden and taste its choice fruits.
>
> Lover
>
> I have come into my garden, my sister, my bride; I have gathered my myrrh with my spice. (Song of Songs 4:16–5:1a)

Because love and passion are depicted here as fruit in a garden, the "little foxes" must be those little things in life that somehow mess up the garden. We've heard different theories on why the little foxes would be a problem, from their eating the fruit to their being so playful with each other that they knock the blooms off the plants, which means no fruit. The latter interpretation seems more consistent with the idea that it's little foxes, not big ones, that are a problem.

What are the little things that nip your physical oneness while it's still in the bud? Surely, one of the most common and powerful destroyers of such connection is conflict. Love needs care to blossom and grow. You need to protect your physical relationship from all the little foxes in life. It's especially critical to keep problems and disagreements off-limits when you have the time to be together for touching or making love.

Communicating Desires

It's a mistake to assume that your partner likes whatever you like or that you can read each other's minds. Would you go out to a restaurant and order the same meal for your partner that you want? Of course not. It's also too easy for some people to assume that their partner *won't* like the things they like. Either way, you're mind reading—making assumptions about what is in your partner's mind. And because many couples have trouble talking openly about their physical relationship, it's really easy for these assumptions to take control. You don't know what your partner's expectations and desires are until he or she tells you—and vice versa. Of course, there are some other ways to tell, if you are paying attention.

Because of your history together, you can often assume correctly, of course, what your partner likes. But that's not enough; people change. We can't tell you how many couples we've talked with for whom it seems that one partner expects the other "to just know" what he or she likes or doesn't like when making love. It's as if people believe that "it just isn't romantic or exciting if I have to tell you what I want. You *should* know!" This is an unreasonable expectation. If you hold this fantasy, you should challenge it for the health of your relationship.

Couples who have the best sexual relationships have ways of communicating both verbally and nonverbally about what they like. Furthermore, there's usually a genuine unselfish desire to please each other. There's a strong sense of teamwork involved, even in lovemaking, where each gives and receives pleasure willingly. This giving spirit, combined with direct communication, leads to great lovemaking.

We recommend that you learn to give your partner clear feedback about what feels pleasurable or unpleasant to you, including while you are touching or making love. We're not, of course, suggesting that you have a Speaker-Listener discussion in the middle of lovemaking. (Though if it really excites you that much, let us know how it goes.)

Although it feels risky at first, open communication is the key. You can consider trying some new ideas to break out of ruts—such as reading a self-help book about improving your sexual relationship. That might help you get started in talking about this sensitive topic. Agree to set one night aside to surprise each other with some of the things you learn. Determine to make lovemaking a time for fun and discovery. Try something new, even if only once. A good discussion in which you explore the sensual and sexual sides of your relationship may relieve many of your concerns about performance and lead you to the discovery of a lot more joy in this area.

We're not saying that every couple can have a perfect physical relationship. Sometimes there are real physical problems that need attention. Or one of you may have to work through sexual mistreatment from the past. But even in these situations, open and clear communication is important to making your relationship the best it can be. You both have to want it, protect it, and nurture it.

●   ●   ●

In this chapter, we've emphasized several keys for keeping your physical relationship growing and vibrant. Now it's up to you.

We don't intend this chapter to be a substitute for sex therapy if you have a history of significant sexual difficulties. Working with an experienced Christian sex therapist can usually accomplish a great deal when there are significant problems. Our focus here has been more on helping couples who have lost some edge or even have some problems that are not too difficult to work through as a couple.

The following exercises can help you enhance your physical intimacy. They have worked successfully for many couples over the years. If you're ready for greater sensual and sexual enhancement, read on.

Doing Your Part

Giver-Receiver Exercise

This is an exercise that has benefited many couples—whether or not they were having trouble in their physical relationship. The purpose is twofold: (1) to keep you "in touch" with sensuality in your physical relationship, and (2) to help you learn to communicate more openly and naturally about what you like and don't like in your physical relationship.

This isn't the time for sexual intercourse. That would defeat the purpose, as we want you to focus on sensuality. Don't be goal oriented, other than to focus on the goal of relaxing and doing this exercise in a way that you each enjoy. If you want to make love following the exercise, that's up to you. But if you've been experiencing feelings of pressure in regard to your sexuality, we'd recommend that you completely separate out these practice times from having sex.

The general idea is that you each take turns giving and receiving pleasure. The first few times, you are either the *giver* or the *receiver* until you switch roles halfway through the time you have set aside. When you are in the *receiver* role, your job is to enjoy the touching and give feedback on what feels good and what doesn't. Your partner does not know this unless you tell him or her. You can give either verbal or hand-guided feedback.

Verbal feedback means telling your partner what actions feel good, how hard to rub, or what areas you like to have touched. Hand-guided feedback consists of gently moving your partner's hand around the part of the body being massaged to provide feedback about what really feels good.

When you are the *giver*, your role is to provide pleasure by touching your partner and being responsive to feedback. Ask for feedback as often as necessary. Be aware of changes in how your partner is reacting—what feels good one minute may hurt the next. You are to focus on what your partner is wanting, not on what you think would feel good.

Begin by choosing roles and then give a massage of hands or feet for about ten to twenty minutes, asking for and giving feedback. We recommend massages of such areas as the hands, back, legs, and feet the first few times to get the hang of the technique. This also helps you relax if there are some issues about sexuality between you. Then switch roles. Repeat as often as you like, but also remember to practice these roles in other aspects of your sensual and sexual relationship.

We recommend that you try the Giver-Receiver exercise over the course of several weeks, several times a week. As you work on the exercise, there are some variations of the technique to work in over time. Assuming all is going well in your exercises, begin to move to other areas for touching. Wherever you want to be touched is great.

Over time, you can drop the rigid emphasis on the giver and receiver roles and work on both of you giving and receiving at the same time—while still keeping an emphasis on sensuality and communication of desires. Or you can vary the degree to which you want to stay in these roles as you wish. If you practice this over time, it will become easier for you to communicate openly about touch. It will also be easier for you to work together to keep physical intimacy vibrant and alive.

Exploring the Sensual
In addition to doing the Giver-Receiver exercise, set aside a specific time for sensual activities together. This works for all couples, regardless of whether they are engaging in sexual activity. Be sure you will not be interrupted.

At the start of this exercise, talk about what's sensual for each of you and what you'd like to try doing to keep sensual experiences in your relationship. Here are some ideas:

(continued)

- Give a massage to your partner, using the Giver-Receiver technique.
- Share verbally with your partner what you enjoy both sensually and sexually.
- Cuddle and hug as you talk to your partner about the positive things you love about him or her.
- Plan a sensual or sexual activity for your next encounter.
- Plan a wonderful meal together. Prepare it together and sit close together—share the meal.
- Wash your partner's hair.
- Spend some time just kissing.

Read to Each Other

Read the Song of Songs aloud, taking turns reading to each other. This could be done a few verses or a chapter a night, or all at once. Set aside time without interruptions (after the children are down for the night). Enjoy sharing one of the most explicit, beautifully written love stories ever written. Try figuring out what some of the imagery is referring to as you go.

Learn from a Good Book

Many couples have benefited from reading a book or two on sexual enhancement. There are many options, including books from both secular and Christian perspectives. There are so many books available that we are reluctant to recommend specific ones because the type of book you might benefit from is likely to be different from what another couple would want to read. Different couples might find the same book too racy or too tame or too Christian or not Christian enough. The key here is to do a little homework so that you can select a book or two that you both are likely to appreciate and that matches your sensibilities. You can do a lot of research online, looking up reviews and descriptions, to get ideas. We've list a few well-regarded books here in order to get you started in your search.

Douglas Rosenau. (2002). *A Celebration of Sex: A Guide to Enjoying God's Gift of Sexual Intimacy*. Nashville: Nelson.

Joseph and Linda Dillow and Peter and Lorraine Pintus. (2004). *Intimacy Ignited: Conversations Couple to Couple: Fire Up Your Sex Life with the Song of Solomon.* Colorado Springs: NavPress.

Any of the books by Clifford and Joyce Penner. Their books are mostly older, but some are classics and highly recommended.

13

Got Your Back

Carrying Each Other's Burdens

> *Carry each other's burdens, and in this way you will*
> *fulfill the law of Christ.*
> GALATIANS 6:2

How do you handle it when your partner is struggling? How do you provide the support that he or she needs? And when *you* are distressed, upset, or concerned about something, how does your partner support you? This chapter is about how you can be there for each other when the challenges and cares of life confront you.

If you and your mate can do what we describe in this chapter, you will likely do very well in your life together no matter what else happens. Being emotionally supportive goes to the heart of meeting some of the deepest needs and desires people have in marriage.

What we have to say here is not as pertinent to situations where the two of you are in conflict. Those are moments when being emotionally supportive can be extremely difficult. However, even if you have some difficult conflicts and issues, there are other times when you can boost your support for each other in genuine ways. This will do a great deal to protect and preserve your connection.

We all need to have reasonable expectations about support in marriage. There are no couples who are always able to be there for each other in loving and helpful ways (although there are some couples who come close). Really being there for each other at the most important times is not easy. We aim to help you do a better job of giving each other emotional support when it is needed.

Backing One Another in Life

The apostle Paul wrote that we should "carry each other's burdens, and in this way you will fulfill the law of Christ" (Galatians 6:2). In the original Greek, the word for burdens means a weight, a load, trouble, or heaviness. Heavy gets right to it. The characteristic of burdens is that they weigh and wear—they push you down and sometimes threaten to crush you. But anything that pushes your partner down also gives you the opportunity to lift him or her up. When you do this, you are fulfilling Jesus' great commandment to love one another.

There are many old windmills in Europe. If you look around the back of one, you'll typically see two very large poles that are supporting the structure from behind. Those poles "have the windmill's back," no matter how strongly the wind is blowing. One of the greatest things that can happen in marriage is for both partners to be able to help the other withstand life's headwinds. And there are many specific strategies for strengthening your marriage in this way.

Some couples are busier playing "get you back" than "got your back." That's too bad. When you are constantly in the negativity of the conflict mode, you are wiping out opportunities to draw close. It doesn't have to be that way. Earlier in Galatians, before the apostle Paul wrote about carrying each other's burdens, he noted that the sum of the whole Old Testament law was to "love your neighbor as yourself," and he said that relationships are destroyed by "biting and devouring" each other (Galatians 5:15). To be emotionally supportive of each other in life, you have to limit corrosive conflicts so that you can pay attention to what weighs down the other's heart.

Almost all couples have some trouble with conflict. When anyone is under stress and strain, they are more likely to be short and snarky with their mate. (*Snarky* is an old term derived from the Greek word for being snippy and shark-like with your mate—just kidding.) So the very times when one of you most needs emotional support and tender loving care, you'll tend to drive the other away. The good news is that although conflicts can eat away at your marriage, the damage from them is much less for those couples who are able to show genuine emotional support for each other on a regular basis. It's a type of love in action that is powerfully protective of your marriage.

The Protective Power of Emotional Support

The topic of social or emotional support in relationships has been one of the major areas of advance in research about couples. A number of researchers at different universities (including Carolyn Cutrona, Joanne Davila, Lauri Pasch, Tom Bradbury, Guy Bodenmann, and their respective colleagues) have produced influential works in the study of social support between partners. Many studies show that social support from a partner is related to personal well-being, especially in the face of stress.

Perhaps even more important, being able to support each other emotionally when there are personal challenges reduces the degree to which conflict and problems damage a marriage. Studies show that among couples in which the partners are not very able to be emotionally supportive, negativity plays a bigger role in how marriages fare. But for couples who are emotionally supportive, the presence of conflict is less associated with marital quality. To be clear, poorly handled conflict is never a great thing. But it's far worse when a couple does not have positive ways to connect and provide support. Emotional support helps preserve all of what's best in your relationship. Think of it as a super anti-cancer vegetable for your relationship.

Wyndol Furman of the University of Denver has studied friendships and romantic relationships for decades. He has noted that the two pillars of success are having a safe haven and a secure base. That means having a foundation of emotional safety. And there is nothing more potent for building that than being emotionally supportive of each other.

Weighed Down

Life can be joyous and fun, but it can also be pretty heavy. Everyone faces some serious struggles in life, and some have to deal with several of them. This is just reality. As we've noted earlier, Jesus said, "in the world you will have trouble." Consider what your mate is concerned about right now—whatever you are aware of that is weighing on his or her mind that is causing worry and stress, or just concern. Do you know what concerns are foremost in his or her mind? Now take a moment to consider what troubles your sense of peace. Has there been something pulling you down all day, even if you haven't been thinking about it all the time? How does it affect you?

Here are some of the big and small kinds of burdens people have to bear:

- Concerns about a child (for example, illness, arranging child care, teen rebellion)
- Job loss, problems at work
- Worries about the future
- Health problems
- Problems with family, friends, neighbors, or coworkers
- Aging parents who need more care and help
- Money, especially not having enough to meet basic needs
- Losing something that creates a hassle, such as a smartphone or driver's license
- Getting into an argument with a service agency (cell phone company, Internet provider, credit card company)

These kinds of big and small stressors are pretty common, and everyone has their own reactions. People vary in how they are affected by stressful events and situations.

Denise and Arturo have been married seventeen years and have seen a lot of life together. They have been blessed with two pretty easy children, and they both have had steady jobs—at least until now. But there is a significant, unrelenting stressor in Arturo's life. He's one of the most valuable employees at the company where he works, but the company is a small business that is not particularly well run. That means Arturo has to focus on doing his job well while worrying that the company will go out of business because of the owner's poor decisions. Stressors that you are aware of but that you feel you have little control over can cause the most damage, psychologically and physically. Although we often hear, "Just turn it over to God," that is much easier said than done. Yes, we should make every effort to do that, but we can also take comfort in realizing that the Bible would not bother to tell us "be anxious for nothing" if it was easy to stay nonanxious.

Denise knows that Arturo is stressed and anxious about the future, and she also knows that he doesn't like talking about it. He doesn't seek her out to discuss it, but she knows he's really bothered when he comes home and sits next to her, sometimes leaning on her or just holding her hand. In fact, they both understand this little ritual so well that each experiences it as a wonderful part of their closeness. She knows he needs her support, and she knows he gets the most out of simply being physically in touch. Sometimes she says, "You're worried about work, right?" and he responds "Yes" or nods his head. This works for them.

What baffles Denise is that there are other types of stress that wear her down that Arturo doesn't seem to be bothered about in the least. Their youngest child, Lupe, has some struggles in school, and neither Denise nor Arturo thinks Lupe's teacher is very helpful. They have had numerous meetings with her and the principal, and Denise comes home drained every time. It exhausts her even to think about the subject. In contrast, Arturo is comfortable talking openly, intently, but kindly with the teacher about it. Denise sees no evidence that this stresses him at all, whereas it is a giant weight within her to think about it or deal with the school about it.

Of course, people are different. But even knowing this, we may expect our mates to process and handle stressors the same way we do. Sometimes what is obvious to one doesn't even show up on another's radar. You won't be much help in providing emotional support to your mate if you don't know what is weighing him or her down and what kind of support would be most helpful. Arturo and Denise didn't really have to talk about how Denise could provide the support that Arturo needed most. They kind of grew into that whole process. But most couples don't just slide into giving each other the kind of support each wants and needs.

Most couples will benefit greatly from talking openly about what kinds of burdens affect them or even when something is being a burden. Perhaps most don't know how to tell each other or what kind of emotional support to ask for. But Denise had shared earlier about what works best for her. What she needed to feel Arturo's support was to be able to talk and know that he was listening. It's not as though they talk about it for hours, but when she's really affected by something, she simply tells him she needs a little time or she brings up the subject while they are doing something like cleaning up after dinner. Sometimes she tells him directly that what she needs at that moment is to just let it out and for him to simply listen, without trying to fix anything.

Capitalizing by Sharing Positives

Most of this chapter deals with providing emotional support to each other when one is burdened. There is another type of emotional support that researchers are finding is a powerful source of connection in relationships—connection that springs from one partner's sharing something positive that happened to them and their partner's listening and responding with excitement and interest.

Christopher Langston conducted an influential study on the effects of sharing positive news with others. He called this "capitalizing" on the positive things that happen in life. He described a kind of positive contagion that can come when good things are shared between friends or partners. Shelly Gable and colleagues conducted further research on this idea and found that sharing positive events and emotions in relationships did have positive effects in relationships and that these effects were more lasting than the impacts of discussing negative events. Essentially, when one person shared positive things that were going on and that person felt that his or her partner was interested and that the partner understood and validated those experiences, there was a lasting positive benefit.

(continued)

Other researchers, led by Nathan Lambert, have shown that people can learn how to better respond to their partner's sharing of positive events. This is an area where upping your game can make a real difference in your marriage.

What can you do? It's not difficult; it just takes presence of mind and the intention to do it: try to notice when your partner is sharing something positive, something they are excited about, something good that happened that they mention or start talking about. When they do this, tune in and get excited with and for your partner. Show interest and positive emotion about what your partner is excited about sharing. Emotional support is not just for the times when there are burdens and stress. It is something powerful you can give when good things are happening for one or both of you. Share and share in those things.

Weight Lifting

We want to help you lift some weight from your mate's heart. To that end, we offer you some strategies for thinking about it and doing it. All of the approaches we cover here will be most effective if they are heartfelt. If you are lacking in genuine desire to help your partner in this way, you can do two things that will make a difference. First, pray that God would give you a heart of growing compassion and understanding for your mate. See Chapter Three for some help in doing that. Second, go ahead and try some of the strategies here with your mate. Put some action into your intention to be more supportive. Feelings can lead to action, but actions can also lead to genuine feelings. Remember, what you have the most control over in your marriage is doing your part.

Noticing and Reaching Out

Let's say one of you is really burdened with something, perhaps a significant worry about the future that hasn't been shared. One of two things has to happen for emotional support to be possible: either the one who feels the burden has to let the other know that something is going on, or the other has to notice that something is up without being told and then ask about it.

Tamia and Marcel have a son with autism. Tamia was not aware, most of the time, just how much she was worrying about her son's future. That may seem strange to you, but some people are a lot more aware than others of what is going on inside their own heart. Marcel would know when Tamia was really upset, though. Over the years, he figured out that she was usually upset about something when she was doing things like turning her ring around and around on her finger and looking off into space. He would notice, and he'd reach out to her by saying something as simple as "Are you doing all right tonight, dear?" That would bring her out of her thoughts, and she would start to share what she was feeling. Usually something had happened that day, such as hearing about the son or daughter of a friend going off to college, and that would start the gears turning in Tamia's head about what kind of future their son would have.

Tamia appreciated these moments. They told her that Marcel was aware of her, that he was thinking of her, and that he knew when something was not right. She did not always feel like talking about what was going on in her mind, but she loved it that he noticed. This was one of Marcel's ways of reaching out to her. Tamia could have let him know directly, but in their relationship, Marcel had the stronger antenna for when either of them was upset or struggling. That's not unusual, and it could be either one of you who is more aware, or both of you might notice certain kinds of things

What's the action point? For most of us, it's that we need to slow down a little and think about what we're going through and about what our partner might be going through. And if something seems to be weighing on either's heart, we need to find a way to bring it up or take action on it.

Touching

Loving and gentle touch is amazingly powerful. It can be one of the most effective agents of healing in human relationships. Medical health professionals are often taught the importance of simple touch as part of establishing connection and lowering anxiety in their patients. Touch can affect every aspect of your being. Our bodies are built to respond to all kinds of touch, including holding hands, hugs, and massage.

Pain, disease, worry, and distress bring powerful emotional experiences. Physical touch can touch your heart, especially if you feel isolated and alone in your worry or pain. It sends a strong message that another is there, caring and concerned and with you. Just as the physical union of Adam and Eve brought about an awareness of oneness from separateness, touch is an expression that you are not just two but one, facing life together.

We sometimes recommend that couples hold hands, even when talking about problems, as a way of saying to each other, "We may disagree and we are going through some hard times, but we are still a team and there for each other." This is not something all couples can do or want to do, but it really works for some. The following example demonstrates both touching and listening.

Lars and Nancy were going through a tough time. They had just had their third child and were fighting about taking the kids all over the place to different activities and about handling household tasks. They had recently moved to the area and hadn't established a support system. They had become very disconnected from others and from each other.

For the tough discussions about kids and chores, they decided to go full-on with the Speaker-Listener Technique. They did not use the full structure and all the rules very often, but this was a conversation they wanted to handle well. They also decided to hold hands while they discussed what had been difficult and divisive issues. Conversations don't always go well even when you do your best, but this approach was great for them. They had a long, deep discussion about what each was feeling, hurting about, and frustrated about. Each was carrying a painful burden related to their marriage and what was best for them and their children.

In their long talk, they broke through. Spontaneously, they also started hugging each other at the end of it. They had worked through the pain that was keeping them apart, and each felt supported and heard. Soon they were taking walks in the warm glow of the setting sun, and the whole family was enjoying swimming lessons. They also devised a game plan for handling the household tasks and decided to work on not getting upset when chores were not done perfectly. The key was reconnecting and finding out that each wanted to get on track and touch the pain the other was feeling.

By holding hands as they talked and by hugging afterward, Lars and Nancy were telling each other something very important, without words: "We can disagree and argue, but we will not allow these tensions to crack the foundation of our relationship and threaten the vision of our future together. We love each other and are there for each other no matter what."

Here are some ways to touch supportively:

- Hug
- Hold hands
- Put your hand on the other's back while sitting together
- Gently massage your mate's neck and shoulders
- Spoon

Chemistry Time

Unless you've been living on an island somewhere, you are likely aware that there is chemistry behind almost everything you feel. Stress and worry are also very chemical. That doesn't mean that chemicals cause everything, but what it does mean is that if you are worried or anxious or stressed, there is something chemical going on in addition to what you are aware of feeling. A team of researchers headed up by Karen Grewen at the University of North Carolina at Chapel Hill was interested in looking at how "warm partner contact" affected chemicals having to do with connection and comfort.

It is now widely understood that the chemical oxytocin is fundamental to feelings of attachment. It's a chemical famous for flooding a woman's body at the time of birth. It helps in managing stress and boosting rapid attachment between mother and child. Although women have more oxytocin than men and may be more affected by it, men have it too. Physical contact, including and especially sex, causes a lot of oxytocin to be released in the bodies of both women and men. People call oxytocin the cuddle hormone.

(continued)

What Grewen and colleagues were particularly interested in was how warm contact between two partners would affect oxytocin levels, blood pressure, and other indicators of relaxation at the chemical level. They had couples come into their labs and go through a series of steps designed to boost these very positive chemical reactions. The researchers had the couples hold hands (if they were comfortable doing so), talk about a time that they felt very close, watch a bit of a romantic video they had previously seen, and hug. What the researchers found was that these simple activities led to significant increases in the blood levels of oxytocin and decreases in stress.

What does this research mean for you? Holding hands, hugging, sitting close together—really simple stuff—can make a big difference in your sense of connection and your body's ability to fight stress. When times are tough, the tough get hugging.

Listening

Listening is another important way to provide emotional support for each other's burdens. Listening accomplishes the same thing that the most potent types of caring touch do: it helps the one who is struggling know that he or she is not alone. When partners pay attention to each other's feelings, they honor their loved one's experience and reassure them that they are not going through it alone.

Jason is married to Cathy. She feels unsupported by him, but from Jason's point of view, he's doing all he can do by working more than sixty hours a week. Cathy also works outside the home, though not for as many hours, and she does most of the housework. Both come home exhausted and don't feel that they can do another thing. Jason is not aware that there is something more that he could do that would make a real difference to Cathy. She needs him to be more supportive in ways besides the doing the "breadwinning thing." Although Cathy may well wish that he'd take responsibility for more of the chores around the house, what would have the greatest impact on her would be for him to take some steps to give her more emotional support.

Jason was brave enough to ask Cathy what he could do to help her feel more supported. When he did this, she told him that it would be great if he'd call from time to time during the day and ask her how her day was going. This would help her know that he was thinking of her and that he cared. She also told him that what would mean a lot to her was for him just to listen to what was on her mind, especially when she was upset or anxious about something.

Cathy and Jason also decided to increase the positive appreciation they expressed to each other. He explained to her that it would feel especially good to him to be reminded a little more often that she appreciated how hard he was working to support their lifestyle. By focusing on how each partner could be more supportive of the other, this couple was able to bring about some powerful changes in their marriage.

What do we mean by really listening? Although paraphrasing (see Chapter Five) helps show that you are listening, we are not suggesting or expecting that you paraphrase every time your partner expresses a thought or feeling. We are also not talking about listening so that you can give your partner advice. Beware of giving advice when that's not what your partner needs or asks for.

When you know you want to share something with your partner to receive emotional support, simply remind him or her that you just want to be heard. You can say something as simple as, "Honey, this is one of those times that I just want you to listen." Of course, if you are burdened or struggling and you want your mate's advice, asking directly for it also can help make things clear about your needs and expectations.

If you are the one seeking to support your mate, you can always just ask, "Is this one of the times when you want me to listen, or do you want some advice, or do you want me to do something to help?" If one or both of you becomes aware that a conversation intended to be supportive starts going off track, you can pause the conversation, clarify what the need is now, and get back on track.

Sometimes we see couples in which one of the partners assumes that the other should "just know" whether the partner needs just be heard or to receive something more. Don't do that to your mate. To expect your mate to read your mind is not fair, and you are less likely to get what you need. Let yourself be blessed by helping your mate understand what you want in the moment, without expecting them to figure it out on their own.

The Special Case of Anxiety and PTSD

Some couples struggle when one partner has PTSD or a serious anxiety disorder. One of the things that experts who work with such couples have learned is that some types of caring behavior by the spouse can make it harder for the other spouse to get better. Avoidance is the hallmark of these types of problems. It can take many forms, but in one way or another, it reduces discomfort or anxiety in the short run but ends up limiting the quality of life in the long run. In an attempt to alleviate burdens and reduce anxiety, a caring partner can do things that foster avoidance over time, which leads to the opposite outcome from what is intended.

Handling these types of problems well is very tricky. The spouse of one who is suffering can either be supportive in ways that make things worse or can be too harsh and impatient about the symptoms. If you are struggling with such a problem in your marriage, consider finding a therapist who specializes in helping couples who face these types of problems. There are effective, research-based strategies that you can try that will boost emotional support and help you strengthen your marriage over time.

Doing

Yes, this chapter is mostly focused on emotional support and connection when one or both of you are feeling burdens in life. So what does "doing" have to do with it? A lot! Sometimes actions speak louder than anything else in reaching into the hurting soul of another.

What kinds of doing are most supportive when one partner is dealing with the tough stuff of life? It's mostly the little thoughtful things that help take the load off. Martha and Phil are at the time of life when their parents' ages and health have become a source stress. Martha's father was diagnosed with stomach cancer, which added to his already growing list of health problems. She started going over to her parents' home several times a week, where before she had been going a few times a month. Phil picked up the slack on the tasks that Martha normally did but was having trouble getting to or finishing. For example, she was normally the one who paid the bills, but when Phil asked what more he could do, she said she'd really appreciate if it he'd start going through the mail and making sure bills were being paid.

Phil's simple action took pressure off of Martha in a way that felt really good to both of them. There were a number of things like this that he was glad to do and that made a difference. Martha could see that he was not going to leave her alone with the extra pressure she was feeling, and he felt good doing things that he knew were relieving that pressure. "Doing" of this sort not only relieves real pressures the other is experiencing but also demonstrates a mate's desire to support the other at a tough time.

Here are some examples of the kinds of tasks that one partner can do to support the other when challenging times arise:

• Do housework
• Pick up the kids
• Make dinner
• Handle logistics, such as figuring out travel plans if a trip is needed for one or both of you
• Search online for some information and organize it for the other
• Assess what the other normally does during the day, and take on some of those tasks

Telling Time

When you feel that you need support or you think that your partner does, it's great to let each other know. Try to notice more often when your partner might need more support, but also make it OK to tell each other when either of you need something extra in the burden-lifting department. Those are "telling times"—times when it would be great to tell each other what would help.

There are two ways to make this happen. One, when you need support, tell your partner about it. Let him or her know that it's one of those times, and briefly explain what would really help you right now. That last point is really important. You are more likely to get the type of support you want most if you can make it clear to your partner what that is. Two, if you notice that your partner is burdened, check in with him or her, and then ask what you can do to help. What do these telling times look like? Here are some examples.

When You Need Some Support

"I'm really upset by something Joe said to me at work. I don't need any advice or problem solving right now, but I'd sure love to just tell you what I'm upset about. That OK now or in a bit?"

"Hi dear. I'm really anxious about my presentation tomorrow. Could I just get a good long hug for a few minutes? That would help."

"I've been worrying more in the past few days about that medical test. I can't stop thinking about it. Could you pray for me to be at peace about it?"

When You Think Your Partner Might Need Some Support

"You look pretty down about what happened with Beth. Do you want to talk about it? Want a hug or for me to just hang out by you? Is there anything I can do to help?"

"Hey sweetie. It sounds like what happened at work today really ticked you off. What can I do right now to help? Do you want me to just listen? Do you want any advice? What would help?"

The idea here is to keep it short and sweet. If this style of openness works for the two of you, make telling time a thing you both regularly do.

Help!

In this section, we address the fact that some situations and some relationships are a lot harder than others. What follows are some suggestions we hope can help if you are in a really tough spot.

The Burdens Are Unrelenting

We want to be realistic about how difficult some burdens are in life. Some troubles go on and on. In a recent show on television, one character noted that what was sometimes so difficult about having children was the "on and on-ness" of it all. Of course, having children is wonderful, and for most couples they add a depth of meaning to life that is profound and that leads to deeper life satisfaction. But the tasks and concerns of parenthood do have an on and on-ness about them.

Some burdens that weigh one or both of you down just don't stop. What do you do, give up? That's obviously not a real option. When a burden goes on and on, it's all the more important for you to find the best ways to carry it together. Yes, this is the hardest time to do it, but you need each other all the more when you have something with unending on-ness going on.

This brings us to a subject that is important but that we will not spend a lot of time focusing on. Sometimes—many times—the support you can provide each other is not going to be all you need. That's when friends, family, your church, and other sources of support become crucial. This is why many couples are more in trouble these days than couples in the past. Research shows that American couples are more "alone" now than at any other time, perhaps, in history. Couples tend to move away from their extended families these days. They are busier than ever and so are less and less likely to be involved in church, community, and neighborhood organizations and activities. This leaves them isolated and less able to receive and give help when it is needed.

If one or both of you are emotionally burdened and under chronic stress, you will need to think seriously about what other sources of support are available. This is especially true for those of you who are caregivers to a spouse who has a chronic illness, mental illness, or some other disability. Whom can you call on to provide relief from the strain you are under? Being there for your mate in sickness and in health is a great expression of love and commitment, but it's not easy or right for you to do it on your own.

Related to this last point, keep the following in mind: one of the most meaningful things you can do as a couple is to be that resource which spells relief for someone else who is bearing a long-term burden with their own mate. For example, you might know a couple in which one partner is disabled. It could be very powerful in your own relationship to work together to help relieve the stress on the caregiver in that relationship. In Chapter Sixteen, we mention this kind of service to others as one of the ways to deepen the spiritual and emotional connection between the two of you.

But My Mate Isn't Great at Doing What I Need Most!

It's time to be very direct. Marriage is one of the most important and valuable relationships in all of life. It's a relationship that is tied to theology throughout scripture and history. But marriage can also be painful, difficult, and disheartening. The kind of support and connection that one partner longs for may not be what the other is able to provide. Here are a few thoughts about that.

No one will get all of what they want or need this side of eternity. Where we are right now is not heaven. Paul described it as a time of "groaning and travailing" as we wait for our redemption along with all of nature (Romans 8:22, 23). You are not yet complete, and neither is your mate. For most people, it's probably easier to see imperfection in a mate than in oneself. Some people have just the opposite problem, however, and are so hard on themselves that they have trouble seeing flaws in others. Our main point here is that marriages are strongest when each tries to be a support for the other. But we want to be realistic in saying this. The level of support from your mate that you might long for most deeply may not be something that he or she will be able to provide—or be able to provide at this time in life.

Difficult situations can sometimes become worse when your partner is not there when you need him or her to be. Sometimes it may seem that the more your mate is trying, the worse things get. But through it all, try to recognize when and how your partner is attempting to give you support, even when it's not the kind you might want most. We want to teach you how to give support of the right kind at the right time and in the right way. But it may never come in the way you want. So it will help for you to recognize and be thankful for how your partner tries to help, even if you wish for more.

You can think of this issue in terms of the spiritual gifts discussed in the New Testament. The clear teaching is that people have different gifts and that all don't have the same gifts. Here's one of the core passages about spiritual gifts.

> We have different gifts, according to the grace given us. If a man's gift is prophesying, let him use it in proportion to his faith. If it is serving, let him serve; if it is teaching, let him teach; if it is encouraging, let him encourage; if it is contributing to the needs of others, let him give generously; if it is leadership, let him govern diligently; if it is showing mercy, let him do it cheerfully. (Romans 12:6–8)

Some people are gifted to be an encouragement to others. Most people are not. Some are gifted in acts of service. Many are not. In some way, grace is involved in all of this. It's true that some people marry a person who happens to be amazingly helpful in providing support and encouragement. Perhaps this is because that spouse happens to have some special gifts in this department.

But we believe that almost everyone can learn more how to help their partner carry the burdens of life. You can find out how your mate wants to be encouraged. You can become more skilled in meeting his or her needs. You can decide to do this rather than just letting things slide. At the same time, don't require your mate to become a superhuman being who knows how to love you perfectly when you need it most. Most people would love to have that. And most couples can do a lot better than they normally do in moving toward it. But the goal is not perfection. The goal is to have a love that is growing to be more than it already is.

Doing Your Part

1. The goal of this exercise is to help the two of you improve your weight-lifting abilities: your ability to lift the weights each of you carries around in your heart and mind—the things that burden you each of you.

    Take out a piece of paper and write down each kind of support we've described. They are listed here. Then rate on a scale of 0 to 10 the degree to which you desire each kind of support when you are burdened, with 0 being "not at all important to me" and 10 being "most important to me." We recommend that you each rate them on separate sheets of paper. That way, if you and your spouse are working through this book together, you can each give your ratings without being affected by what your partner says about his or hers.

    Note that these categories can overlap, just as we showed in some of the examples we gave. There is nothing magical about this list, though we think it covers a lot of bases. Feel free to add to it because we may have left off something super important to you or your mate.

    - Noticing and reaching out
    - Touching
    - Listening
    - Doing

    Next, think about or write down some thoughts in answer to these questions:

    - How do you let each other know you need support?
    - What kinds of touch help? What works for each of you? Hugging, holding hands, massage?
    - How do you let each other know that you need the other simply to listen?
    - How can you tell when your partner is supporting you? Maybe you can ask him or her to let you know.

The rest of this weight-lifting exercise is pretty obvious. Sit down and talk together about what you can do to increase the emotional support you give each other now and in the future.

2. Look for those times when your partner is sharing something good that happened to them. Notice the moments when they are excited about something and sharing it with you. Tune in and get into the flow of their positive emotions. Show your partner you are interested in their joy and share in it with them.

PART FOUR

The Promise
Is Lasting

14

The Power of Commitment

Love ... is not self-seeking ... love ... always hopes,
always perseveres.
1 CORINTHIANS 13:5–7

A simple question says it all: Are you sticking together, or do you just feel stuck? In the book *The Power of Commitment* (by coauthor Scott), these words are used to describe two paths on which couples find themselves. What path do you want to be on together? Because you are reading this book, we assume you want to stick, which means to really thrive in your journey together. We also know that many of you feel that you are closer to stuck than to sticking. Many of you are in danger of stopping altogether—getting a divorce and moving on.

If you are sticking strong, we want to help you keep it that way. If you relate more to being stuck, we want to help you get sticky again—even if you've become discouraged.

Jesus Said

In this book, we make no attempt to present a theological treatise on divorce, reasons for divorce, separation, and implications for remarriage. All of that is important, but not what this book is for. We are much more focused here on helping couples flourish in marriage and prevent divorce. Further, to be clear, we do not believe that two people should remain together no matter how destructive or dangerous their marriage has become. If you have questions about such matters, we encourage you to seek further knowledge and advice. We do, however, want to come back to Jesus' teaching about marriage that came in response to a question from the Pharisees about divorce. In his answer, Jesus focuses on the heart of what God had in mind about commitment in marriage.

> "Haven't you read," he replied, "that at the beginning the Creator 'made them male and female,' and said, 'For this reason a man will leave his father and mother and be united to his wife, and the two will become one flesh'? So they are no longer two, but one. Therefore what God has joined together, let man not separate." (Matthew 19:4–6)

The word translated as "united" here is from the Greek *kollao*, which means to "join fast together" or "to glue." This gets right to what commitment is all about—it's the glue that holds two people together. Jesus went on to connect commitment to oneness, driving home the point that the potential of marriage—God's ideal—comprises two people in a relationship of unbroken oneness.

As we will now explore, the glue that keeps a marriage together and thriving is a complex blend of forces and dynamics, the most important having to do with your will, decisions, and determination.

The Complexity of Commitment

To consider the complexity of commitment, let's look at two marriages. Both reflect commitment, but the type of commitment is very different. Notice what's similar and what's different as you compare the commitment in these two marriages.

Ethan and Madison Bennett: Feeling Trapped in Their Relationship

Ethan and Madison married thirteen years ago. They have a four-year-old son and a seven-year-old daughter. Ethan manages the meat department in a large grocery store, and Madison works part-time as a secretary in a medical office. Like most couples, they started out feeling very much in love. But the normal strains of life, especially the stress of a major job change for Ethan, have left both of them feeling distant and weary of trying to make things better.

Madison has considered divorce on more than a few occasions, and finds herself thinking about leaving Ethan. Ethan also feels unhappy with the marriage, but hasn't considered divorce as often as Madison. He hopes for more, but hasn't told Madison this, and he thinks trying to get closer just isn't worth it or even possible. When he does try to do something positive, he feels that his efforts go unrecognized by Madison. He's become anxious about the thought of her leaving and has become afraid to rock the boat, thinking, "Maybe things will get better when the kids leave home."

Madison and Ethan both work around others they find attractive. Larry, a handsome single man at Madison's work, has been sending signals of interest in her. It used to be that people more widely perceived someone who was married as strictly off-limits, but not so much anymore. Hungry for connection, Madison has been seriously contemplating an affair and finds herself thinking more and more about Larry.

Madison is deeply disappointed in her marriage and has come to the conclusion that Ethan will never be the kind of lifelong partner she had hoped for. Furthermore, she feels that she has put a lot more into the marriage than Ethan has, with little in return. When he does make some effort to move toward her, she doesn't trust it, and usually thinks, "Too little too late, pal." Like Ethan, she is thinking that it's just not worth the effort to try anymore.

As Madison thinks about leaving Ethan, difficult questions plague her. First, she has strong beliefs that divorce is not right and is not OK with God. She also wonders how a divorce would affect the kids. Would they ever get over it? Would Ethan want custody? She also asks herself about how hard it would be to get a divorce. Would Ethan try to stop her? She wonders about whether she could support herself and the kids on her income alone, about who would get the house, and about whether another man would accept the children if she did want to remarry.

For Madison, thinking about all the costs of divorce lead her to conclude that staying is better than leaving, at least for now. She's in pain, but she balances this against the pain and stress a divorce could bring. Ethan has thought about many of these same questions, but he is not as unhappy as Madison, so he thinks less about all the "what ifs." He assumes that their marriage will continue for the long haul, but it's not really an idea that gives him comfort. A feeling of despair hangs over each of them.

Sophia and Thomas Turnlington: Constraint and Dedication

Sophia and Thomas were married fifteen years ago. They have one girl, age thirteen, and two boys, ages eleven and seven. Although they have had their stressful times, both Sophia and Thomas have consistently valued their life together. They met when they worked for a large insurance company, he in sales and she as manager of the claims department. They are also quite involved in their church as a couple and as a family.

Their kids present some real challenges. The younger boy has a serious learning disability and requires a lot of attention and support. Their daughter is beginning to show more signs of rebellion than they had ever anticipated, and this too causes concern. Despite this, Sophia and Thomas both feel the commitment and support of the other in facing their struggles.

Thomas does occasionally become aware of his attraction to women he meets at work. However, because of his commitment to Sophia, he has decided not to daydream about "what if." He chooses not to dwell on thoughts of being with someone else. Everyone has regrets at times in marriage, but for Sophia and Thomas, these times are few. They genuinely respect and like each other, do things for each other, and talk fairly openly about what they want out of life and marriage. Because of their spiritual convictions, they each resist thinking about divorce and do not see it as any kind of solution, even when they do get very frustrated with each other. Not only is their commitment strong on all levels, but each is willing to help the other reach for what he or she desires in life. Simply put, they feel like a team.

What Is Commitment?

There are many ways to think about commitment, and two broad themes make up what researchers who study commitment tend to consider. The commitment of *personal dedication* refers to the desire to maintain or improve the quality of the relationship for the mutual benefit of both partners. Personal dedication is characterized by a desire (and actions) not only to continue in the relationship but also to improve it, sacrifice for it, invest in it, link it to personal goals, and seek the partner's welfare, not just one's own.

In contrast, *constraint commitment* refers to forces that keep individuals in relationships whether or not they're dedicated. Constraint commitment may arise from either external or internal pressures. Constraints help keep couples together by making ending the relationship more costly—economically, socially, personally, or psychologically. If dedication is low, constraints can keep people in relationships they might otherwise want to leave.

Ethan and Madison have a commitment characterized by constraint. Madison in particular is feeling a great deal of constraint and little dedication—the essence of feeling stuck. She feels compelled to stay in a dissatisfying marriage for a host of reasons: their kids, money, family pressure, and so on. Ethan also has high constraint commitment and little dedication, though he's less dissatisfied with their day-to-day life.

Like Ethan and Madison, Sophia and Thomas have a good deal of constraint commitment, but they also have a strong sense of dedication to each other. Any marriage will generate a significant amount of constraint over time. That's normal. Happier, more dedicated couples are just as likely to have considerable constraints as less satisfied, less dedicated couples at similar points in life. In fact, today's dedication becomes tomorrow's constraint. You fall in love, so you get engaged. You stay in love, so you get married. You're still together, so you have kids, buy a house, and so on. These things become the constraints that help hold you together.

Dedicated couples choose to have more constraints as they move through the stages of marital and family life together. In fact, dedication is what leads you to choose to give up options and be more constrained on a deeper path. If you've been married for a while, the odds are that your dedication has led you to build some pretty deep foundations for your marriage. Happier couples just don't think a lot about constraints, and when they do, they often draw comfort from them. When you are sticking, you don't feel stuck; you feel good about where you are and where you're heading.

Constraints: The Binds That Tie

Our definition of commitment includes two kinds: dedication and constraint. What constitutes the overall constraint commitment people have depends on who they are, what they value, and what their circumstances are. Here is a list of factors that are commonly part of the constraints that keep a person in his or her marriage.

- Social pressure from friends and family
- Financial considerations
- Concerns for children's welfare or fear of loss of contact
- The difficulty involved in the process of leaving
- Moral factors, such as a belief that divorce is generally wrong or that a person should always finish what he or she has started
- Poor quality of alternatives

You could think of constraints this way: all other things being equal, the greater the number of them, the more likely it is that a person will choose to stay in the marriage, even through tough times. In fact, research by Galena Rhoades, Scott Stanley, and Howard Markman at the University of Denver demonstrates what theory predicts. Couples with more constraints are more likely to stay together; it is not only dedication that makes a difference in how relationships go.

We believe that without constraint commitment, most couples would not make it in marriage beyond a few years, because of the normal ups and downs in satisfaction in life together. Although the concept of constraints sounds negative,

> for most married couples, there are a lot of constraints that the two partners do not think about day-to-day. Constraints only become an issue when they make it hard for someone to leave a relationship.

How Does Commitment Develop?

Dedication usually starts to build between two partners early in their relationship, as two partners spend more time together and find joy and satisfaction in the relationship. Think about the earlier days of your relationship. As your dedication to one another became more apparent, you may have noticed that you became more relaxed about the relationship. But just before that, in most relationships, there's an awkward period during which the desire to be together—and your attachment—is great, but the commitment is unclear. That produces anxiety about whether or not you'll stay together. This increase in wanting to be together is important for all couples, but especially important for couples in which one or both partners have a tendency (for reasons in their past) to be insecure about their relational attachments.

Almost all forms of commitment can be understood as symbols of security. It is only with a deep sense of security about the future of the relationship that two people can fully experience the wonder, mystery, and potential of their connection.

The Importance of Keeping Dedication Strong

What happens to kill dedication for some couples over time? For one thing, if a couple isn't handling conflict well, satisfaction with the marriage will steadily decline. Because satisfaction fuels dedication, dedication begins to erode along with satisfaction. Both partners try less, both see their partner as trying less, and soon their relationship feels as though it is in danger of dying.

Maintaining the kind of deeper dedication that allows a marriage to thrive requires ongoing decisions and action. Sliding won't cut it. Although constraint commitment can add a valuable stabilizing dimension to your marriage, it can't give you a great relationship. It can, however, keep you from doing immensely impulsive, stupid things when you are unhappy in the short term. It can help you not to bail out when you are unhappy for a season and help you see the wisdom of nurturing dedication. But it is dedication that builds and deepens the best things in a marriage. More dedicated couples report not only more satisfaction with their relationships but also less conflict about the problems they have and greater levels of openness. Dedication helps provide the deepest level of security that makes it safe to connect. The rest of this chapter focuses on what you can do to foster and deepen dedication.

Dedication and Agape

In the most famous passage in scripture about love (1 Corinthians 13), the Greek word for "love" is *agape*. Agape is considered the most central type of love in Christian thought. Agape is committed love. As the apostle Paul wrote,

> Love is patient, love is kind. It does not envy, it does not boast, it is not proud. It is not rude, it is not self-seeking, it is not easily angered, it keeps no record of wrongs. Love does not delight in evil but rejoices with the truth. It always protects, always trusts, always hopes, always perseveres. Love never fails.
> (1 Corinthians 13:4–8)

The apostle John wrote these lines about agape: "There is no fear in love. But perfect love drives out fear, because fear has to do with punishment. The one who fears is not made perfect in love" (1 John 4:18). If you read the context of this marvelous verse, you'll find that John is talking about the love of God shown to us by Christ on the cross—perfect love and perfect commitment.

John is also laying out a more general principle. Although neither you nor your mate can love perfectly, if agape permeates your marriage, it will drive out fear of rejection. What is described as agape in the New Testament is, in essence, the same concept researchers describe in defining dedication. It is dedicated love that promotes deeper levels of oneness and intimacy.

The Power of Dedication: Choices, Couple Identity, Sacrifice, and the Long-Term View

Many aspects of commitment relate to the choices you make and how you handle the alternatives you do not choose. In essence, commitment involves making the choice to give up other choices. Any commitment you make requires that you choose from among several options. Some of these decisions involve setting priorities. Some involve how you handle your attraction to others. Part of dedication is being so committed that you develop an identity as a team moving through life together. All of these aspects of committed love—of dedication—involve sacrifice. And it is the totality of dedication to one another that produces the long-term investment that makes for lasting, genuine love in marriage. Those are the themes we turn to now as we explore what it takes to live out true dedication in your marriage.

Every aspect of dedication we describe here represents a whole category of ways you can put one of the three keys—decide don't slide—into action.

Keeping Priorities

When people need to make decisions involving competing time and resources, those who are more dedicated to their partners are more likely to make decisions that protect the relationship. For example, early on in the relationship, most people will move mountains to spend time with their partner. But as the cares and hassles of life take over, too many people allow their relationship to take a backseat. A great relationship is a front-seat deal.

To some degree, problems with priorities can reflect overinvolvement elsewhere as much as a lack of dedication at home. Unfortunately, as people get busier and busier, too many end up doing what Scott, in his book *The Power of Commitment*, calls "no-ing" each other rather than *knowing* each other: "No, I don't have time to talk tonight." "No, I promised Fred I'd help him put up that new fence." To protect your relationship, you've got to be willing to say no to less important things so that you can say yes to the things that are important to your partner and good for your marriage.

"Yes" Takes Too Much Time

Before coauthor Scott's son Luke turned six, he uttered profound words about acting on priorities. From his earliest days of talking, "no" had been a word that came easily to his little lips. One day, Scott asked him to stop playing with his toys and get ready for dinner. Surprise, Luke said no. But Scott felt like ribbing him some about it, and the conversation went something like this.

DAD: Luke, let me hear you say "yes." You can do it; it sounds like this: "Yeesssss."

LUKE: (*giggling*) No.

DAD: (*playfully*) Oh, come on—you can do it. Let me hear you say "yes."

LUKE: No.

DAD: You are such a "no" boy, let's try being a "yes" boy. It would be fun!

LUKE: (*laughing*) No.

DAD: Yes, yes, yes!

LUKE: (*on the ground in hysterics*) No, no, no!

Scott was not looking for anything serious in this conversation, but something serious popped out of Luke's mind and mouth.

DAD: Luke, how come you say no all the time?

LUKE: Because "yes" takes too much time.

What Luke said was really the essence of acting on priorities. Luke knew early on that when someone asked him to do something that was not high on his list of priorities, he should say no rather than yes, because yes just takes too much time from what matters most. What do you need to be saying no to more often, to keep your marriage a high priority?

Handling Attractive Alternatives

Just because two people make a choice to give up other choices, that does not mean that all others disappear from the planet. In our research, we talk about "alternative monitoring," which is a technical way of referring to how much you keep an eye out for other potential partners in life. The more you are tuned in to other potential partners, the less your personal dedication to your mate.

Do you find yourself frequently or seriously thinking about being with people other than your spouse? This aspect of dedication is the one that is most sensitive to your current level of happiness. In other words, when unhappy with their partners, people tend to start thinking about the "what ifs." What if I had married her instead? What if I was no longer married to him? You can "what if" yourself to a place of despair and resentment if you choose to do so.

One study showed that people who are highly dedicated actually mentally devalue attractive potential partners. This research amplifies a point written hundreds of years ago by Malachi, following the verse in which God says He hates divorce.

> So guard yourself in your spirit, and do not break faith with the wife of your youth. (Malachi 2:15)

People who are more dedicated are more likely to "guard their spirit" by thinking in ways that protect their marriage. The word for "guard" in the Hebrew means to put a hedge around something. We're not talking wimpy little hedges here, either, but really strong, large boundaries around something to protect it. Setting up these boundaries is something you have control over. You can choose not to dwell on tempting alternatives, and—when you are aware of attractive options—you can choose to look for what is not so good about those options. You can choose to look less at attractive alternatives and think less about them. This amounts to focusing on why that grass on the other side of the fence really isn't greener.

Couple Identity: The Story of Us

Couples vary in the degree to which they view the relationship as a team rather than as two separate individuals. In the happiest and strongest marriages, "we" transcends "me" in how the partners think. If a couple doesn't have this sense of being a team, conflict is more likely, because the spouses see problems as "me against you" instead of "us against the problem." Our research clearly shows that couples who are thriving in their marriages have a strong sense of "us." We aren't suggesting that you should merge your identities, but a great marriage will have two individuals coming together to form a team in life.

One couple, Melissa and Will, had a pretty stable and harmonious life up until the emptying of their nest. As happens with many couples, some of the glue that had bound them together weakened with the departure of their children. They drifted for some time, experiencing increasing distance and conflict—developing lives that were largely independent from one another. One day, they started to turn it all around.

Consider the power of a talk like this, and the humility required of both partners. They were at the breakfast table together.

WILL: *(looking up from his smartphone)* Can we talk a second?

MELISSA: *(putting her magazine aside)* Sure, what's up?

WILL: Well, something . . . um, something important.

MELISSA: *(nodding and listening)*

WILL: I've been thinking that we're at a big point in life here. What we do in the next year might lay down the pattern for us for the next thirty years. I'm not sure I like the path we're on, and I've been thinking that maybe we should really plan for the kind of relationship we want in the future. You know, to be very intentional about where we go from here.

MELISSA: *(barely suppressing a smile)* I love that idea. I've been wondering—actually worrying a bit, too—about where we're headed. I'd like us to be really close and not just share a house in the years ahead.

WILL: Me too, but I'm thinking that if we're not careful, we'll only be roommates for the next thirty years. I want to be best friends and lovers.

MELISSA: What do you think we should do next?

WILL: How about we go away for a weekend? Maybe to that cabin. No TV, no distractions. Just us. We can talk and play and plan for our future. What do you think?

MELISSA: Sounds perfect. Let's look at the calendar.

The strategies we suggest throughout this book are most powerful if you make these kinds of decisions together. Many couples have nurtured and protected their couple identity from the start. If you have it, work at keeping it. If not, take this time to openly discuss and plan for how you will express your "we" in the years ahead.

Sacrifice

Our culture encourages devotion to self above all. Notions of sacrifice, teamwork, and placing a high priority on your partner and your relationship don't receive much positive press. In fact, our society seems to glorify self and vilify whatever gets in the way of our self-seeking. Selfishness may sell in our consumer-oriented culture, but it doesn't bring lifelong, happy marriages. Godly love is the kind of love that leads us to serve another. It works powerfully against the tendency to use our partner for our own good, as if he or she were just another product to be consumed (see Galatians 5:13–15).

Our research has shown that people who are happiest in marriage actually gain some sense of satisfaction from doing things that are largely or solely for their partner's benefit. We aren't recommending psychological martyrdom of some sort, but rather seeking to find real joy in giving to your partner in important ways.

The Bennetts (the stuck couple) have stopped giving to each other. Ethan doesn't think he'll get anything back if he gives more, and Madison already feels that she's given more than her share for a lifetime. Neither feels like sacrificing anything at this point. They've lost the sense of "us" that promotes giving to each other without resentment. Neither is going to give much at this point, perhaps waiting for the other to do so. That could be a very long wait.

Relationships are generally stronger when both partners are willing to make sacrifices. The key is to think about not only what you do for your partner but also why you do it. Do you do things with the attitude, "You'd better appreciate what I'm doing"? Do you often feel that your partner owes you? There's nothing wrong with doing positive things and wanting to be appreciated. There *is* something wrong with believing that you are owed. Studies have long shown that the sense that one is owed in return for doing kindness toward one's mate—a form of keeping score—leads to less quality in relationships. In couples who are doing well, you'll find two partners who give freely to each other and who are grateful for what is given. It's a beautiful form of teamwork.

We do not want to leave you with the impression that someone should choose to be a doormat and give everything to some selfish lout of a partner in order to fulfill their hope of having a strong and happy marriage. Some people are truly selfish or caught in destructive habits and sins, and sometimes the most loving thing one mate does for the other is to confront them effectively about their behavior and why it needs some serious examination—but in a loving way if at all possible. If you think you might need to push your mate about some pattern of unacceptable behavior, pray for guidance and consider seeking counsel from wise and caring people in your life.

At the end of this chapter, there are a number of activities you can do to think about your commitment and how to deepen it. If you do nothing else, check out the last section, "Give a Little Love." It is a powerful way to boost your positive sacrifice on your own, and you can do it no matter what your partner is doing.

The Long-Term View

When people are more dedicated to their partners, they want and expect the relationship to last. They want to grow old together. This is a core part of dedication and plays a critical role in the day-to-day quality of marriage, because no relationship is consistently satisfying. What gets couples through tougher times is the long-term view that commitment brings. How? When you actively decide that you will be together no matter what, you can safely deal with the curveballs life throws at you. The long-term view stretches out the time perspective, making it easier not to overreact to the small annoying events in day-to-day life together.

We're not saying everybody should devote herculean effort to save his or her marriage, no matter how abusive or destructive. However, for the great number of couples who genuinely love each other and want to make their marriages work, a long-term perspective is essential. It encourages each partner to take risks, disclose deeper feelings and desires, and trust that the other will be there when it really counts. In the absence of a long-term view, almost everyone tends to focus on the immediate payoff. This is only natural. If the long term is uncertain, you're going to concentrate more on what you're getting in the present.

What we have called the hidden issue of commitment (Chapter Eight) is easily triggered when the future of the relationship is uncertain. When commitment is unclear, partners don't feel accepted—a core issue for everyone—and instead feel pressured to perform. The message is, "You'd better produce, or I'll look for someone who can." Most of us resent feeling that we could be abandoned by someone from whom we expect to find security and acceptance. People generally do not invest in a relationship with an uncertain future.

The Turnlingtons, our example of a highly dedicated couple, do not have the perfect marriage (who does?), but they have a strong belief in their future. They talk about plans for life together. For couples like them, the long-term view allows each partner to cut the other some slack, leading to greater acceptance of weaknesses and failings over time. Whereas the Bennetts experience anxiety or resentment around the core issue of acceptance, the Turnlingtons feel the warmth of a secure commitment—each conveying the powerful message, "I'll always be here for you." That's the essence of what commitment is about: believing not only that you will be there for each other in the future but also that you can count on each other through the ups and downs of life.

Sometimes commitment becomes a weapon in a fight. When such a weapon is wielded, it's like an atomic bomb that leaves unparalleled devastation in its wake. Despite Ethan and Madison Bennett's low level of commitment, they aren't going to get a divorce anytime soon. Still, the topic comes up more and more often in their arguments.

ETHAN: Why does this house always look like a pigsty?
MADISON: Because we have two big dogs, and I'm at work every day.

ETHAN: I end up having to clean up all the time, and I'm tired of it.

MADISON: Oh, and like I don't clean up all the time after the kids? When you're here, you usually disappear into your shop. I'm the one cleaning up constantly—not you.

ETHAN: Yeah, yeah, I disappear all the time. You don't even know what really happens in this marriage. I don't even know why we stay together.

MADISON: Me neither. Maybe you should move out.

ETHAN: Not a bad idea. I'll think about it.

By the end of the fight, each was trying to convince the other that they weren't committed. If you're trying to keep your marriage on track, don't bring up the topic of divorce, period. Don't trash the long-term view.

The Principle of Least Interest

In 1921, E. A. Ross defined the law of personal exploitation: "in any sentimental relation, the one who cares less can exploit the one who cares more." Willard Waller described this as the "principle of least interest." In any relationship, deal, or negotiation, the one with the least interest has the most power. This fits in with commitment theory; the one who is less committed has more power—at least in a negotiation or dispute.

Have you ever told someone, "I couldn't care less"? Often when we say something like this we're trying to say to the other, "I have more power here because I don't really care how this turns out." When you and your partner are really stuck over some repeated problem, challenge yourself as to whether you are messing around with how committed you are as a means of having control.

Jesus demonstrated a radically different kind of power: the power of being the most committed, not the least. As he said before he ascended to heaven, "surely I am with you always, to the very end of the age" (Matthew 28:20).

But All We Have Is Constraint Commitment!

This section is for those of you whose marriage might be in serious trouble. If that's not you, you can skip to the activities at the end of the chapter.

Many couples are like Ethan and Madison Bennett. All they have is constraint, with little of the sense of companionship they both wanted. Our primary focus in this book is to prevent marriages from getting to that point. But even if yours has, we don't think you have to stay there. If that's where you are, it's not too late to turn things around, especially if both of you are willing to do the work.

What can you do if you find yourself in a marriage characterized by constraint without much dedication? How do you redevelop dedication?

First, you need to believe that it's possible, especially with the Lord's help. We cannot predict the future of your relationship, but we find that couples can repair and strengthen even lifeless marriages. Second, you must really be willing to work at it, because it will take *sustained* work before the feelings of dedication return. You will have to work against your present feelings and some tendencies that now exist in the relationship.

If you want to breathe life into your marriage, follow the pattern in what Jesus Christ advised for the church at Ephesus. He told the Ephesians that all they were doing was wonderful, but that they lacked one thing—they had forsaken their first love for Christ (Revelation 2:1–7). Here, as in other key passages, the word for love is agape, and that is very like dedication. Note what He suggested they do about it:

> Remember the height from which you have fallen! Repent and do the things you did at first. (Revelation 2:5)

Jesus says to *remember, repent,* and *do the things you did at first.* Although the Lord is talking about our dedication and love for Him in this passage, the process applies to restoring one's love in marriage as well. Remember, when we are talking about dedication in commitment research, we are talking about what the Bible calls agape. That's the kind of love Christ is talking about regaining here. So consider these steps in light of that simple message.

They will be most powerful if you sit down together and really think them through as a couple.

1. *Remember* **what you used to have together.** Spend some time reminiscing together about the good old days. What was it like when you first met? What attracted you to each other? What did you do on your first date? What did you used to do for fun? Do you still do any of these things?

    It's nearly impossible to recapture the euphoria that many couples feel early on, but you can recapture some of the good feelings that once characterized your relationship. There was a spark there, a delight in getting to know each other. In some ways, this step is an attempt to regain an appetite or desire for the relationship again—to light the fire again.

2. *Repent:* **decide to turn things around.** You can do this whether or not your partner is willing to, although making a commitment to do it together is far better. Repentance means to change your mind and your direction. Asking God to help you with this would be one of the smarter prayers you could make.

3. *Do* **the things you did at first.** Early in a relationship, couples talk more as friends and do more fun things together (see Chapter Eleven), are more forgiving (see Chapter Fifteen), are more likely to look for the good and not the bad in the other (see Chapters One, Two, and Three), and usually do a better job of controlling conflict (see Chapters One through Six).

    Commit yourself to becoming less self-centered and more other-centered. Where you have been selfish, admit it to yourself and decide to turn the pattern around. The things that you can do to restore dedication in your marriage are the same things that couples can do to prevent marital distress and divorce in the first place. This book is filled with concrete tips on the "doing" part. What you must supply with the Lord's help is the willingness to act.

The reason these steps can work is that they involve doing the things that allow dedication to grow early in the relationship. We believe you can do this if you are both committed to the task.

Doing Your Part

If you do only one of the activities in this section, we suggest that you skip to the last one. It is the most powerful.

Assessing Dedication Commitment

These next items will help you gauge your level of dedication. Use this 7-point rating scale: 1 = strongly disagree, 4 = neither agree nor disagree, and 7 = strongly agree. Jot down your responses on a separate piece of paper.

1. My relationship with my partner is more important to me than almost anything else in my life.
2. I want this relationship to stay strong no matter what rough times we may encounter.
3. It makes me feel good to sacrifice for my partner.
4. I like to think of myself and my partner more in terms of "us" and "we" than "me" and "him [or her]."
5. I am not seriously attracted to anyone other than my partner.
6. My relationship with my partner is clearly part of my future life plans.
7. When push comes to shove, my relationship with my partner comes first.
8. I tend to think about how things affect us as a couple more than how things affect me as an individual.
9. I don't often find myself thinking about what it would be like to be in a relationship with someone else.
10. I want to grow old with my partner.

To calculate your score, simply total your ratings. In our research—with a sample of people who were mostly happy and dedicated in their relationships (including some who had been married for over thirty years)—the average person scored about 58 on this scale. If you scored at or above 58, we'd bet you're pretty highly dedicated. Your dedication may be quite low, however, if you scored below 45. Whatever your score, think about it. Does your score suggest anything to you about how well you are doing your part in your marriage?

(continued)

Considering Priorities

An important way to look at dedication is to consider your priorities. How do you actually live your life? What does this say about your commitment?

Divide a piece of paper into three columns. In the first column, list what you consider your top five priorities in life, with number one being the most important. Possible priority areas might include work and career, your partner, adult children, religion, house and home, sports, future goals, education, possessions, hobbies, pets, friends, relatives, coworkers, television, and car. Feel free to list whatever is important to you. Be as specific as you can.

In the second column, list what you think your partner would say are your top five priorities. For example, if you think your partner would say that work is your top priority, list that as number one. In the third column, list what you believe are your partner's top five priorities.

When both of you have completed your lists, compare them. Don't be defensive. Consider how your priorities, and your perception of your partner's priorities, have impacted your relationship. Use the Speaker-Listener Technique if you think it will help. If you see a need to make your relationship a higher priority, talk together about specific steps you can take to make this happen. You might find it helpful to use the problem-solving process you learned in Chapter Six. The chapters on enhancing your relationship provide additional suggestions of ways to make it a higher priority.

Give a Little Love

Almost all of us know of easy things we could do that would make a positive difference in our marriage. These can be thought of as little sacrifices for your mate or your relationship. Our emphasis is on the "little things," and that is very important. Life can get in the way of doing big things on any given day. Big things are great to do from time to time, but big sacrifices require big opportunities that you cannot (or should not) try to make happen. Small sacrifices do not require big opportunities. They are readily and routinely doable.

THE POWER OF COMMITMENT

Here's a little exercise for you. Take a few minutes to think about things you can do or have done in the past that fit these characteristics:

1. It's something under your control.
2. It's something small that you can decide to do just about any day or week you want.
3. It's something that you know is good for your relationship and that your partner tends to like.
4. It's something you are not otherwise likely to do today or this week, even though you very well could.

It's the last of these four characteristics that makes this action a small but meaningful sacrifice. To perform the action, you have to do something other than what you'd naturally do: you have to decide to do it and follow through.

Go ahead and write down a few ideas that fit the listed characteristics.

Now it's challenge time: commit to yourself to perform one or two of these actions in the coming week. Not ten, just one or two. Develop a way to remind yourself and get after it. Don't tell your partner what you are doing. Just do it! Your partner may or may not notice all of these small sacrifices, but he or she will notice some of them, and your relationship will be stronger for it.

15

Forgiveness and Restoration

Bear with each other and forgive whatever grievances
you may have against one another. Forgive as the
Lord forgave you.
COLOSSIANS 3:13

Someone once likened two people in a marriage to Alaskan por-
cupines. When winter comes and the snow begins to fall, they
draw close to get warm. But their quills begin to stick one another.
When they separate, they become cold again. They want to stay
close, but they don't want to keep getting hurt. Marriage is like
that. In order to keep warm, you have to endure getting hurt from
time to time. That's why you and your mate have to learn to
forgive each other.

Many things can cause hurts, some major and some minor.
Offenses can range from affairs and addictions to something as
simple as forgetting an important appointment. Couples cannot
hope to overcome the damage from sin and imperfection without
forgiveness. Forgiveness is the oxygen that keeps the flame of love
from going out.

That Hurt!

You will hurt each other at times. Neither you nor your mate is
perfect or capable of perfectly loving each other, no matter how
deep your commitment and care. Sometimes one hurts the other
because of thoughtlessness, sometimes because of the very human

inability to love another perfectly. And at times, one mate will do something with intent to hurt the other—most often by saying something cutting or nasty when frustrated or angry. Marriages that thrive are testaments to grace, expressed in acts of forgiveness and forbearance.

Some wrongs are greater than others. Some people rarely do anything that would cause their mate to even think about forgiveness; others do so fairly frequently. Sometimes a person does something so egregiously wrong that forgiveness can be given but reconciliation may not be possible. We will look at many important distinctions in this chapter because we believe that offering forgiveness can be hard to do even when it is properly understood, and that doing so is virtually impossible when poorly understood.

Let's look at two couples who need forgiveness. Both examples demonstrate the need for forgiveness, but the infractions are very different: one's minor, and one's major. And they have very different implications.

I Forgot

Mary and Tony met each other in a church support group and later married. Each had been married once before, and both had primary custody of the children from their first marriages, in which both had been painfully betrayed. They found they had much in common, not only in pain but in joy and the capacity for love. There had been nothing remarkable about their blended family except that they had done a great job of it. They both felt and expressed thankfulness for finding each other. They had handled the many stresses of blending two families, and had forged a loving new family. They had their ups and downs, but they dealt with their problems with love and respect.

Tony, an engineer with a construction firm, had saved the company from financial disaster by catching a critical design flaw in the company's plans for a high-rise. If he had missed the problem, it could have led to the building's collapse. For this, Tony was to be honored as employee of the year at the firm's annual awards luncheon. He was proud of the award and happy to receive the substantial bonus that came with it. Tony asked Mary to attend the big event; he was proud to be honored, and wanted his wife to celebrate the occasion with him, and she said she'd be glad to. He had told his boss and fellow workers that she would be coming, and a place was saved for her at the front table, right beside Tony.

Mary, a real estate broker, got distracted on the big day while showing a newly listed house, and she completely forgot about the luncheon. Tony felt totally embarrassed. He was also a little worried, as it was unlike Mary to forget something so important. He left her a message and a text, but Mary rarely answered the phone when with a client. She forgot to check her phone, and Tony sat through the luncheon with her empty chair beside him. He tried to make the best of it by saying, "She must have gotten hung up at the doctor's office with one of the kids." Afterward, he started to feel angry about it, but he didn't call her. He wanted to see if she'd remember on her own.

As soon as Tony walked in the door that evening, Mary remembered that she had forgotten:

MARY: *(distressed)* Oh no! Tony, I just remembered—

TONY: *(with some pain and anger in his voice)* Where were you? I have never been so embarrassed. I really wanted you there.

MARY: I know, I know. I'm so sorry. I really wanted to be there with you.

TONY: So where were you? I tried calling.

MARY: I was showing a house that just came open, and I felt it was going to go fast, so I jumped on it, and I, um, I really just completely forgot the luncheon. I feel terrible.

TONY: So do I. I didn't know what to tell people, so I made up something about you maybe being at the doctor's office with one of the kids.

MARY: Please forgive me, dear.

Should he? Of course. It's not such a big deal for him to be forgiving in this context. What happened hurt and was embarrassing, but it's not going to derail their marriage. Now consider a very different example—one in which forgiveness is a much more complicated matter.

The Grass Looked Greener

John and Megan have been together twenty years. They met in high school, marrying right after graduating. John had worked his way up in a department store chain to become a department manager. Megan had become an office manager for an accounting firm. After they had been married for about ten years, they decided that Megan would stop working while their children were young. Money was tight, but they both wanted to try to make it work. Everything sailed along just fine until the fourteenth year of marriage. Megan noticed that John was gone more and more. His job demanded a lot, but she wondered, "Does he really need to be gone this much?" She became suspicious because something just didn't feel right to her. They had drifted in their relationships with God, their church, and each other. Everything felt less connected, and Megan wondered if she was the only one noticing.

She began to suspect that John was having an affair. She'd make phone calls to the office when he was supposed to be working late. He was rarely there, or, at best, he didn't answer the phone. When she'd ask him about this, he'd say he must've been down the hall, in the copy room, or talking with a colleague. Even when she called his cell phone, there were more times that he just didn't pick up than she could remember in the past. Excuses about missing calls didn't compute with Megan. She became so suspicious that she talked with her best friend about it and even went to see their pastor for ideas about what to do. He suggested that she and John come in for some counseling to alleviate her fears, but John would not have anything to do with that.

Megan got sick and tired of being suspicious, so she took matters into her own hands. One night when John said he'd be working late again, she arranged for a friend to come over to watch the kids. She borrowed her friend's car and sat outside the building where John worked, waiting to see if he left the office. He did, and she followed him from a distance. She followed him right to an apartment complex, noting the door where he went in. She sat in the car for three hours before she got up her nerve to look at the name on the mailbox—Sally Something-or-Other.

"Not good, this is not good," she said to herself. Her stomach was in knots. Now what? She decided to knock on the door. After fifteen minutes, Sally came to the door in her bathrobe.

SALLY: *(seeming tense)* Can I help you?

MEGAN: *(calm but falling apart on the inside)* Yes. Please tell John I'm out here in the car and I'd like to talk to him.

SALLY: *(gaining composure)* John? Who's John? I'm alone. Perhaps you have the wrong address.

MEGAN: *(sarcastically)* Perhaps I could take a look.

SALLY: I don't think so. Look, you have the wrong address. I don't know what your problem is, but you should leave or I'll call the police. *(closing the door)* Good-bye!

MEGAN: *(yelling as Sally closes the door)* Tell John I'll be at home—if he remembers where it is!

John rolled in an hour later. He denied everything for about three days. Megan didn't back down. She told him to get out. "An affair is bad enough, but if you can't even admit it, there's nothing left for us to talk about." Now it was John's turn to fall apart. He began drinking and disappeared for days at a time. He stopped by the house briefly every now and then to touch base with the kids, all of whom were very attached to him. Megan felt even more alone and betrayed. The children had no idea what was happening, but they were scared. Although Megan still loved John, her anger and resentment grew. She told her pastor, "I thought I could trust him. I can't believe he would leave me for someone else!"

The longer John was alone with his thoughts, the more God worked on his heart. His denial finally crumbled, but his sense of shame was so great that he was afraid to deal with Megan head-on. Yet he really did love her, and started to panic about losing her. "Is it really over?" he wondered. He felt terrible and knew he'd done to Megan exactly what his ex-wife had done to him. In a way, he found new respect for Megan. There was no begging or pleading from her, just strength and determination. He had been attracted to Sally, but she wasn't even his type. He really didn't want to leave Megan. She was the one for him, and he knew it. And he knew he had been colossally stupid.

Of course, Megan didn't feel tough at all. She was in agony. But she was very clear about what she saw at Sally's. She alternated between feeling anger and intense grief. Although she was not sure whether she wanted to stay or leave, she had a sense of what it would take to go forward if John decided to come back. There was no chance she'd go on with him unless he came clean with her and God, and truly repented. She also decided that he'd have to go to counseling with her if they were going to have a chance. This was too much to work through alone. The pastor had given her the name of a therapist who he said was really wise in helping couples recover from severe damage to trust. But she was not totally sure she wanted to work it out.

One night, Megan dropped the kids off at her friend's house for a sleepover so that she could take a break from everything. She came back home to find John sitting at the kitchen table with a terrible look of pain and fear on his face.

JOHN: *(desperately)* Please forgive me, Megan. I don't know . . . I'll get help. I don't know . . . I'm not sure what happened.

MEGAN: *(cool outside, angry and sad inside)* I'm not sure what happened either, but I think you know a lot more than I do.

JOHN: *(looking up from the table)* I guess I do. What do you want to know?

MEGAN: I'd like to know what's been going on, without you hiding anything.

JOHN: *(tears welling up)* I've been having an affair. I met Sally at work, we got close, and things sort of spun out of control.

MEGAN: I guess they did. How long?

JOHN: What?

MEGAN: *(voice raised, with some anger coming out)* How long have you been sleeping with her?

JOHN: Five months. Since the New Year's party. Look, I couldn't handle things here at home. There's been so much distance between us—

MEGAN: *(feeling hot about what he said)* So what! What if *I* couldn't have handled it? I didn't go looking for someone else. I don't want you here right now. Just go! *(turning away, heading into the next room)*

JOHN: If that's what you want, I'll go. I'll call our pastor and talk with him.

MEGAN: Right now, that's just what I want. I need to think about this. Just let me know where you'll be, for the kids' sake.

JOHN: *(despondent)* I'll go to my parents' place. That's where I've been staying lately.

MEGAN: *(without much emotion)* OK. I figured that's where you probably were.

JOHN: I'll leave. Please forgive me, Megan. I know I've been unfaithful to you. I've asked God to forgive me, and I hope you'll be able to.

MEGAN: I don't know if I can.

Megan went upstairs while John slipped out the door. It was the loneliest night of her life. At this point, she had some big decisions to make. How could she forgive John? She'd already known that she'd have trouble trusting him again. He seemed to acknowledge his fault in what had happened, and he wanted to come back. But how could she trust any of that?

What do you think?

Making Forgiveness Last

Virginia Holeman at Asbury Theological Seminary in Kentucky has worked extensively with couples on matters of forgiveness. She finds that it doesn't matter so much which partner takes the lead in the path to forgiveness, as long as both partners are on the path. Further, she finds that couples who are committed to change are the ones who make change happen. And in doing so, they actually see growth in their commitment, fueled by forgiveness. She also finds that couples who heal from major wounds are those who make reconciliation the "central organizing theme" of their marriage. They change whatever in their lives they need to change because they are in it together. They move forward no matter what.

What Is Forgiveness?

Webster's New World Dictionary has a clear definition of forgiveness: "1. to give up resentment against or the desire to punish; . . . 2. to give up all claim to punish or exact penalty for (an offense); . . . 3. to cancel or remit (a debt)." The picture of forgiveness is a canceled debt. Forgiveness is a decision to give up your perceived or actual right to get even with, or hold in debt, someone who has wronged you.

Forgive is a verb. It's active. It's something you must decide to do. When one of you fails to forgive, you will be less able to function as a team because one of you is kept in a "one-down" position. You cannot walk hand in hand through life if you are not on the same level.

The lack of forgiveness is the ultimate in scorekeeping, with the message being, "You are way behind on my scorecard, and I don't know if you can ever catch up." In that context, resentment builds, conflict increases, and bitterness grows deep roots. The real message is, "Maybe you can't do enough to make this up." People often walk away from debts they see no hope of paying off.

What Motivates You to Forgive?

There are a number of scientists who have delved deeply into forgiveness, including whether forgiveness is more likely when you do it for personal benefit or for the benefit of the other. In a number of studies, Everett Worthington, Michael McCullough, and colleagues have found evidence that both kinds of motivation can promote forgiveness. That both motives are in the mix is in keeping with passages in scripture like Mark 11:25 and Colossians 3:12–14. In the first, Jesus says to forgive others so that we will also be forgiven. In the second, Paul emphasizes forgiving others to reflect the love of Christ to us.

What Forgiveness Is Not

Infractions can be small or large, with the accompanying sense of debt being small or large as well. In the earlier examples, Mary has a much smaller debt to Tony than John has to Megan. John and Megan have a vastly more complex task ahead of them if their marriage is going to make it. We believe that to make forgiveness work in your marriage, you have to understand what forgiveness is not. When people are confused about what forgiveness requires, it's very hard for real forgiveness to occur.

Forgiveness Is Not Forgetting

We've all heard the phrase "forgive and forget," but the two words have very little to do with one another. The memory of a painful offense against you is just not something that will go away. Do you think Christ has forgotten the cross? Of course not! Yet are we forgiven? Of course! Fortunately, when people say "forgive and forget," they usually mean that you need to put the infraction in the past. That is a more reasonable understanding than expecting memories to just disappear. Forgiveness is deciding to stop using the memory to remind the offender of his or her failure and the debt we're owed.

Another misconception related to the forgetting myth is the belief that if a person still has feelings about what happened, he or she has not really forgiven. We believe that you can perfectly forgive the person who hurt you and still feel the pain, anger, and grief that the offense has caused. Forgiveness doesn't mean you stop feeling the effects of what happened.

Megan may come to a point of completely forgiving John. She may work through and overcome her anger and her desire to lash out and hurt him back. It is very understandable that she would want to have him feel some of the pain and humiliation that his behavior has caused her to feel. If she is able to forgive him fully, what happened will leave her with wounded trust and a grief that will remain for many years. Tony and Mary's case is far less severe and is not nearly as likely to leave lasting damage. As it turned out, Tony forgave her completely, and fairly rapidly. He didn't dwell on what happened, and he didn't need to grieve about it.

However, when he is reminded of her missing the event, such as when there are other company events, he will remember and feel a twinge of pain. That doesn't mean that he's holding it over Mary or trying to get even. And that is the essence of forgiveness. He has no desire at all to do something in return, such as skipping out on something important to her.

It will take some serious work and a long time for Megan and John to feel as though things are level between the two of them. And getting back to being level is the goal for a marriage that is going to last and reflect the grace and love of God.

Forgiveness Does Not Mean the Offender Is "Off the Hook"

The question comes up all the time: "Does forgiveness mean that a person who did something wrong is no longer responsible for what they've done?" No! The one who did wrong is responsible for the wrong they did, period. No excuses. The offender is accountable to God and sometimes to others. The offender's responsibility is to sincerely repent, humbly seek forgiveness, and turn from the hurtful behavior. Whenever possible, the offender should also make amends for the damage they've done.

Who is responsible for what? It turns out that both the one who has offended and the one who has been hurt or wronged have responsibilities. It is the offender's job to take full responsibility and accept the consequences for what they've done. But the person who has been hurt also has responsibilities. Forgiveness is not optional if you want to live as an obedient Christian. We are commanded to forgive others throughout the New Testament, even as God has forgiven us (Matthew 6:12; Matthew 18:21–35; Colossians 3:13) and sometimes again and again (Matthew 18:22). It's a very high standard, achievable only by God's enabling grace. It is the forgiver's responsibility not only to forgive but also to seek peace and, where possible and wise, reconciliation. (As we shall cover in the next section, forgiveness does not always mean that the relationship can be restored.) Romans 12:18 says, "If it is possible, as far as it depends on you, live at peace with everyone." It's not always possible to live at peace with another, but the offended person is responsible for the part they have control over—"as far as it depends on you." Further, we are to leave punishment up to God, who may deliver it through others, such as by discipline of the church or by government authorities.

You can forgive your partner completely for something harmful or for a problematic pattern of behavior, but that does not mean that you should not challenge him or her to change where there needs to be change (unless, of course, it is unsafe to confront the offender). In 1 Corinthians 5, Paul tells the Corinthians to withdraw fellowship from a fellow believer who had failed to repent for a heinous sin. But the purpose of the seemingly harsh action was not for rejection or humiliation. The purpose was to help that believer turn his life around. Later, he did repent. So Paul urged the church to welcome him back into their fellowship. This passage in 1 Corinthians, therefore, clarifies the meanings of forgiveness, responsibility, and restoration.

To summarize: if you have been wronged by your partner, it's up to you to forgive. And if you've wronged your partner in some way, it's your job to take responsibility for your actions and to take steps needed to see that you don't commit that wrong again. It's up to you to seek forgiveness, to apologize, and, where needed, to change. The point of scripture is that we each do everything we can to make forgiveness happen and to seek reconciliation and protect oneness. Both the offended and the offender have responsibility for their part. Only then is healing and reconnection fully possible.

These perspectives on forgiveness assume that the infraction is clear and that you are both humble and mature enough to take responsibility for doing your part. But what if two partners do not agree that something harmful has happened or that whatever has happened was serious? How can you move forward then? For one thing, if you are the one who feels harmed, you must be open to examining the possibility that your partner really didn't intend to do anything wrong. There can be a sincere difference in the interpretation of what happened and why.

Pippa and Oggie, for example, experienced such an event. When Pippa was away visiting her sister for a week, Oggie cleaned out the garage. He knew Pippa was often bothered because she couldn't use the garage for her car; he worked hard and threw out a number of old boxes, thinking this would make his wife really happy. When she returned, she was very pleased, just as Oggie thought she'd be. In fact, she was ecstatic about it, and let's just say that they had a very fine weekend. You never know what's going to spark some serious passion.

The trouble started a few days later, when Pippa started wondering about a box of mementos she had saved from her high school days. It turns out that in his zeal for making space, Oggie had accidentally thrown out a box containing Pippa's mementos. It was a total accident. He'd even noticed the box and thought he'd put it aside to protect it. But that hadn't happened, and it got thrown away for good.

When Pippa realized the box was gone, she went into orbit. She was more upset than Oggie had ever seen her. In her initial anger and frustration, she accused Oggie of being "stupid, insensitive, controlling, and domineering." As is often the case, when one does something that hurts the other deeply, intended or not, the one who's been hurt can do some serious damage in response. Forgiveness often ends up needing to go both ways. What happened was unfortunate. Pippa had every right to be upset. Those things meant a lot to her. But it really was a mistake. Pippa was being unfair in accusing Oggie of intentionally hurting her—directly challenging his integrity. This was a very negative interpretation of his intentions. Oggie felt awful about it, but when she called him stupid, he lashed out with his own choice words. Now they were both digging a hole big enough to park both cars in.

When harmed in the way Pippa was, it's more than OK to expect an apology—not because your partner intended to hurt you, but because the mistake did hurt you. Oggie can apologize to Pippa without agreeing that he meant to do it. But she has a long wait ahead if she expects to hear him say, "You're right. I threw out your things because I'm a control freak, and I think I should be able to do whatever I want around here. I can see how this is a deep flaw in my character, and I promise I will work to make deep, lasting changes in who I am and how I treat you." He can't say that, or anything remotely like that, because it's not true. Effective apologies and attempts to make amends need to be genuine.

Not Feeling It?

Do you have trouble feeling like forgiving others? It's really powerful to feel compassion for the person who has hurt you, but sometimes that just does not come easily. How can you feel genuine compassion and thereby add to the power of forgiving another? Jesus had some thoughts on that in Luke 7:36–50. The passage describes the time when Jesus went to dinner at a Pharisee's house, and the Pharisee became scandalized that a woman who was such an admitted sinner touched Jesus, wiping his feet with her hair and tears and applying costly perfume. Jesus challenged the Pharisee for his lack of love, noting that "he who has been forgiven little loves little." Those who are lacking in love and forgiveness for others may be lacking a deep appreciation for the forgiveness they have received. Do you want to be more forgiving from the heart? Ask God to help you become more aware of the wonder of His forgiveness of your faults.

Whether or not you both agree on the nature of the infraction, you can still move ahead and forgive. The alternative is bad for your marriage and even for your own health. It takes humility to give up the need you may feel for your partner to completely agree with you about what happened. Of course, we are not talking about sweeping some very serious problem under the carpet, but rather suggesting that with lesser things, you figure out a way to let them go. The Bible calls this forbearance. The long-term good of your marriage and life together depends on it.

Forgiveness Does Not Assure Restoration of the Relationship

Forgiveness and restoration usually go hand in hand, as with Tony and Mary. Their connection was not seriously threatened and was quickly restored. What we mean by restoration is that the relationship is repaired and ready for renewed intimacy and growth. Restoration means that instead of moving ahead with one owing the other, the two are fully reconciled. But what about the much more difficult situations? Suppose it's very clear to you that your partner did something quite wrong and isn't going to take any responsibility for it, as could have been the case with John and Megan. Suppose that instead of owning up to what he did wrong, John had continued to deny that anything had even happened, or that it was somehow Megan's fault that he became tempted. That would be an insurmountable obstacle to reconciliation. She could still forgive, but it would be unwise to reconcile in that case. If their marriage was going to have any chance of moving forward, John had to own up to what he had done.

In the case of many affairs, both spouses are responsible to some degree for letting their marriage drift. John and Megan had grown very distant, and neither was more to blame than the other for that. However, the affair was entirely John's fault. He, not Megan, was responsible for that action. If he tried to defend himself by emphasizing both of their failings, he'd do more damage than he already had done because he would be blaming her for what he did wrong.

When John showed up in the kitchen asking for forgiveness, the worst thing Megan could have done would be to go on as if everything had returned to normal. It had not. You can't sweep things like this under the rug. It may have been a struggle for Megan to forgive him, but that decision is separate from the question of whether or not she should allow full restoration of the relationship. Here's what we mean:

When John came back to the house that night, Megan didn't know what level of responsibility he was taking for the affair. "What if he really blames me for it? What if he thinks it's my fault for not being more exciting and more available sexually?" If he felt justified or was not serious about taking responsibility, why would she even think it remotely possible that they could have a good future? It would be an unwise risk to take him back. In fact, even if he handled things as perfectly as possible, it was still going to be very hard to restore the relationship.

Here is what actually happened. John and Megan had some very intense talks on the phone, and it was easy to escalate. But John persistently stated his desire to rebuild the marriage. Megan asked him to come to the house one night to talk about it. She poured out her anguish, pain, and anger. He just listened. She focused on how his behavior had affected her. He made a sincere apology, complete with deep sorrow. This enabled her to believe that there was a chance they could get through this. They talked for a couple of hours. The highlights of the conversation went like this:

JOHN: I made a very selfish choice that hurt you so very deeply. It was wrong of me on every level to allow it to happen.

MEGAN: I appreciate the apology. I needed to hear it. I love you, but I can't pick up where we left off. If we can make this work, it's going to take a lot of time and hard work.

JOHN: I understand. We're not going to be able to just move forward like nothing happened. What can I do that would help the most?

MEGAN: I don't really know. I don't know which way is up. I just know that I needed to hear you say you'd done something very wrong and mean it.

JOHN: Megan, I did do something horribly wrong. I know it. It's also very clear to me . . . clearer than it's been in years . . . that I want our marriage to work. I want you, not someone else.

MEGAN: I'd like to make it work, but I'm not sure I'll ever be able to trust you again.

JOHN: I understand. I'll have to earn your trust.

MEGAN: That's what I want. I want to make it, and I want to trust. With God's help, I can work on it. It's going to take me a while. I also need some way to believe it won't happen again.

JOHN: I know we'll need some help. *(pausing)* Megan, I'd like to come back home. I could sleep in the guest bedroom.

MEGAN: That's OK with me, but I need to know we'll go and get help to get through this.

JOHN: Like our pastor or a Christian counselor?

MEGAN: Yes. I'm not sure what to do next, and I don't want to mess this up. If you'll agree to that, I can handle you coming back home, but I don't see any kind of intimacy happening for some time. Do you understand that?

JOHN: I do. I don't see how it could be otherwise, in fact. That makes sense.

MEGAN: I can't handle it if you expect me to go on like nothing's happened. I'm very, very angry with you right now. I have a gigantic pile of pain and hurt.

JOHN: I know, and I won't pressure you to act like nothing happened. We're going to need help on how to deal with a lot of stuff.

MEGAN: OK.

As John validated her pain and anger, Mary really opened up. He didn't get defensive or act as though nothing bad had happened. If he had, she was prepared to work on forgiveness but end the marriage. Both realized that it would take some time. They also realized they needed help.

John did the best he could under the circumstances. Next day, he called their pastor for an appointment. His taking action showed Megan that he was serious. It gave her evidence that he meant what he had said. They met with the pastor, who got them connected with a counselor who understood what they needed to do. They started seeing her the next week, and the forgiveness work took a clear direction.

Megan and John got through this serious breach of trust. It took time, but they worked hard. Megan never forgot what had happened, but the ache in her heart became weaker over the years. They rebuilt trust and commitment. They made their marriage stronger than it was before.

Regaining Trust

We're often asked how you regain trust when it's been severely damaged. That question is not as relevant for minor offenses. There was no loss of trust in what happened between Tony and Mary. Pippa had some loss of trust in Oggie for a while, but that didn't last. For Megan and John, regaining trust took a lot of time, but it was worth it. Trust is essential for a marriage to thrive.

How do you regain it? There are two key points:

1. **Trust builds slowly over time.** Trust builds as you gain confidence in someone's being there for you. Although research shows that people vary in their general trust for others, deep

trust comes only from seeing that your partner is there for you over time. Megan can only regain her trust slowly. The best thing that can happen is for a considerable amount of time to go by without a serious breach. That takes commitment to new ways of living together. John and Megan can't afford to let the same kind of distance build up again. But if he has another affair, it will be nearly impossible for her to trust him again.

2. **Trust has the greatest chance to be rebuilt when each partner takes appropriate responsibility.** The greatest thing John can do to regain Megan's trust is to take full responsibility for his actions. If she sees him doing all he can do without her prodding and demanding, her trust will grow. In seeing his dedication-based effort, she will more easily gain confidence that things can get better—not perfect, but really better.

Megan can also help rebuild John's trust. For one thing, he'll need to see that she won't hold the affair over his head forever. If she reminds him about it, especially during arguments, he won't be able to trust that she really wants to move ahead and grow closer again.

Easier Said Than Done: "I Forgive You"

Frank Fincham is a university-based researcher and scholar who has studied forgiveness extensively. He discourages partners from too quickly using the words "I forgive you" when there has been significant harm or betrayal. What he recommends instead is to say something like, "I am working toward forgiving you." The essence of the idea here is that it is very rare for someone to say the simple words "I forgive you" and have those words actually match reality. Forgiveness is a decision, but it is also a process that takes time and effort. Some of the most challenging work needs to happen within each person, both in the one who did something wrong and in the one who was hurt, and this just cannot be rushed if it's going to be truly lasting.

Keys to Forgiveness and Restoration

In this section, we briefly highlight key principles for making forgiveness a reality.

1. Make forgiveness a central characteristic of your marriage. Cultivate an atmosphere of grace and forgiveness. Think regularly about how to extend lavish grace to your mate, even for minor annoyances.
2. If you have hurt your partner, take full responsibility for your actions, whether or not you meant to hurt him or her. You validate your partner's pain and loss by doing so. When you have sinned, ask God to forgive and cleanse you (1 John 1:9). Apologize. Apologies motivated by genuine sorrow make forgiveness easier. Change where change is needed. Ask for forgiveness, but do not expect it immediately. Give your partner space and time to work on it. Consider ways of making amends. By that, we do not mean that you are paying off a debt as much showing good faith and a desire to make things right. (Paying off a debt implies that your partner intends to hold you in debt, which would not be forgiveness.)
3. Don't mistake natural feelings of grief and anger for a lack of forgiveness. Allow your partner and yourself to have strong feelings about what has been lost. Empathy is critical for full restoration.
4. If something deeply damaging has happened, get help to deal with it. Ask your pastor for guidance. Seek counseling from someone who knows how to help with the kind of problem you are facing (see suggestions in Appendix A, "Getting More Help with Serious Problems").
5. If you want to fully forgive and restore your relationship when your partner has hurt you in some way, try to put yourself in your partner's shoes. That means trying to understand what he or she may have been going through that was part of whatever happened. This does not mean making excuses for your partner; it means pushing yourself to be understanding where possible. This can be very difficult if what happened was deeply hurtful, and will certainly require the Lord's help. If you can gain some empathy for your partner as part of your

effort to move forward with forgiveness, you make reaching complete restoration of your relationship more possible. Research on forgiveness has shown this very clearly.

6. If you have forgiven your partner for something or you are working on it, never bring up the forgiven acts as a weapon in an argument. Never use the memory of painful hurts to gain leverage or to hurt your partner when you are hurting. If you need to talk it through more, sit down and do that—but keep it safe. Use the communication skills we described in Chapter Five.

7. Expect forgiveness and full restoration to take time in proportion to the damage done. You might have completely forgiven your partner for whatever happened but then wake up tomorrow feeling more grief and anger. Accept that forgiveness can be a process, and trust that God is eager to help you along the way.

Doing Your Part

Pray and think about ways you may harbor resentment, bitterness, and a lack of forgiveness in your relationship. Do you still hold old wrongs against your partner? Do you bring up past events in arguments? How long have you had these feelings? Are there patterns of behavior that continue to offend you? Are you willing to push yourself to forgive? Do you need to seek outside help, perhaps by asking a friend or a pastor to hold you accountable?

Pray and think about the times you have hurt your partner. Have you taken responsibility for them? Have you apologized? Have you taken steps to change any recurrent, harmful patterns? Just as you may be holding on to some grudges, you may be standing in the way of reconciliation if you've never taken responsibility for your own offenses.

16

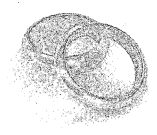

Spiritual Blessings and Intimacy

Unless the LORD builds the house, its builders labor in vain. Unless the LORD watches over the city, the watchmen stand guard in vain.
PSALM 127:1

We have covered many key areas of marriage. We've left the most mysterious topic for last. Spiritual oneness and intimacy may be the most elusive and fragile kind of intimacy for most couples. Because it can be fragile, it is most likely to thrive when you are managing many of the more mundane matters of marriage well. But all the rest of your marriage may work most smoothly when the two of you have a spiritual connection, with God at the center. To have that, you need the kind of trust, safety, and security that are born of commitment and respectful handling of issues and problems in your relationship. That's why we've waited until now to discuss spiritual intimacy.

For those of you in marriages in which you do not share the same faith as your mate, much of what we have to say in the rest of this chapter will be harder to work out. We acknowledge that some kinds of spiritual oneness are going to be far more difficult, if not impossible, when core spiritual differences are great. However, if that is the case for you, we still believe that rather than ignoring deeper beliefs or having conflicts over them, you can strengthen your marriage by giving careful consideration to what is possible. So you might find that the principles we have covered—especially in the chapters on friendship and expectations—can help you strengthen your connection even if you have important differences in beliefs. We also cover some considerations for couples with faith differences in a section later in this chapter.

For those who *do* share the same faith and spiritual orientation, there are still fine lines to walk as we enter this topic. For example, we don't want to raise unrealistic expectations that every marriage can easily achieve some kind of mystical soul-mate status. There's great potential for blessing, but many couples do not find it all that easy to attain deep levels of spiritual connection. Do not let unreasonable expectations spoil what elements of spiritual connection might work for the two of you.

Does being more "spiritual" or faithful always make it easier for relationships? It hardly seems so, at least from considering famous characters in the Bible. The Old and New Testaments provide many examples of great men and women of God. However, from what we are told in scripture, many of them were not exactly easy to relate to as people, and many had significant problems at home (for example, Adam and Eve, Genesis 3; Abraham and Sarah, Genesis 12; Moses and Zipporah, Exodus 24:24–26; David and Michal, 2 Samuel 6:20–23). Our point is that each of you can be very spiritual people and still struggle in your marriage. Nevertheless, if you are growing in the various ways we have been discussing, you're ready for exploring how to deepen your spiritual connection.

Failing to Enter the Promise

The Israelites were in captivity for many years in Egypt. When they were finally released, God directed them toward the land of blessing that He had promised. When Moses and his people came up to the edge of the land God had promised, they stopped. God told them to first send some spies into the land to check things out. The spies brought back a description of the land as a place "flowing with milk and honey." It was a land of great promise, but the Israelites did not enter into the promise that God had for them because of fear and unbelief.

Listen to the fear as the returning spies gave their report:

"But the people who live there are powerful, and the cities are fortified and very large. We even saw descendants of Anak there. The Amalekites live in the Negev; the Hittites, Jebusites and Amorites live in the hill country; and the Canaanites live near the sea and along the Jordan."

Then Caleb silenced the people before Moses and said, "We should go up and take possession of the land, for we can certainly do it." But the men who had gone up with him said, "We can't attack those people; they are stronger than we are." And they spread among the Israelites a bad report about the land they had explored. They said, "The land we explored devours those living in it. All the people we saw there are of great size. We saw the Nephilim there (the descendants of Anak come from the Nephilim). We seemed like grasshoppers in our own eyes, and we looked the same to them." (Numbers 13:28–33)

The last sentence is very telling. They seemed like grasshoppers in their *own* eyes. They didn't see themselves as being able to handle what God had promised. You very likely know the rest of the story. The ten spies who did not want to enter the land talked the people into staying out. So the Israelites wandered in the desert for forty years until that unbelieving generation died off.

Marriage is like this. God has given us a land of great spiritual promise in his design for marriage, but many do not fully enter into it. Whether from unbelief or from fear of not being up to the task or from a lack of knowing which way the marital promised land lies, too many couples do not take hold of the rich blessing God intends for their marriage. If you are intimidated by the task, you may not even try. And if your marriage is not safe for intimacy in other ways, you won't feel secure enough to try. Intimacy and deeper connection can be a scary place to go in a marriage. This is a fear you must conquer if you are to fully experience the potential blessings. Much of what we've been trying to teach in this book is about ways to act in love and cast out fear. If you want to go deeper in terms of spiritual intimacy, we have some suggestions for which way to head.

What Is Spiritual Intimacy?

You might have hoped we'd be giving you the five magical steps to spiritual oneness. We're not going to do that. It's not that we wouldn't like to, but we truly believe in what we said at the outset, in the first chapter: oneness is mysterious, and spiritual oneness is probably the most mysterious part of all. We don't want to offer any simple formulas. (These might actually inhibit you from developing your own unique spiritual connection.) But we do want to offer you some ideas. In fact, you can think of what follows as a kind of brainstorming. Our aim is to help you think about this topic, and to encourage you to move on into this kind of intimacy in your marriage. We don't know exactly what will help you draw closer together spiritually, but we have some ideas about approaches that have helped other couples.

Sharing Your Walk

Spiritual intimacy speaks to some ability to share in each other's spiritual life. That could mean many things. Many couples who are growing in their spiritual oneness have learned to share together about their personal walks with Christ. This is a kind of "as you go" sharing of thoughts about God, struggles in faith, answered prayer, and so forth. This is sharing spiritually as friends. What moves you at the deepest levels of your soul? When have you felt closest to the Lord? What are you most afraid of in your spiritual life?

Colton and Elena have cultivated this kind of connection in their marriage. They married seventeen years ago, and neither was very spiritually involved at the time. However, as they have gone through the trials of life and the joys and pains of parenthood, they have increasingly turned their hearts to God. Now they are actively involved with the Lord and with others in their church. Only in recent years have they have begun to talk more openly about their thoughts and struggles in their faith. For example, Colton has always been more on the skeptical side of life, asking why and why not, a lot. Elena doesn't have as many questions, but does struggle more personally with God at times.

When the child of one of their best friends died from liver disease at the age of three, it led to a spiritual struggle for both of them. For Elena, the struggle boiled down to anger at God for allowing her friend's child to die. This was not so much a crisis of faith for her but a very personal issue with God about what had happened. For Colton, there was much emotion in this event, but it was also a real crisis of faith: Why would God allow such a thing? Maybe God isn't who I think He is. Maybe He doesn't even exist. Such spiritual struggles are not uncommon for deep-thinking Christians. The rewarding aspect of this sad event was that Colton and Elena began talking much more openly about these deeper matters that they had kept inside in earlier years. This cultivated a spiritual friendship based in the sense of being one in the Spirit. It was about the only thing they could feel thankful for in the midst of the awful loss that had occurred.

Many people don't feel comfortable sharing their deeper experiences with their mate. Perhaps most fear rejection. For others, it's a matter of privacy. We've met many people who hold this view. Still others find it difficult to put into words what their spiritual experience with Christ is like, making it hard to talk about with another. These examples illustrate why it is so important for the two of you to find ways of connecting spiritually that work for both of you. This may mean pushing yourself through the discomfort to share what you can. Or it may mean being content to accept your partner's reluctance in this area and to wait for him or her to open up.

Connected in Giving: Serving Others Together

Some couples find greater spiritual closeness in serving the Lord together. And we believe that just about all Christian couples could boost their spiritual connection and sense of meaning and purpose in life by regularly doing something along these lines together.

One couple we know, Lucas and Joan, have been married for more than thirty years. They have tried praying together, scripture reading, and so on, but none of these more typical ways of connecting spiritually have worked smoothly for them. But over the years they have noticed how much guests who come to their home seem to enjoy their hospitality. Now, they think about creative ways to use their home to reach others, enjoying preparing for an event together and cleaning up and talking about it afterward. As a result, they have begun carving out more frequent times to use their home for ministry to younger families, neighbors, and work associates. This has created a new joy and a spiritual closeness they had not known before.

Ministry may be one of the most important ways you can express your oneness in marriage, though we know this will be a new thought for many couples. As a matter of fact, when Christ was praying for us to become one, he twice emphasized the purpose of our oneness: "so that the world may believe that you have sent me" (John 17:20, 21). When you minister together as a couple, you are looking beyond yourselves to the world you are called to reach. Your own relationship struggles can seem less important. Your marriage can take on a larger meaning that gives you a stronger sense of oneness as well as happiness. You are perfecting your oneness as a light to the world. We cannot think of too many ideas here that are more powerful than this one. Give it some serious thought.

Sharing Spiritual Insights and Thoughts

Some couples are drawn together by sharing their thoughts about and reactions to passages of scripture. This could mean reading the same passage together and then simply talking about it. What brings closeness is the sharing of what the Lord is impressing on the heart. For some, this comes easiest if they use a devotional guide. One of the great advantages of using such a tool is that it takes the pressure off of either of you to teach the other, and allows you both to be taught by the devotional. There are many excellent couple's devotionals on the market these days, as well as many devotionals not directed toward couples that would be fine choices for helping you cultivate this kind of sharing.

For other couples, spiritual intimacy is fostered by listening to Christian radio together or watching on the Internet a teacher or pastor that both partners like. This is similar to talking together about a sermon you just heard or about something a teacher in your church taught that really hit home for you. The key idea here is sharing what you are hearing in the messages from scripture.

Another couple, Ginger and Josh, tried many times over the years to study scripture together. Nothing seemed to work. Ginger had been a Christian for years before Josh entered the faith, so he felt threatened by her greater knowledge. Not only did they have the typical problems of making time for this, but when they did have the time, it would sometimes lead to conflict. As it turns out, both were very twitchy on hidden issues of control. So when either one would assume a teacherly tone or manner, conflict would erupt: "Who made you the spiritual genius?" "What makes you think you understand that passage correctly?"

Ginger and Josh finally found something that really worked well for them, a blog where the writer regularly posted deep and fascinating points about Christianity. Both appreciated the author a lot, and they found it easy to go out and get a cup of coffee once a week to talk about what they had read on the blog that week. The trust they each had for the writer helped them keep their own control issues at bay.

There is a passage in the Old Testament that has most often been interpreted to be simply about learning the Torah (literally, "direction from God"), but much more is implied:

> Love the LORD your God with all your heart and with all your soul and with all your strength. These commandments that I give you today are to be upon your hearts. Impress them on your children. Talk about them when you sit at home and when you walk along the road, when you lie down and when you get up. (Deuteronomy 6:5–7)

The heart of this passage is about parenting and raising children to love the Lord by helping them grow in their understanding of Him and His will. In family life, the picture here is one of frequent talking about scripture in the various contexts of daily life. It has to do with cultivating a regular conversation about the sayings of God. It is noteworthy that the regular discussion of God's desires (which are most clearly revealed in scripture) is so clearly linked to loving God with our whole heart.

Another implication of this passage is that one's spiritual life is not to be compartmentalized in religious activities but to permeate all of life. When your spiritual lives are more openly and regularly shared in this way, you will experience one facet of spiritual intimacy. Still, your particular style may vary greatly from what other couples do.

Shared Meaning and Action

Studies have shown that people who are more religious on average do *slightly* better in their marriages. The research tends to be on "religiosity" measured simply rather than on deeper nuances of faith. Further, most of the relevant findings are based on samples in which being more religious means being more traditionally religious from a Christian perspective. Researchers find that those who are more religious are more likely to remain together and more likely to have *a bit* higher quality relationships. The emphasis we place on "slightly" and "a bit" is important. Those who identify more strongly with a faith have some edge in marriage, on average, but it's no panacea for peace and harmony. What does it take for faith to really matter? Mutual involvement.

One scholar who studies how faith and relationships intersect is Annette Mahoney at Bowling Green State University. She studies faith from a psychological perspective rather than from the perspective of a particular religion, such as Christianity. In 1999, she published an important study on how and when faith is associated with stronger and happier marriages. What she found was that, compared to the impact of the religious activities of each individual in marriage, the real impact of faith on marriage is found in what the two individuals do together. The couples who practice their faith together—and see their faith as a core aspect of their union—were those who showed clear marital strengths associated with faith. For example, although the religious practices of individuals mattered in marriage, what mattered far more were praying together, talking together about God and how His will relates to their marriage, talking about personal spiritual issues, attending church together, engaging in rituals of the faith together, and so forth. Mahoney's

work strongly suggests that a deeper involvement based on
shared belief and meaning does something important and
good for a marriage.

If the two of you share the same faith but have not developed ways to practice your faith more deeply together, this is
one of the most important things you can do to create a marriage of true lasting promise.

Praying Together

We don't know how many Christian couples pray together regularly. It seems less common than a lot of people assume. We're
not talking about praying together at dinner. Although many
families do not do that, many other families find that practice
pretty manageable. But to actually sit (or kneel) down and pray
deeply together, regularly? We think that this is not a common
experience for Christian couples. For some, it's just a matter of
the time not working out. But for others, praying together is
something hard to bring about because when we pray, we are
capable of being at our most vulnerable and authentic; therefore,
for many people, this is a level of openness, even with their mate,
that they are just not able to manage.

Praying together can be an important part of experiencing
spiritual intimacy in your marriage. However, you should not
assume that it's something the two of you are regularly going to
be able to manage. But if you are both open and interested in
making this happen, there are many ways to get there. You could
pray openly or quietly or silently, for long periods or short. There
is no rule book on how to pray together in marriage. One approach
to praying together lies in sharing needs and prayer requests with
each other and then taking the time to pray together for those
issues and concerns you each raised. Sharing needs in this manner
also will promote a sense of oneness in your walk with Christ. By
praying for each other, you are sharing each other's burdens in a
very intimate and real way (recall Galatians 6:2, which we discussed in Chapter Thirteen).

Note that in this chapter, we are discussing praying together.
Be sure to think and act on the ideas in Chapter Three that focus
on the importance of your praying regularly and effectively, as an

individual, for your mate and your marriage. No matter how interested or able the two of you are in praying together regularly, you also can do your own part by praying for your marriage.

Worshiping God Together

Much has been made in recent years of the fact that couples and families eat fewer meals together than they used to. This decrease in relaxed time together diminishes opportunities for sharing our lives. Likewise, many couples do not regularly worship together. Worship, of course, can take a variety of forms: attending church services, giving thanks (Hebrews 12:28, 29), and singing praise songs together (Colossians 3:16). You can probably think of other ways as well.

One couple we know of has a tradition of singing praise hymns together as they travel. This is a great example of sharing in worship and communion with Christ. Singing together may or may not be your cup of tea, but that's our key point: find out what your cup of tea is when it comes to spiritual intimacy. God has left you great room for the expression of your creativity in marriage. As we said at the beginning of this chapter, we do not want to tell you what to do in this area so much as stimulate you to consider some ways you might grow together spiritually.

Taking Communion Together

Before Jesus was crucified, he instituted the ritual we know as communion as a way to remember Him and what He has done for us on the cross (see Mark 14:22–24; John 13; 1 Corinthians 11:20–34). The key concept here has to do with the idea of sharing our deepest fellowship with the Lord. Communion is to be one of our most personal, deepest acts of relating to Him. Although this is a very personal experience, we are instructed to do it corporately.

Communion is another deep spiritual experience you can share together. It's not an opportunity for talking so much as an opportunity to be side by side in this powerful remembrance. It is a symbol of your spiritual oneness. Because of the many demands of life, even life at church, many couples are not regularly together for communion. One couple, Janis and Quint, have small children and are very active in children's ministry. Therefore, it has become fairly hard for both to take communion at the same time. Often, one is holding down the class of preschoolers while the other slips into the service. Taking communion together will require them to ask a friend to watch the kids while they both leave to attend the service. It might add a special blessing to your marriage to make it a higher priority to share communion together from time to time. It's hard to imagine how that could not be the case.

Making and Protecting the Time

We think two of the very most important ideas in this book are contained in Ground Rule 2 (see Chapter Four): set aside times for the great things and learn to protect those times from conflict and issues. As we conclude this discussion of spiritual intimacy, we can't think of any other area where this advice is more important. You can want to make spiritual time together, you can think it's a great idea, but if you don't plan for it in some way, it will not happen.

Just as important, when you have set aside some time for enhancing spiritual oneness, you must protect this time from conflict and issues. It's not that struggling together can't foster spiritual growth, but if you end up struggling much of the time when you are trying to draw together spiritually, you won't end up being closer. Use the other skills and strategies we've been talking about to protect this crucial part of your marital oneness.

There's great spiritual promise in your marriage. But you must take hold of it. Being deeply connected spiritually does not just happen any more than the other aspects of a great marriage just happen. Seek the Lord in prayer for the unique ways that the spiritual fullness of your marriage may be developed.

For Those Who Do Not Share the Same Faith

If you and your partner do not share the same faith and beliefs, it will be more difficult to achieve the kind of unity and connection in faith that we are focusing on here. Nevertheless, there are other principles that maybe beneficial for the two of you to consider related to the themes of this chapter. We have two specific points for you to think about. Both are based on our belief that your marriage matters. We know that you would not be reading this book if your marriage did not matter to you and those around you. And because this is a Christian book on marriage, we are also going to assume that you are likely a Christian and that your mate either does not share your faith at all or does not consider it as important as you do.

First, give regular thought to how your own walk in your faith impacts your marriage in this context of unshared faith. Research suggests that when faith is not shared, one mate's being very active in his or her faith can make it more likely that the marriage will fail. Yes, *more* likely, not less. It may already be obvious to you why this could be the case. When faith is not shared and one spouse is extensively involved, he or she can easily spend a tremendous amount of time and energy away from his or her mate doing things that the mate has little or no interest in doing. Does that sound like you? If so, we have no idea how God would like you to handle this. Clearly, you should not abandon your faith in God through Christ. But if you are extremely involved in activities because of your faith, it is worth asking yourself whether God wants you so involved at church (for example) that you risk having your marriage fail. There is some balance point you may need to consider—related not to the depth of your faith or your allegiance to God but to how you act out your faith in light of the difference between you and your mate.

The second point we make here is about strengthening connection in your marriage in important ways even when you may not share this most central belief about life. We appreciate that a substantial difference in faith and beliefs places limitations on connecting spiritually. However, any couple could do some of what we have discussed in this chapter and, in doing those things, gain greater strength and connection in married life.

Both Alice and Nick were born and raised in Asia (both were from families of Chinese decent, she from Taiwan and he from Singapore). They met when both were attending college in Hawaii, where, within months, they were planning a life together. In almost all ways, their marriage has been exceptionally strong.

They settled in Taiwan after they finished college and married, and from there, they have been able to travel and regularly stay in touch with his family as well as hers. They are fortunate to have the means to do this.

About five years into their marriage, Alice became a Christian. Nick has been supportive of Alice's faith, but does not share it. Whereas Alice has a calm, settled, and deep faith, Nick tends to have an unsettled mind about what to believe in life, never finding real peace in any one set of answers. Alice is involved in a church in Taipei, but Nick has not joined her. As an example of how strong a couple they are, they recognized that this issue of unshared faith had some potential for creating distance in their marriage. Not being prone to sliding when it comes to important matters in their marriage, they talked about how to handle the issue in ways that would protect rather than threaten their marriage.

One of the things Alice and Nick decided to do was to get involved as a couple in a local community group that provided a place for the elderly in their neighborhood to gather with others and eat together. Isolation of the elderly is a growing concern in many countries, and these types of services are one way that caring people are trying to address the issue. This is something that both Alice and Nick could really get into together. In fact, both had strong feelings about respecting and caring for the older generation, and this service had deep meaning and purpose for both of them. Caring for others in this important way transcended issues of faith and helped them increase their closeness.

The key point we leave you with here is that there is a broader way to view much of what we have covered in this chapter: even if you do not share the same faith in Christ, you can strengthen your shared life together around activities that matter to you both, thereby deepening connection in marriage. Your marriage will benefit.

o   o   o

We remind you to think of what we have covered here as a type of brainstorming. There are many ways to deepen your spiritual oneness in your marriage. Try some out. Seek answers. Be creative. Ask God to show you some pathways.

Doing Your Part

Our recommendations here are quite simple, but potent. We suggest that you talk together about two things. First, take some time together to discuss what you have read here. Discuss your desires, your fears, and your concerns about spiritual oneness. It might help to talk about how you were each raised in this regard. What have you observed? Second, spend some time brainstorming together about what you might try as ways to increase your spiritual intimacy. You could go back through the list of ideas we have presented here and talk about each type of shared spirituality that we have discussed. What of any of those things sounds worth pursuing in your marriage? What are you open to trying? The key here is that you are looking for ways to strengthen this connection that work well for both of you. We also recommend that you try not to do everything but to try one new thing. Sometimes when trying to set spiritual goals, people talk themselves into doing so much that they end up doing nothing because it becomes overwhelming. Starting a little something new is far more important than promising to do everything new.

Pray for God's blessings individually and, if you are comfortable doing so, as a couple. May God bless you with a deeper spiritual connection in your marriage.

17

Onward

You could think of this book as providing a recipe for a lasting, happier, and healthier marriage. The ingredients are in place, and now the key is for you to blend these ingredients with your commitment in order to live out the lasting promise of your marriage.

You may begin using these ideas for a while, only to fall back into some of your old patterns. That's normal. Most successful couples experience setbacks from time to time. Many times, couples try a new strategy that works well, but then slack off and slide back into old patterns that are not so great. During those times, it's easy to feel as though you have not made any progress at all. But that's not true. Don't trust those feelings. Most of us take two steps forward, one—and sometimes two—steps back. It's a lot like all of spiritual life and the process of sanctification—it's not one smooth path to the top. What's most important is not to quit, and to keep moving forward. Passages throughout the Bible make it pretty clear that we all struggle with this dynamic. Instead of losing heart and giving up, just keep moving forward by trying a few of the ideas we've presented that seem most important to what you believe your marriages needs.

One way to get things moving in the best direction again is for the two of you to hold a meeting to tighten up your game as a team. You might even find it valuable to schedule such a meeting once a year, or at whatever interval makes the most sense for you as a couple. Use this meeting to talk over what steps you want to take next in keeping your marriage on track. That's a very powerful way to decide about your future rather than slide your way through it.

In his classic book *Mere Christianity*, C. S. Lewis wrote the following line about making changes, asking God for help, failing, asking for forgiveness when needed, and trying again: "Very often what God first helps us towards is not the virtue itself but just this power of always trying again." Lewis is saying that real change comes from continuing to try. That is encouraging because, in his wisdom, Lewis is acknowledging the difficulty of making lasting changes. We are all flawed, and, despite our best intentions, we all fail to stay on the better path. You are human, and it is unrealistic to expect constant peace and continual growth, with no setbacks, over years together in marriage.

To get the most out of the strategies we have presented here, you have to keep trying. That does not mean trying everything, but it does mean doing your part to continue doing the things that matter most in your marriage. When you've let things slide and your connection has been neglected for a while, decide to get back in the game. When you've fallen off the path, get back up, check your heading, and move forward.

We know of some couples who reread this book once a year in order to keep their marriage on track. What a great idea. One of the advantages of it is that there are some very powerful strategies here that you are likely to forget. Do you remember every useful piece of information from any class you have ever taken? Same goes for reading a book like this. Review is good. We all learn better when we go over key concepts again and again. Furthermore, sometimes the strategies that didn't seem needed or valuable at one point in your marriage will be just what you need most at another point along the way.

For the purposes of review, go back and read the sections you may have highlighted. None of the strategies and ideas are all that complicated, but some need to be mastered if they are to be most useful to you. This is especially true in regard to changing patterns of communication and how you handle conflicts. These patterns are usually deeply ingrained, starting from childhood and past relationships and then sometimes existing in deep ruts of behavior in your own marriage. If you have patterns you want to change for the better, you will have to work at it. For example, if the two of you tend to escalate when you try to talk about issues, you need to master some form of Time Out. Likewise, if you want to communicate more effectively, you need to practice using the Speaker-Listener Technique until the underlying principles become second nature. You cannot wish the negative patterns away. You have to drive them away by replacing them with new behaviors and attitudes. If we haven't said it enough, practice the specific strategies that seem to be most useful for your marriage—not everything, but the ones you see here that address some need or desire and that work best in your marriage.

We've detailed our approach in this book. We've provided tools you can use to build a relationship that brings long-term fulfillment and to protect your relationship from naturally occurring storms. But, like anything else, once you have the tools, what you do with them is up to you. You can make a difference in your marriage. Ask God to help you do that.

We close by weaving together some thoughts on love.

Many waters cannot quench love;.

Rivers cannot wash it away . . .

so

Serve one another in love.

The entire law is summed up in a single command:

"Love your neighbor as yourself."

for

There is no fear in love. But perfect love drives out fear.
(from Song of Songs 8:7; Galatians 5:13, 14; and 1 John 4:18)

Appendices

Appendix A

Getting More Help with Serious Problems

There are many situations in which people need a lot more help than what can be gleaned from a book or a marriage education class. Because you are taking this time to think more about your life and relationships, it may also be a good time to think about additional services that you or others you care about may need. Even if your main goal right now is to improve your marriage or relationship, difficulties in other areas can make it that much harder to make your relationship work. Likewise, if you are having severe problems in your relationship, they can make dealing with any of these other problems more difficult. This appendix discusses some areas where seeking additional help could be really important for you and your family.

Specific Challenges

In each of the categories here, we give you some ideas for how to seek other help and services. We also list some resources, such as national hotlines and websites, following this section.

Financial Problems
- Serious money problems make everything else harder.
- Job loss and unemployment can be key sources of conflict and stress for couples.

- Although this book can help you as a couple work more as a team, you may need more help in learning to manage your finances or in finding a job.

There are two types of needs that a couple can have in this category. One major problem for some is simply not having enough money or job security to pay all the bills. When the troubles are severe enough, there are various government resources that you may qualify for (for example, country welfare services, sometimes going by a name such as the Department of Human Services). There are also food banks that can help out in times of serious need. Those can usually be found by searching on the Internet. As with so many types of help, you can always turn to people at your church or other churches in your area to find out what they know about local services.

The second major type of problem couples have with finances has less to do with not having enough money or income but is more directly related to difficulties managing money well as a couple. There are many resources available to help those who want to learn more how to manage money well. For example, many churches around the United States sponsor financial management workshops somewhat regularly. This may not be something that your own church offers, but if you live in a larger city, there is likely to be some other church in the area that does offer such help. (You don't have to change churches to get help at another church!)

There are also various national experts who offer all sorts of resources, workshops, and online information. One expert in this area who is well appreciated by many is Dave Ramsey. He has a daily radio show, a website containing lots of information, and materials for teaching adults and children how to deal with money; he also regularly works with churches in putting on workshops. Ramsey's work is just one example of the many resources that are available if you are ready to get help.

Serious Marital or Other Family Problems or Stresses

- If you have serious marital or adult relationship problems that require more help than can be provided in this book, you can seek counseling from someone who specializes in working with couples.

- Coping with a serious, life-threatening, or chronic illness or disability in a child or adult can place a lot of stress on caregivers and their family relationships. Community resources often exist to assist families with these kinds of issues.

If you have serious difficulties in your relationship and decide to seek counseling, ask a number of people for ideas of whom you could go to for counseling. Doctors, pastors, and friends can be good sources of information about couple's counselors who are respected in your area. If you do see a counselor for your marriage, we also recommend that the two of you talk together after a couple of sessions to see whether you both feel that the person you are seeing has the ability to help you. If you live in a large community, there are many people you could work with. If after a couple of sessions you do not have confidence that the person you are seeing understands you and has a plan that makes sense to you, try seeing someone else. Sometimes a particular counselor is just not the right fit for a couple, and it is important that you have confidence in the person you are seeing.

Substance Abuse, Addictions, and Other Compulsive Behaviors

- No matter what else you have to deal with in life, you will find it harder if you or your partner, or another close family member, has an addiction or substance abuse problem.
- Drug or alcohol abuse and addiction rob a person of the ability to handle life well, have close relationships, and be a good parent.
- Alcohol abuse can also make it harder to control anger and violence.
- Other problems families sometimes face include eating disorders, sexual addictions, and gambling.

You need to decide to get help with these problems to improve your life and the lives of those you love. It will make it easier if your partner or spouse supports this decision.

There are multiple types of services and supports to help people struggling with substance abuse in their own life or in that of a loved one. If you are involved in a church, your pastor or others at your church may well know some excellent local resources. There are Alcoholics Anonymous groups in virtually every city in the United States (and likely around the world). There are similar groups for dealing with other types of substance abuse and addiction, as well as groups like Al-Anon for helping family members cope.

If you have the resources, you might find it particularly valuable to work with a couple's therapist who specializes in helping with addictions. The research evidence is clear that when there are two willing partners, couple-based approaches can be particularly effective. Therefore, with some types of addictive behavior, part of the services can include both of you in ways that make the counseling more effective. However, that depends on your ability to find a therapist who really understands this area well and is used to working with two partners together.

Mental Health Problems

- Mental health problems come in many forms, from anxiety to depression to schizophrenia, and serious mental health problems place a great deal of stress on couple and family relationships.
- Depression is particularly common when there are serious relationship problems. (See Chapter Seven for more specific information about depression and marriage.)
- Having thoughts of suicide is usually an important sign of serious depression. Seek help if you struggle with such thoughts.

The good news is that there are now many effective treatments for mental health problems, with services available in all counties, including options for those with limited means of paying. In the United States, every county has a community mental health center. Some larger churches have counselors on staff who can help you get the help you need. Pastors and doctors often know of skilled therapists in their communities whom they have found helpful to those who are struggling. If possible, seek out a therapist or other mental health professionals who have a good amount of experience in addressing the specific kinds of struggles you are having.

Domestic Aggression and Violence

- Although domestic aggression and violence of any sort is wrong and dangerous, experts now recognize different types. For example,
  - Some couples have arguments that get out of control, with frustration spilling over into pushing, shoving, or slapping. This can be dangerous, especially if you don't take strong measures to stop the patterns from continuing.
  - The type of domestic violence that is usually the most dangerous and the least likely to change occurs when a male uses aggression and force to scare and control a woman. Verbal abuse, threats of harm, and forced sexual activity can be part of this pattern.
- This book is not a treatment program for physical aggression. If you are dealing with aggression and violence in your relationship, you need more help than this book can provide. That might mean seeking marital or relationship counseling or seeking the advice of local or national domestic violence experts.
- If you have any questions about the safety of your relationship or the safety of your children, you should contact a domestic violence program or hotline, especially if you feel that you or others are in danger of being harmed.

The bottom line is that you must do what you need to do to ensure that you and your children are safe. If you ever feel that you are in immediate danger from your partner or others, call 911 for help or contact a local or national domestic violence hotline. The national number for the United States is listed in the next section.

Where to Get More Help

If you, your partner, or your relationship experiences any of these special problems, we strongly recommend that you get more help.

As noted earlier, there are many ways to find out about resources local to you. You can ask a therapist in your community or contact a local counseling center or community mental health center. Also, members of the clergy and family physicians are usually well aware of resources for meeting various needs in their communities, so consider asking them for suggestions.

There are community mental health centers in all areas of the United States. Other counseling centers and mental health professionals are often available as well (both nonreligious and religious).

The following are some national hotline numbers and a website that may be useful to some readers:

National Resources
Domestic violence hotline: SAFELINE, 1-800-799-7233
Website with links for help with substance abuse and mental health issues: www.samhsa.gov/public/look_frame.html
Hotline for referrals to substance abuse treatment: 1-800-662-HELP
Suicide prevention hotline: National Hopeline Network, 1-800-SUICIDE (784-2433)

Appendix B

Resources from PREP®

We mentioned the Prevention and Relationship Enhancement Program (PREP) in the introduction. PREP is a research-based approach to helping couples build and maintain strong and happy marriages. Many of the specific strategies we have presented in this book are based on PREP. PREP is also a company that produces various programs and materials for couples. Most of the products from PREP are designed for those who work with couples, but there are some that are also directly available to couples who are interested.

Whether you are seeking greater meaning in your own relationship or you wish to work with others in your community, this section describes an array of resources available from PREP.

Self-Help

PREP does not produce a lot of materials that are made for distribution directly to individuals and couples, but there a number of PREP resources that you may want to consider.

Prayer Journal: Like a Tree Planted by Water

A number of the key ideas in Chapter Three were based on this well-designed journal that was built to help you pray consistently and wisely for your mate and your marriage. The journal is designed to help your marriage thrive like a tree planted by water

(Jeremiah 17:8). The teachings, passages used, and personal journaling are designed to help you more fully invite God into your relationship and to invite Him to lead you on a path of growth and development in your marriage. The journal is designed for the individual. It is for you and your prayer life; it is not designed for spouses to use together. You can use this journal whether or not your partner is also interested in doing so.

The prayer journal was developed and is published by Christian PREP, and can be ordered at www.PREPinc.com by clicking on Shop → Books.

Calming Skills Audio CD

The *Calming Skills* audio CD helps people practice various methods of physical and mental relaxation to improve stress management. This inexpensive CD includes several different guided relaxation routines. You can play this CD at home or work and use it to practice relaxation skills such as those we discussed in Chapter Seven. As is true of so many other areas we touch on in this book, practice can make a real difference in your quality of life.

To order a copy of this audio CD, just go to www.PREPinc.com and click on Shop → Audio & Video.

Books

In addition to this book, there are many other titles from various authors associated with PREP that may help strengthen your relationship. You can learn more about any of our books by visiting www.PREPinc.com and clicking on Shop → Books.

Many of these books can also be purchased through your local bookstore, and any of them can be ordered on the Web. Here are a few suggestions:

The Power of Commitment: A Guide to Active Lifelong Love
> Scott M. Stanley
> Best-selling marriage expert Dr. Scott Stanley shows couples the way to active, lasting love through an understanding of what commitment can do for a relationship. Like *A Lasting Promise*, this book contains a blending of core teachings from scripture along with solid ideas based on research.

Fighting for *Your Marriage: A Deluxe Revised Edition of the Classic Best-seller for Enhancing Marriage and Preventing Divorce, 3rd Edition*

Howard J. Markman, Scott M. Stanley, and Susan L. Blumberg

This is the best-selling secular book based on the internationally recognized PREP approach for couples. Like the book you are holding, it is filled with practical suggestions and advice for helping couples build lasting, loving marriages.

12 Hours to a Great Marriage: A Step-by-Step Guide for Making Love Last

Howard J. Markman, Scott M. Stanley, Susan L. Blumberg, Natalie H. Jenkins, and Carol Whiteley

This clear, self-guided book provides busy couples with practical steps on how to make their love last. You could think of this as a methodical or condensed version of *Fighting* for *Your Marriage*.

You Paid How Much for That?! How to Win at Money Without Losing at Love

Natalie H. Jenkins, Scott M. Stanley, William C. Bailey, and Howard J. Markman

This book unveils deeper, often hidden meanings of money and helps conquer the issues of finances as they relate to relationships.

The *Fighting* for *Your Marriage* DVD Collection

The *Fighting* for *Your Marriage* DVD collection is the perfect complement to our books that deal with communication and conflict management (such as the one you hold in your hands). Couples can curl up on the couch and get further instruction and ideas about how to use the communication skills. The videos include footage of real couples demonstrating the Communication Danger Signs and also the skills we described in this book to do things a better way.

To order these DVDs, just go to www.PREPinc.com and click on Shop → Audio & Video.

Understanding Commitment DVD

In 2004, PREP professionally recorded a talk by Scott Stanley on commitment, given to a large audience of couples who were attending a weekend workshop. This DVD contains the informative talk which highlights Scott's most powerful points about commitment (and a lot of humor). The video can help an individual couple or a group to better understand the real power that comes from acting on loving commitment in marriage.

To order this DVD, just go to www.PREPinc.com and click on Shop → Audio & Video.

Helping Others: Instructor Materials

PREP and Christian PREP provide training and materials for those who work with couples in marriage education workshops or in counseling. The variety of tools and strategies available from PREP continues to grow over time. An increasing number of resources do not require training and can be ordered by anyone desiring to help couples. To learn more about the resources available, check out www.PREPinc.com.

For example, PREP offers separate, self-contained modules for use in teaching couples important concepts and strategies. These modules are freestanding, meaning that they can be used separately or along with other marriage education workshop materials. There are modules on many topics—for example, communication skills training, understanding personality differences in marriage, handling anger and stress, relaxation strategies, understanding how one's own history affects marriage, issues and events, and fun.

Appendix C

Research and Scholarly References

What follows here is a *very* abbreviated list of the studies we rely on to inform the recommendations we have for couples. If you would like to peruse a much larger list, please contact PREP at info@prepinc.com and ask for Scott Stanley's master reference list. Stanley also has a blog at www.slidingvsdeciding.com, where he covers topics ranging from practical insights for relationships to discussions of new studies, public policy, and trends about marriage and families.

Allen, E. S., Atkins, D., Baucom, D. H., Snyder, D., Gordon, K. C., & Glass, S. P. (2005). Intrapersonal, interpersonal, and contextual factors in engaging in and responding to extramarital involvement. *Clinical Psychology: Science and Practice, 12,* 101–130.

Allen, E. S., Stanley, S. M., Rhoades, G. K., Markman, H. J., & Loew, B. A. (2011). Marriage education in the Army: Results of a randomized clinical trial. *Journal of Couple and Relationship Therapy, 10,* 309–326.

Amato, P. R. (2000). The consequences of divorce for adults and children. *Journal of Marriage and Family, 62,* 1269–1287.

Amato, P. R., & Previti, D. (2003). People's reasons for divorcing: Gender, social class, the life course, and adjustment. *Journal of Family Issues, 24,* 602–626.

Baucom, D., & Epstein, N. (1990). *Cognitive behavioral marital therapy.* New York, NY: Brunner/Mazel.

Baumeister, R. F. (2002). Yielding to temptation: Self-control failure, impulsive purchasing, and consumer behavior. *Journal of Consumer Research, 28,* 670–676.

Beach, S.R.H., Hurt, T. R., Fincham, F. D., Franklin, K. J., McNair, L. M., & Stanley, S. M. (2011). Enhancing marital enrichment through spirituality:

Efficacy data for prayer focused relationship enhancement. *Psychology of Religion and Spirituality, 3,* 201–216.

Beach, S.R.H., Sandeen, E. E., & O'Leary, K. D. (1990). *Depression in marriage: A model for etiology and treatment.* New York, NY: Guilford Press.

Bodenmann, G., & Shantinath, S. D. (2004). The Couples Coping Enhancement Training (CCET): A new approach to prevention of marital distress based upon stress and coping. *Family Relations, 53,* 477–484.

Carroll, J. S., Willoughby, B., Badger, S., Nelson, L. J., Barry, C., & Madsen, S. D. (2007). So close, yet so far away: The impact of varying marital horizons on emerging adulthood. *Journal of Adolescent Research, 22,* 219–247.

Christensen, A., & Heavey, C. L. (1990). Gender and social structure in the demand/withdraw pattern of marital conflict. *Journal of Personality and Social Psychology, 59,* 73–82.

Clements, M. L., Stanley, S. M., & Markman, H. J. (2004). Before they said "I do": Discriminating among marital outcomes over 13 years based on pre-marital data. *Journal of Marriage and Family, 66,* 613–626.

Conger, R., Elder, G. H., Lorenz, F. O., Conger, K. J., Simons, R. L., Whitbeck, L. B., Huck, S., & Melby, J. M. (1990). Linking economic hardship to marital quality and instability. *Journal of Marriage and the Family, 52,* 643–656.

Cordova, J. V., Gee, C. G., & Warren, L. Z. (2005). Emotional skillfulness in marriage: Intimacy as a mediator of the relationship between emotional skillfulness and marital satisfaction. *Journal of Social and Clinical Psychology, 24,* 218–235.

Cummings, E. M., & Davies, P. (1994). *Children and marital conflict.* New York, NY: Guilford Press.

Cutrona, C. (1996). *Social support in couples: Marriage as a resource in times of stress.* Thousand Oaks, CA: Sage.

Davila, J., Karney, B. R., & Bradbury, T. N. (1999). Attachment change processes in the early years of marriage. *Journal of Personality and Social Psychology, 76,* 783–802.

Emery, R. (1982). Interparental conflict and the children of discord and divorce. *Psychological Bulletin, 92,* 310–330.

Emmons, R. A., & McCullough, M. E. (2003). Counting blessings versus burdens: An experimental investigation of gratitude and subjective well-being in daily life. *Journal of Personality and Social Psychology, 84,* 377–389.

Fincham, F. D., Beach, S.R.H., Lambert, N., Stillman, T., & Braithwaite, S. R. (2008). Spiritual behaviors and relationship satisfaction: A critical analysis of the role of prayer. *Journal of Social and Clinical Psychology, 27,* 362–388.

Fincham, F. D., Hall, J. H., & Beach, S.R.H. (2005). 'Til lack of forgiveness doth us part: Forgiveness in marriage. In E. L. Worthington (Ed.), *Handbook of forgiveness* (pp. 207–225). Hoboken, NJ: Wiley.

Furman, W., & Collins, W. A. (2008). Adolescent romantic relationships and experiences. In K. H. Rubin, W. Bukowski, & B. Laursen (Eds.), *Handbook of peer interactions, relationships, and groups* (pp. 341–360). New York, NY: Guilford Press.

Gable, S. L., & Reis, H. T. (2010). Good news! Capitalizing on positive events in an interpersonal context. In M. P. Zanna (Ed.), *Advances in experimental social psychology* (vol. 42, pp. 195–257). San Diego, CA: Elsevier Academic Press.

Gottman, J. (1994). *What predicts divorce? The relationship between marital process and marital outcomes.* Hillsdale, NJ: Erlbaum.

Grewen, K., Girdler, S., Amico, J., & Light, K. (2005). Effects of partner support on resting oxytocin, cortisol, norepinephrine, and blood pressure before and after warm partner contact. *Psychosomatic Medicine, 67,* 531–538.

Halford, W., Markman, H. J., Kline, G. H., & Stanley, S. M. (2003). Best practice in couple relationship education. *Journal of Marital and Family Therapy, 29,* 385–406.

Hawkins, A. J., Blanchard, V. L., Baldwin, S. A., & Fawcett, E. B. (2008). Does marriage and relationship education work? A meta-analytic study. *Journal of Consulting and Clinical Psychology, 76,* 723–734.

Johnson, M. P., Caughlin, J. P., & Huston, T. L. (1999). The tripartite nature of marital commitment: Personal, moral, and structural reasons to stay married. *Journal of Marriage and Family, 61,* 160–177.

Kiecolt-Glaser, J. K., & Newton, T. L. (2001). Marriage and health: His and hers. *Psychological Bulletin, 127,* 472–503.

Lambert, N. M., Fincham, F. D., & Stanley, S. (2012). Prayer and satisfaction with sacrifice in close relationships. *Journal of Social and Personal Relationships, 29,* 1058–1070.

Langston, C. A. (1994). Capitalizing on and coping with daily-life events: Expressive responses to positive events. *Journal of Personality and Social Psychology, 67,* 1112–1125.

Larson, J. H., Crane, D. R., & Smith, C. W. (1991). Morning and night couples: The effect of spouses' wake and sleep patterns on marital adjustment. *Journal of Marital and Family Therapy, 17,* 53–65.

Larson, J. H., & Holman, T. B. (1994). Premarital predictors of marital quality and stability: An applied literature review. *Family Relations, 43,* 1–10.

Lilienfeld, S. O., Lynn, S. J., Ruscio, J., & Beyerstein, B. L. (2009). *50 great myths of popular psychology: Shattering widespread misconceptions about human behavior.* Hoboken, NJ: Wiley-Blackwell.

Mace, D., & Mace, V. (1980). Enriching marriages: The foundation stone of family strength. In N. Stinnett, B. Chesser, J. DeFrain, & P. Knaub (Eds.), *Family strengths: Positive models for family life* (pp. 89–110). Lincoln, NE: University of Nebraska Press.

Mahoney, A., Pargament, K. I., Jewell, T., Swank, A. B., Scott, E., Emery, E., & Rye, M. (1999). Marriage and the spiritual realm: The role of proximal and distal religious constructs in marital functioning. *Journal of Family Psychology, 13,* 321–338.

Manning, W. D., & Smock, P. J. (2005). Measuring and modeling cohabitation: New perspectives from qualitative data. *Journal of Marriage and Family, 67,* 989–1002.

Markman, H. J. (1981). The prediction of marital distress: A five-year follow-up. *Journal of Consulting and Clinical Psychology, 49,* 760–762.

Markman, H. J., Floyd, F., Stanley, S. M.,, & Jamieson, K. (1984). A cognitive-behavioral program for the prevention of marital and family distress: Issues in program development and delivery. In K. Hahlweg & N. Jacobson (Eds.), *Marital interaction: Analysis and modification* (pp. 396–428). New York, NY: Guilford Press.

Markman, H. J., & Hahlweg, K. (1993). The prediction and prevention of marital distress: An international perspective. *Clinical Psychology Review, 13,* 29–43.

Markman, H. J., Renick, M., Floyd, F. J., Stanley, S. M., & Clements, M. (1993). Preventing marital distress through communication and conflict management training: A 4- and 5-year follow-up. *Journal of Consulting and Clinical Psychology, 61,* 70–77.

Markman, H. J., & Rhoades, G. K. (2012). Relationship education research: Current status and future directions. *Journal of Marital and Family Therapy, 38,* 169–200.

Markman, H. J., Rhoades, G. K., Stanley, S. M., Ragan, E., & Whitton, S. (2010). The premarital communication roots of marital distress: The first five years of marriage. *Journal of Family Psychology, 24,* 289–298.

McCullough, M. E., Kilpatrick, S., Emmons, R. A., & Larson, D. (2001). Is gratitude a moral affect? *Psychological Bulletin, 127,* 249–266.

McCullough, M. E., Worthington, E. L., Jr., & Rachal, K. C. (1997). Interpersonal forgiving in close relationships. *Journal of Personality and Social Psychology, 73,* 321–336.

Ohayon, M. M., Carskadon, M. A., Guilleminault, C., & Vitiello, M. V. (2004). Meta-analysis of quantitative sleep parameters from childhood to old age in healthy individuals: Developing normative sleep values across the human lifespan. *Sleep, 27,* 1255–1273.

Pasch, L. A., & Bradbury, T. N. (1998). Social support, conflict, and the development of marital dysfunction. *Journal of Consulting and Clinical Psychology, 66,* 219–230.

Rehman, U. S., Rellini, A. H., & Fallis, E. (2011). The importance of sexual self-disclosure to sexual satisfaction and functioning in committed relationships. *Journal of Sexual Medicine, 8,* 3108–3115.

Rhoades, G. K., Stanley, S. M., & Markman, H. J. (2009). Couples' reasons for cohabitation: Associations with individual well-being and relationship quality. *Journal of Family Issues, 30,* 233–258.

Rhoades, G. K., Stanley, S. M., & Markman, H. J. (2009). The pre-engagement cohabitation effect: A replication and extension of previous findings. *Journal of Family Psychology, 23,* 107–111.

Rhoades, G. K., Stanley, S. M., & Markman, H. J. (2010). Should I stay or should I go? Predicting dating relationship stability from four aspects of commitment. *Journal of Family Psychology, 24,* 543–550.

Rhoades, G. K., Stanley, S. M., Markman, H. J., & Ragan, E. P. (2012). Parents' marital status, conflict, and role modeling: Links with adult romantic relationship quality. *Journal of Divorce and Remarriage, 53,* 1–20.

Riek, B. W. (2012). The antecedents and consequences of interpersonal forgiveness: A meta-analytic review. *Personal Relationships, 19*, 304–325.

Ross, E. A. (1921). *Principles of sociology*. New York, NY: Century.

Rusbult, C. E. (1980). Commitment and satisfaction in romantic associations: A test of the investment model. *Journal of Experimental Social Psychology, 16*, 172–186.

Scott, S. B., Rhoades, G. K., Stanley, S. M., Allen, E. S., & Markman, H. J. (2013). Reasons for divorce and recollections of premarital intervention: Implications for improving relationship education. *Couple and Family Psychology: Research and Practice, 2*, 131–145.

Smock, P. J., & Manning, W. D. (2004). Living together unmarried in the United States: Demographic perspectives and implications for family policy. *Law & Policy, 26*, 87–117.

Stanley, S. M., Allen, E. S., Markman, H. J., Rhoades, G. K., & Prentice, D. (2010). Decreasing divorce in Army couples: Results from a randomized controlled trial of PREP for Strong Bonds. *Journal of Couple and Relationship Therapy, 9*, 149–160.

Stanley, S. M., Lobitz, W. C., & Dickson, F. (1999). Using what we know: Commitment and cognitions in marital therapy. In W. Jones & J. Adams (Eds.), *Handbook of interpersonal commitment and relationship stability* (pp. 379–392). New York, NY: Plenum.

Stanley, S. M., & Markman, H. J. (1992). Assessing commitment in personal relationships. *Journal of Marriage and Family, 54*, 595–608.

Stanley, S. M., Markman, H. J., & Whitton, S. (2002). Communication, conflict, and commitment: Insights on the foundations of relationship success from a national survey. *Family Process, 41*, 659–675.

Stanley, S. M., Ragan, E. P., Rhoades, G. K., & Markman, H. J. (2012). Examining changes in relationship adjustment and life satisfaction in marriage. *Journal of Family Psychology, 26*, 165–170.

Stanley, S. M., Rhoades, G. K., Amato, P. R., Markman, H. J., & Johnson, C. A. (2010). The timing of cohabitation and engagement: Impact on first and second marriages. *Journal of Marriage and Family, 72*, 906–918.

Stanley, S. M., Rhoades, G. K., & Markman, H. J. (2006). Sliding vs. deciding: Inertia and the premarital cohabitation effect. *Family Relations, 55*, 499–509.

Stanley, S. M., Rhoades, G. K., & Whitton, S. W. (2010). Commitment: Functions, formation, and the securing of romantic attachment. *Journal of Family Theory and Review, 2*, 243–257.

Stanley, S. M., & Trathen, D. W. (1994). Christian PREP: An empirically based model for marital and premarital intervention. *Journal of Psychology and Christianity, 13*, 158–165.

Stanley, S. M., Trathen, D. W., & McCain, S. C. (1996). Christian PREP: An empirically based model for marital and premarital intervention. In E. Worthington (Ed.), *Christian marital counseling: Eight approaches* (pp. 135–158). Grand Rapids, MI: Baker Books.

Storaasli, R. D., & Markman, H. J. (1990). Relationship problems in the early stages of marriage: A longitudinal investigation. *Journal of Family Psychology, 4,* 80–98.

Troxel, W. M., Robles, T. F., Hall, M., & Buysse, D. J. (2007). Marital quality and the marital bed: Examining the covariation between relationship quality and sleep. *Sleep Medicine Reviews, 11,* 389–404.

Vohs, K. D., Baumeister, R. F., & Schmeichel, B. J. (2012). Motivation, personal beliefs, and limited resources all contribute to self-control. *Journal of Experimental Social Psychology, 48,* 943–947.

Waller, W. (1938). *The family: A dynamic interpretation.* New York, NY: Gordon.

Whisman, M. A. (2001). The association between depression and marital dissatisfaction. In S.R.H. Beach (Ed.), *Marital and family processes in depression: A scientific foundation for clinical practice* (pp. 3–24). Washington, DC: American Psychological Association.

Worthington, E. L. (2008). Prayer and marital intervention: Can it be long and strong enough to matter? *Journal of Social and Clinical Psychology, 27,* 686–692.

Wright, P. J. (2013). U.S. males and pornography, 1973–2010: Consumption, predictors, correlates. *Journal of Sex Research, 50,* 60–71.

Zak, P. J. (2008). The neurobiology of trust. *Scientific American, 298*(6), 88–95.

Notes

Introduction

1. Stanley, S. M. (1997). What's important in premarital counseling? *Marriage and Family: A Christian Journal, 1*, 51–60.
2. Stanley, S. M., & Trathen, D. (1994) Christian PREP: An empirically based model for marital and premarital intervention. *Journal of Psychology and Christianity, 13*, 158–165.

Chapter 7: Jars of Clay

1. Centers for Disease Control and Prevention. (n.d.). About us. http://www.cdc.gov/sleep/about_us.htm.

Chapter 10: Protecting "Us" in iWorld

1. Carroll, J. S., Padilla-Walker, L. M., Nelson, L. J., Olson, C. D., Barry, C. M., & Madsen, S. D. (2008). Generation XXX: Pornography acceptance and use among emerging adults. *Journal of Adolescent Research, 23*, 6–30.
2. Kenrick, D. T., Gutierres, S. E., & Goldberg, L. L. (2003). Influence of popular erotica on judgments of strangers and mates. In S. Plous (Ed.), *Understanding prejudice and discrimination* (pp. 243–248). New York, NY: McGraw-Hill.
3. Wright, P. J. (2013). U.S. males and pornography, 1973–2010: Consumption, predictors, correlates. *Journal of Sex Research, 50*, 60–71.
4. Maddox, A., Rhoades, G. K., & Markman, H. M. (2011). Viewing sexually-explicit materials alone or together: Associations with relationship quality. *Archives of Sexual Behavior, 40*, 441–448.
5. See, for example, Bleakley, A., Hennessy, M., Fishbein, M., & Jordan, A. (2008). It works both ways: The relationship between exposure

to sexual content in the media and adolescent sexual behavior. *Media Psychology, 11*, 443–461; Brown, J. D., & L'Engle, K. L. (2009). X-rated: Sexual attitudes and behaviors associated with U.S. early adolescents' exposure to sexually explicit media. *Communication Research, 36*, 129–151; Peter, J., & Valkenburg, P. M. (2006). Adolescents' exposure to sexually explicit online material and recreational attitudes towards sex. *Journal of Communication, 56*, 639–660.

6. See, for example, Regnerus, M., & Uecker, J. (2011). *Premarital sex in America: How young Americans meet, mate, and think about marrying.* New York, NY: Oxford University Press.

About the Authors

Scott Stanley, Ph.D., is one of the original developers of PREP (the Prevention and Relationship Enhancement Program), and cofounder, with Howard Markman, of the PREP companies, which develop (and distribute worldwide) research-based tools and programs for couples and those who work to help them. Stanley is a research professor and codirector of the Center for Marital and Family Studies at the University of Denver. He has published extensively, including scientific journal articles, book chapters, and works for couples, with a focus on commitment theory, communication, conflict, and sacrifice. Stanley is a popular conference speaker and the author of *The Power of Commitment* and coauthor of *Fighting for Your Marriage* and many other books for couples. He regularly appears in both print and broadcast media as an expert on marriage, including appearances on CNN, *Fox News*, *The Today Show*, *Family Life Today*, *Focus on the Family*, and many others, and his research is regularly cited in articles in *USA Today*, the *Washington Times*, the *Wall Street Journal*, *Psychology Today*, *Redbook*, *Ladies Home Journal*, *Marriage Partnership*, and many others.

Stanley maintains a blog at www.slidingvsdeciding.com, where he covers topics ranging from practical insights for relationships to discussions of public policy and trends in marriage.

Daniel Trathen, D.Min., Ph.D., is a psychologist in private practice in Parker, Colorado. In addition to his clinical background of four decades, he served in the U.S. Navy during Vietnam and is also a retired army officer. He has been a visiting professor of marriage and family therapy and a graduate school adjunct professor. In addition to his contributions to Christian PREP, Trathen has taught as a counseling instructor in the graduate departments at Simpson College and Moody Bible Institute. He has presented Christian PREP workshops in churches, seminaries, and for the military throughout the United States. He also has contributed numerous articles for several journals.

Savanna McCain, Ph.D., is a psychologist in private practice in Fayetteville, Arkansas. McCain has conducted outcome research on the effectiveness of PREP with the team at the University of Denver and has worked on aspects of PREP with Markman, Stanley, Blumberg, and colleagues since the early 1990s. She also conducted PREP and Christian PREP workshops for many years. In addition to her contributions to Christian PREP, McCain has been working on the implementation of the program in local church settings, especially with a focus on mentor couple models.

Milt Bryan, M.A., is a therapist in private in Denver, Colorado. He has been a counselor to couples for over twenty-five years and has presented Christian PREP workshops in cities across the United States and in Europe. Bryan and his wife, Jeannie, are missionaries with Cadence International, a ministry dedicated to winning and making disciples from among the nation's military across the world. They provide counseling to Cadence missionaries, serving as team members in the Pastoral Care Department.

Index

Scripture Index

335